HOW
NATURE
WORKS

Watching the underground life of earthworms in a wormery

Calibrating a jar to measure lung capacity

Changing over the sound
received by the ears

Testing peripheral
vision

HOW
NATURE
WORKS

David Burnie

Mapping taste-buds on the tongue

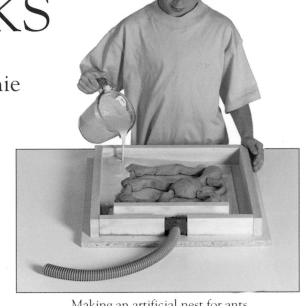
Making an artificial nest for ants

Investigating soil animals with a
Baermann funnel

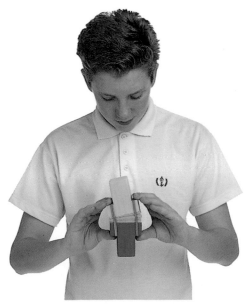
Seeing how joints work

Reader's Digest

The Reader's Digest Association, Inc.
Pleasantville, New York • Montreal

A READER'S DIGEST BOOK
designed and edited by Dorling Kindersley Limited, London

Project Editor	Sharon Lucas
Art Editor	Sally Ann Hibbard
Designer	Gurinder Purewall
DTP Designer	Joanna Figg-Latham
Production	Vivienne Frow
Managing Editor	Carolyn King
Managing Art Editor	Nick Harris

Consultant Editor	Linda Gamlin
Educational Consultant	Richard Scrase

Library of Congress Cataloging in Publication Data

Burnie, David.
  How nature works : 100 ways parents and kids can share the secrets
of nature / David Burnie.
    p.   cm.
Includes index.
ISBN 0-89577-391-0
1. Natural history—Experiments—Juvenile literature.   2. Nature
study—Juvenile literature.   I. Title.
QH55.B87 1991
508—dc20   91-12432

READER'S DIGEST and the Pegasus logo are
registered trademarks of The Reader's Digest
Association, Inc.

Reader's Digest Fund for the Blind is publisher of
the Large-Type Edition of *Reader's Digest*. For
subscription information about this magazine,
please contact Reader's Digest Fund for the Blind,
Inc., Dept. 250, Pleasantville, N.Y. 10570.

Printed in Singapore

Contents

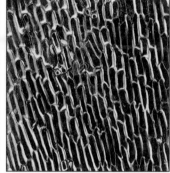

*Looking
at life*

*The world of
plants and
fungi*

Birds

Life in water

Reptiles

Insects and other invertebrates

Mammals

INTRODUCTION

HOW DOES A BIRD FLY? Why do plants need light? How does a tadpole turn into a frog? Because the living world is all around us, human beings have always been fascinated by questions like these. Centuries ago, people used their imagination as much as their eyes to come up with answers. To them, the living world was a place of mystery. Stories of strange creatures from distant lands gave rise to tales of dragons, unicorns, and monsters of the seas. Closer to home, many people believed that living things could appear suddenly out of lifeless matter, or that some plants could turn into animals and fly away.

Since those times, the science of life — called biology — has revealed much about the way things really live. Many of the world's most important biologists have started out as amateur naturalists, equipped only with a great interest in what makes living things "tick." They made their discoveries by experiments and by careful observation, and this book is designed to help you to find out about the living world in the same way.

The experiments featured in this book don't require masses of complicated equipment, and they include things that you can

try both out of doors and at home. They have been devised so that the whole family can join in. Many of them can be safely carried out by young children, but where an adult's help or supervision is needed, this is clearly stated. Some of the experiments produce results straight away. Others, including ones that involve growing plants or raising insects, can take longer. You will need to keep an eye on these experiments day by day, to make sure that there is enough water or food. With these experiments, it helps to think ahead when deciding on the best time to start.

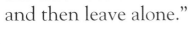

We live in a world that is rapidly changing. Many living things that were once numerous are now threatened by human activities, from farming to driving cars. So it is very important that when investigating plants and animals, you don't damage them. Many of the living things on our planet are beautiful, intricate, and amazing. After collecting anything that is living, put it back where you found it. Remember that the true naturalist's motto is "Look, learn, and then leave alone."

The home laboratory

ALTHOUGH YOU CAN LEARN a lot about nature using just your eyes, a simple home laboratory will help you to discover even more. Most of the experiments in this book can be carried out on a windowsill or worktop, or in the yard, using everyday materials found around the home. Here are some of the items you might find useful. If you don't have everything or the exact item, try something similar — it may work just as well.

■ Naturalist's equipment

A good hand lens is one of the most valuable tools for the would-be naturalist, as are pencil and paper and a sharp knife or scalpel. (A purpose-made dissecting kit will contain many of these items and more.) Remember that scalpels are *very* sharp, and *should only be used if an adult is present.* A microscope is useful, but not essential.

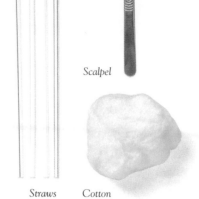

Scalpel

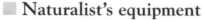

Straws

Cotton wool

Notepad

Pencils

Flashlight

Crayons

Corks

Hand lens

Microscope slides

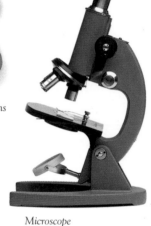

Microscope

■ Everyday measures

Accurate measurements are needed in many everyday activities as well as scientific experiments. In your kitchen, for instance, you will find measures for volume (measuring jugs) and mass (weights and scales). You will probably be able to find a ruler, tape measure, and calculator elsewhere in your house. Most scientists now use the International System (SI) for measures, with meters for length, kilograms for mass, and seconds for time. But if your measures show other units, use these. Where possible, we have listed appropriate conversions. When making equipment that has many pieces (for example, the breeding cage on pp. 102-103), it is important to follow *one* system of measures throughout.

Ruler

Calculator

Tape measure

Thermometer

Dropper bottle

Measuring jug

Measuring cylinder

Funnel

▪ Kitchen utensils and useful tools

You will find all sorts of useful tools in the kitchen (remember to ask first before taking them!). It is important not to contaminate kitchen utensils with anything you use in an experiment — animals, plants, soil, pondwater, or chemicals. Keep a set just for your experiments, or wash them thoroughly in hot water before putting them back where they came from.

Scissors

Metal spoons

Plastic spoons

Saucepan

Tweezers

Seeker

Sieve

▪ Simple materials to buy

For some experiments, you will need to buy small amounts of planed wood and plywood. Be conservation-minded, and make sure that the wood you use comes from a sustainable source. You should be able to buy the materials and objects shown here from a hardware store.

Heavy wood

Sandpaper

Modeling clay

Paper glue

Balsa wood

Tissue paper

Plastic tubing

Paintbrush

Paints

Wood scraps

9

■ Fasteners to find

Try to collect a range of different fasteners for the experiments and projects in this book, from adhesive tape to nails and screws. Collect a variety of fasteners for your home laboratory. If you do not have the precise fastener specified in an experiment, you can usually adapt another kind.

Screws

Panel pins

Nails

Thumbtacks

Stapler

String

Rubber bands

Adhesive tape

Cotton

Quick-drying glue

Wood glue

Wire

Angled lamp

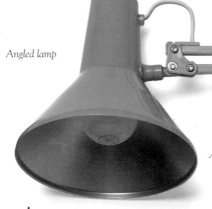

Wire

Bulb

■ Electrical equipment

A few of the experiments in this book need an electric light or bell. An angled lamp is very helpful when you are examining specimens, and can also be used in some of the experiments.

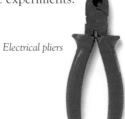

Electrical pliers

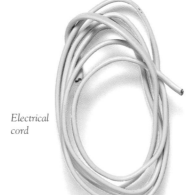

Electrical cord

Bulb holder

■ Some tools to borrow

For a number of experiments, you will need basic woodworking tools, such as a screwdriver, G-clamp, and saw. Some projects also require power tools such as an electric drill or jigsaw. *Ask an adult to use these if they are needed.*

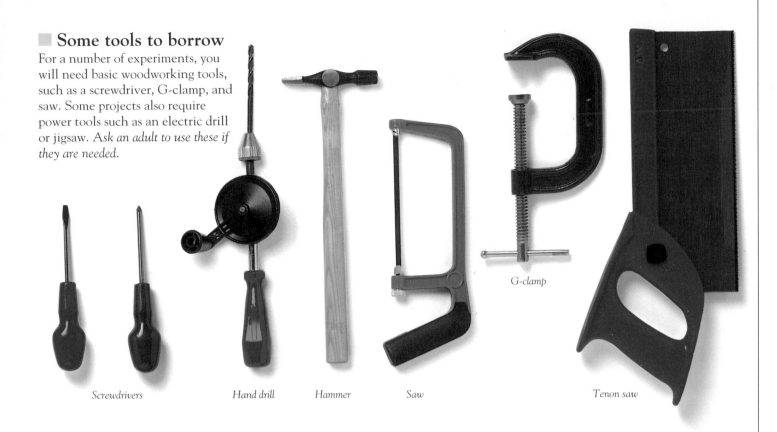

Screwdrivers

Hand drill

Hammer

Saw

G-clamp

Tenon saw

■ Types of container

Jars are some of the most useful items in the home laboratory. Try to collect as many as you can, with screw-top lids if possible. You will also need a few heatproof containers, such as test tubes and laboratory beakers, or metal mugs. NEVER put chemicals in any containers where they might be mistaken for food or drink items.

Jar

Petri dish

Heatproof glass beaker

Test tubes

Jar with screw top

Plastic cup

Glass bowl

Mug

Glass

Plastic bowl

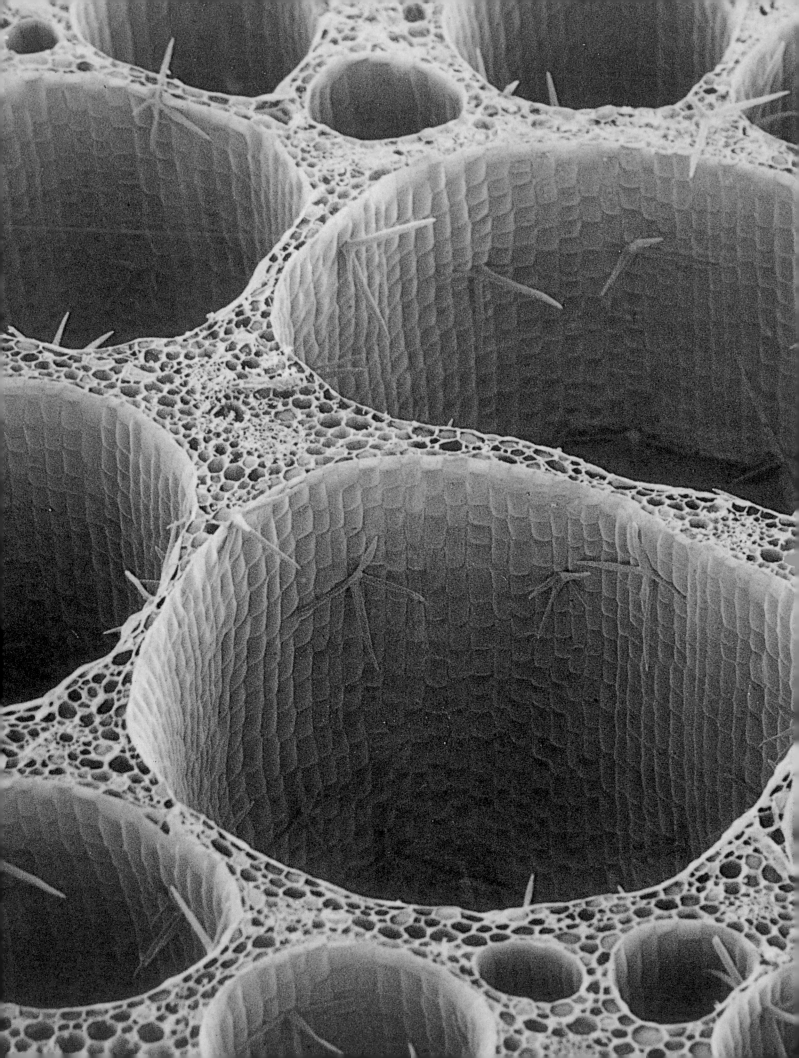

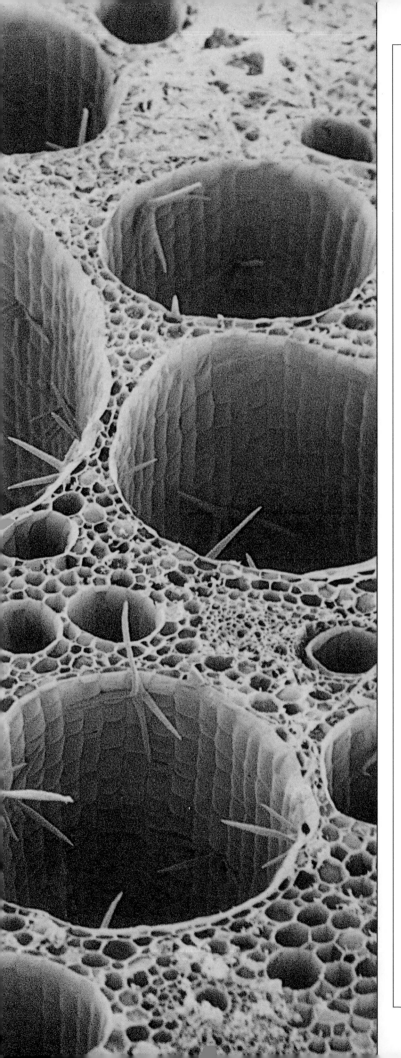

Looking at LIFE

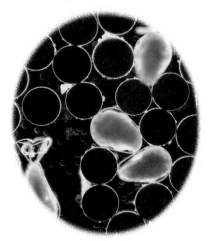

Life in close-up
Well lighted and under magnification, the eggs
and larvae of brine shrimps (above) are a mass of
glowing blobs. Magnified by an electron
microscope, the inside of the waterlily's leaf stalk
(left) becomes a landscape of giant tubes, lined
with countless cells.

WHAT MAKES SOMETHING ALIVE?
When did life first appear on
Earth, and how has it changed
since then? To answer
questions like these, biologists
need to look far into the
Earth's past, studying the fossils
of creatures that became
extinct long ago and looking
for clues to the evolution of
their successors. They also
have to investigate the
chemistry and structure of the
living things that surround
us today.

WHAT IS LIFE?

FOSSILS SHOW THAT LIFE EXISTED on Earth nearly 3.5 billion years ago, about a billion years after the planet was formed. Scientists believe that, from their simple beginnings, carbon-based molecules gradually became more and more complicated. Eventually they became able to reproduce, and at that point, life itself was born.

In the early 1950s, chemist Stanley Miller performed an experiment that looked backward into the remote history of our planet. He filled a glass sphere with a mixture of gases thought to be like that of the Earth's early atmosphere. The sphere was connected to a jar containing boiling water, which imitated an ocean bubbling from the Earth's heat. Vapor from the "ocean" mixed with the "atmosphere" and then passed through a cooled pipe to make it fall back as "rain." To make the simulation complete, sparks jumping between two wires created "lightning" like that occurring during the thunderstorms that raged incessantly on the early Earth.

After checking that the apparatus was completely sealed, Miller let the steamy mixture bubble away for a week before switching it off to see what was now inside. His results were remarkable. In addition to the chemicals he had originally included, many others had now appeared. Among them were amino acids — carbon-containing substances that are among the building blocks of life.

Within each moss cell
there is a tiny, stable environment where the chemical processes of life can take place.

■ How life began

Miller's experiment suggests — but does not prove — that the chemicals on which life is based might have arisen quite by chance, billions of years ago, in the Earth's seas. It is a long jump from simple amino acids to a living cell (p. 16), but, given time, this transformation could have taken place. This is how most scientists think life arose — by the gradual development of complex chemicals that could replicate by using the simple chemicals around them.

A simple experiment
with potatoes shows how water flows in and out of cells.

More than 100 different chemical elements are known on Earth. Of these, only about 20 are essential for life. One, carbon, has the important ability to form chains, or rings of atoms. These can hold together and combine with other elements, such as hydrogen and oxygen, producing chemicals with different properties. The amino acids formed in Miller's experiment contained no more than five carbon atoms, but a living organism could add these together to make chains hundreds or thousands of carbon atoms long.

These giant chains of amino acids make up proteins (p. 18) — substances that are crucial to all forms of life.

■ Characteristics of living things

All living things — from bacteria to elephants — share a number of characteristics that we sum up as "being alive." They take in food, and the chemical energy from food drives their chemical processes and enables them to grow. To obtain the energy from food, they "burn" it, usually by combining it with oxygen and producing carbon dioxide and water as waste products (p. 42). They can respond to the world around them, and, importantly, they produce offspring that grow up to be like themselves.

After reading this list, you might think it is quite easy to tell if something is living or non-living. But what about a virus?

When people get a cold, we often say they have caught a "bug." In fact, they have caught a virus, a minute package of chemicals that has infected the cells that line the nose and throat. The virus "hijacks" these cells, forcing them to make copies of itself. Its duplicate viruses then spread to other people when the first victim sneezes.

So far, the virus sounds very much alive. But a virus does not grow,

Nobel Prize-winning
biologists James Watson (left) and Francis Crick with their model showing the structure of DNA.

and it can only reproduce itself in living cells. Outside them, it appears quite lifeless, and it can be crystallized just like a chemical and stored on a shelf for years. On being brought into contact with living cells, it springs into "life" once more.

The answer to this puzzle is that viruses are descended from living things, but they have lost many of the features of other living things because they are parasites. Since they hijack the reproductive machinery of other cells, they do not need any of their own. They are rather like a car with the wheels taken off. A car is defined as "a wheeled vehicle," so one without wheels is, logically speaking, not a car. However, if you saw it, you would still refer to it as a car. And so it is with viruses.

■ Chemicals that copy themselves

All living things — even the very largest — start out life as a single cell. A blue whale's egg cell, which is too small for you to see, contains all the instructions needed to build and maintain the whale's 150-ton body. As the egg cell grows and divides, the instructions it holds have to be handed on to millions of other cells, so that all the substances needed by the whale's body can be made in the right quantities, at the right time, and in the right place. How does this happen?

Over a century ago, biologists noticed threadlike structures called chromosomes that appeared in cells just before they were about to divide. They also noticed that every species of plant or animal had a characteristic number of

chromosomes — humans have 23 pairs. From this, it seemed likely that chromosomes had something to do with controlling cells, but without the benefit of electron microscopes or modern methods of chemical analysis, they could go no further with this.

We now know that chromosomes are part of the control system of every cell. They are made of proteins and a substance called DNA — deoxyribonucleic acid. The DNA in a chromosome is extremely long — up to 10,000 times longer than the chromosome itself — but is tightly coiled so it fits into a small space.

DNA is made up of two coiled strands that wind around each other — the "double helix." The strands carry four types of chemical, called bases, and it is these bases that are at the heart of the cell's control system. The bases are arranged in a particular sequence, like a computer program, and they make up an almost endless list of instructions, known as genes, for making proteins. These proteins, in turn, make or control every other chemical needed in the cell.

DNA has the extraordinary ability to copy itself. When a cell divides, the

A light microscope can be used to look at cells. Viruses and some bacteria are so small that they can only be seen with a more powerful electron microscope.

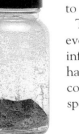

The bubbles show an enzyme is at work.

People once thought that complete living organisms could be "generated" by nonliving matter. Experiments by Louis Pasteur (1822–1895) showed that this did not happen.

two strands that make up the DNA gradually pull apart. In a process called replication, the order of bases on one strand is used to build a copy of the other strand. Each one forms a complete double helix once again. The information in the DNA can therefore multiply itself many times — making it the cornerstone of life.

■ Order out of chaos

If you look at the living world around you, what you see is the product of chemical information. The beautifully sculpted shell of a mollusk (p. 90) is made from the simplest of raw materials, calcium carbonate, shaped according to the information held in DNA. The petals of a flower (p. 47) are made by harnessing sunlight and using it to build up substances in a precise way, according to the plant's chemical program. In the same way, the display feathers of a peacock (p. 132) and the structure of your eyes (p. 166) are all coded by DNA and handed down from one generation to another.

Through the process of evolution (pp. 20-21), information held by DNA has become more complex as different species struggle to survive and reproduce. It is this complexity that makes nature so fascinating the closer you look at it.

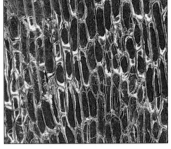

By peeling away layers on the inside of an onion, you can produce a thin skin that is just one cell thick.

Cells

OVER 300 YEARS AGO, the English mathematician and inventor Robert Hooke peered at a thin slice of cork through a simple microscope. What he saw was "a great many little boxes, separated ... by certain diaphragms." He called the boxes "cells," a name that we still use today.

Cells are the building blocks of living things. The inside of a cell is a carefully controlled environment where the chemical processes of life can be carried out. Simple living things, such as bacteria, consist of a single cell, while others — including ourselves — are made up of many billions. Where there are many cells, there is usually specialization: different types of cells carry out different kinds of work.

■ Looking at cells

Cells are far too small to be visible to the naked eye. You can see some plant cells with a hand lens, but you will need a microscope to see animal cells. Biologists use chemical stains to make transparent cells more visible.

■ Animal cell

An animal cell is like a tiny, fluid-filled bag. Inside this is the nucleus, which controls the cell, and the cytoplasm, a jellylike substance that contains many types of tiny structures called organelles. Organelles called mitochondria are the cell's power stations — they burn food to provide energy.

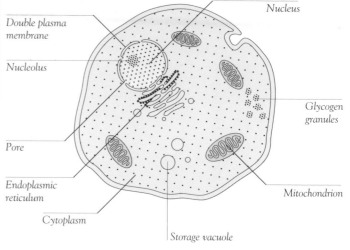

Double plasma membrane

Nucleolus

Pore

Endoplasmic reticulum

Cytoplasm

Nucleus

Glycogen granules

Mitochondrion

Storage vacuole

A group of animal cells
The "bag" around each one is a flexible membrane made up of two layers.

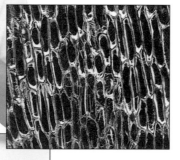

Exposing moss cells
Take a small piece of moss, and place it on a drop of water on a microscope slide. Place a coverslip over the specimen (the moss and the water), put it on the microscope stage, and then focus the microscope.

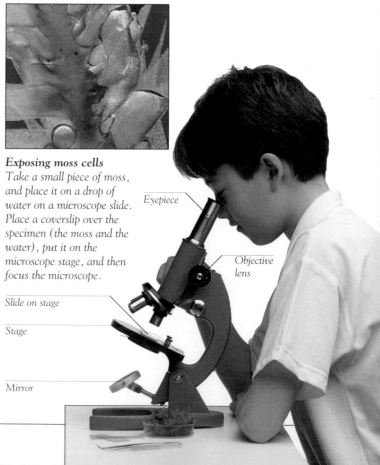

Eyepiece

Objective lens

Slide on stage

Stage

Mirror

Exposing onion cells
Slice a square out of an onion, and peel away the inner surface, so you have an onion skin that is just one cell thick and thinner than tissue paper. Now press it onto a windowpane so it sticks in position. Using a hand lens, you should be able to see the cells.

■ Plant cell

Plant cells have rigid walls made up of cellulose, and most of the space inside the walls is taken up by a fluid-filled vacuole. The fluid presses outward, keeping the cell rigid. The cytoplasm contains organelles, called chloroplasts, that harness the energy of the Sun through photosynthesis (pp. 40-43).

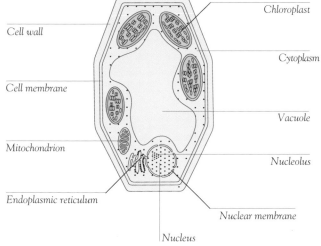

Chloroplast

Cell wall

Cytoplasm

Cell membrane

Vacuole

Mitochondrion

Nucleolus

Endoplasmic reticulum

Nuclear membrane

Nucleus

A group of plant cells
Each of these "tiny boxes" has a double membrane, inside a cell wall of cellulose.

■ DISCOVERY ■
Theodor Schwann

Although cells were discovered in the seventeenth century, it took nearly 200 years for their true importance to be understood. The German biologist Theodor Schwann (1810–1882) was one of the first scientists to realize that cells are the building blocks of animals as well as plants. The "cell theory," which he helped to develop, states that cells are the smallest things that are truly alive, and that all organisms are made up of one or more cells. It also states that cells are produced only by the division of other cells.

Although Schwann's theory was largely correct, there are no true cells in fungi (pp. 64-69). Higher fungi have divisions resembling cells, but they are not actually separate because the membranes between them have holes connecting each division with its neighbors.

EXPERIMENT
Observing osmosis

Adult supervision is advised for this experiment
Water enters a cell from the outside, traveling through the cell's membranes by a process called osmosis. These special membranes let water through, but not salts and sugars. The water crosses the membrane if there is more salt or sugar on the other side — thus equalizing the concentration on either side.

You can observe osmosis at work by using potatoes as models of cell membranes. Cut two potatoes into equal halves. Discard one piece. Remove a $1/2$ in (1 cm) strip of peel around the base of each one, and cut a small hollow in the curved side. Put two potato halves flat side down in dishes of water. Boil the other potato half for 10 minutes to kill the cells.

You Will Need
● *2 potatoes* ● *sugar* ● *3 dishes*
● *spoon* ● *knife*

Potato 1
This is the "control" potato. Leave it as it is, and compare it with the others at the end of the experiment.

Potato 2
The cooked potato shows how water moves through dead cells. Place it in a dish, and put a spoonful of sugar in the hollow. Examine after one day to see what has happened.

Potato 3
This potato shows how water moves through living cell membranes. Leave it in the dish, but put a spoonful of sugar in the hollow. Examine after one day to see what has happened.

Water on the move
By osmosis, water has moved through the cell membranes of potato 3. During this process, water always moves in a set direction — from the side where it has less substances dissolved in it to the side where it has more. What happens without the sugar, or when the cells are dead?

The chemicals of life

IMAGINE A GIANT CHEMICAL FACTORY. Now make it more complicated, speed it up millions of times, and then shrink it until it is invisible. You now have something like a single cell. Many of the cell's chemicals fall into groups. The largest groups are the nucleic acids, the carbohydrates, fats, and proteins. Carbohydrates are used mainly to store energy. Fats also store energy and form membranes. Proteins have many uses — some build up the cell; others, called enzymes, speed chemical reactions.

1 POUR THE UNDILUTED hydrogen peroxide into the jar. Add the liver, and loosely seal the jar with the lid.

BEWARE!
This experiment uses hydrogen peroxide and the one on the opposite page uses caustic soda, which can harm the skin. YOU MUST WEAR RUBBER GLOVES AND WASH YOUR HANDS AFTERWARD. *An adult* MUST *be present during both experiments.*

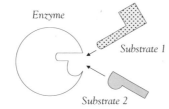

2 CATALASE IN THE LIVER immediately starts to break down the hydrogen peroxide. Bubbles stream to the surface during the reaction, and the gas is kept in by the lid.

Watching an enzyme in action

Adult supervision is advised for this experiment
Your liver is like a factory that produces thousands of different chemicals. To do this, it uses many enzymes. One of these is catalase, an enzyme that breaks down hydrogen peroxide. This experiment lets you see the enzyme at work.

YOU WILL NEED
● *small piece of liver* ● *hydrogen peroxide (available from pharmacists)* ● *jar with a lid* ● *wooden splint or toothpick*

3 LIGHT THE SPLINT'S END, blow it out, unscrew the lid, and then put the splint in the jar. It will burst into flame, as there is more oxygen in the jar than in the air around you.

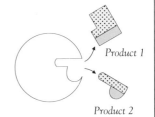
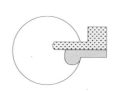

The reigniting splint proves that oxygen is a product of the reaction

---

■ Enzymes at work

Enzymes are proteins that speed chemical reactions, making life possible. They bring together specific chemicals, or "substrates," and make them react. This diagram shows, in a very simplified way, how enzymes are thought to work. Each enzyme controls just one chemical reaction.

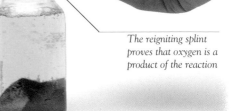

Enzyme
Substrate 1
Substrate 2
Product 1
Product 2

Stage 1
The two substrate molecules slot into the enzyme's "active site." This brings them close together.

Stage 2
A chemical reaction occurs between the two substrate molecules, because the enzyme creates the right chemical conditions around them.

Stage 3
The two substrates change into two new molecules, which leave the enzyme. The enzyme works on two more substrate molecules.

EXPERIMENT
Testing for starch, fat, and protein

Adult supervision is advised for this experiment

Find out if a food contains starch, fat, or protein by carrying out these tests. Use foods that are almost pure: cornstarch (starch), vegetable oil (fat), and egg white (protein). The chemicals used here are all available from pharmacists.

You Will Need
- *cornstarch* ● *vegetable oil* ● *egg white*
- *iodine solution* ● *surgical spirit or alcohol*
- *caustic soda solution* ● *copper sulfate solution* ● *cup* ● *test tubes* ● *water*
- *rubber gloves*

1 WORK ON A SURFACE that you can wipe clean. Ask an adult to make a small amount of copper sulfate solution, and of dilute caustic soda solution. The caustic soda should be added to water.

2 YOU SHOULD CARRY OUT each test twice — once with the substance that you are testing, and once without it. The second test is a "control," which you do to show what happens if starch, fat, or protein is absent.

Testing for starch
In a cup, mix up one tablespoon of cornstarch with enough water to make it runny. Half-fill a tube with this, then add a drop of iodine solution, and shake the tube. The starch in the cornstarch will turn the iodine blue-black. In the tube without starch, the iodine stays orange-yellow.

Testing for fat
Pour some alcohol or surgical spirit into the tube until it is one-third full. Add a drop of vegetable oil, and shake the tube until the oil dissolves. Add a few drops of this solution to another tube containing water, and shake. The fat will produce an "emulsion" of white droplets.

Testing for protein
Pour egg white mixed with water into a test tube until it is one-third full. Wearing protective gloves, add 10 drops each of caustic soda, and copper sulfate solution. Shake the tube. (Keep the solution away from your face.) The protein in the egg white will turn the mixture violet.

Starch absent   Starch present   Fat absent   Fat present   Protein absent   Protein present

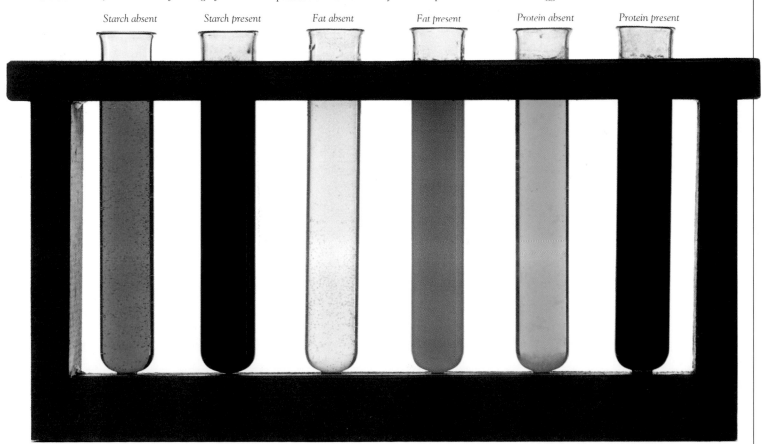

EVOLUTION

THE LIVING WORLD IS FULL OF CHANGE. Though plants and animals seem the same from year to year, evidence shows that all living things change as one generation succeeds another. This process is called evolution. The existence of evolution and the mechanism behind it were revealed by one of the world's greatest naturalists — Charles Darwin.

"The natural history of these islands is eminently curious," wrote Charles Darwin of the Galápagos, a group of islands that he visited in 1835, during a round-the-world voyage on HMS *Beagle*. "Most of the organic productions [plants and animals] are found nowhere else ... yet all show a marked relationship with those of America, though separated from that continent by an open space of ocean, between 500 and 600 miles in width. Considering the small size of these islands, we feel the more astonished at the number of their aboriginal [unique] beings."

At the time, most people believed that all living things had been created in their present form by God, who had specifically designed them for the place they inhabited. But why should so many new species have been made for the Galápagos alone? Why should there be tortoises and lizards, but no frogs or toads? Why should 13 kinds of finch have been created for these islands, but few other birds? And — importantly — why should the plants and animals of the Galápagos be related to those in nearby South America? To Darwin, the idea that they had been created specially did not make sense.

Charles Darwin (1809–1882), whose world voyage revolutionized our understanding of the natural world.

The marine iguana
of the Galápagos, a unique lizard that dives into the sea to graze on seaweed.

■ Long journey across the sea

Charles Darwin decided there was a simple explanation. It was clear that the Galápagos had been formed by volcanoes erupting under the sea, so they would have started out as bare, lifeless rock.

Suppose the new islands were colonized by plants and animals from South America. Plant seeds and birds could have been blown there by the wind, while other animals could have drifted across the sea.

This sea journey would explain why there were reptiles, such as lizards and tortoises, but no frogs or other amphibians, and no native mammals. They simply could not make the sea crossing. Lizards and tortoises are cold-blooded (p. 144) and have thick, waterproof skins. They can go for long periods without food and survive being splashed with salty water. After a violent tropical storm, uprooted trees might have been washed out to sea with a few small reptiles still clinging to them. If the tree reached the Galápagos within a week or two, its reptile passengers would still be alive. But a warm-blooded mammal needs sustenance to keep going — it could not

survive that long without food or water. And an amphibian would die when the seawater soaked its delicate skin.

■ Survival through adaptation

The animals that survived the sea crossing would have found very different conditions from those in South America. There would be much more food to eat, because few other animals would be there to compete for it. But many of the foods would be new — to eat them, they would have had to adapt in some way.

Darwin saw evidence of this adaptation in the Galápagos finches. Some had much larger beaks than normal finches, while the beaks of others were very small. At one extreme, there was a finch with a very large parrotlike beak for cracking big, hard seeds, and at the other, a finch with a tiny, sharp beak like that of an insect-eating bird. Neither parrots nor small insect-eaters such as warblers had reached the Galápagos, and these finches were taking their place. There were even finches taking the place of woodpeckers, probing tree trunks for insects using a cactus spine held in the beak.

A flower and a bee — two living things that have evolved a partnership from which both benefit.

■ A gradual development

Darwin was beginning to have his doubts about Creation, and, in his account of the *Beagle*'s journey, he gave his readers a hint of what he was thinking about the Galápagos finches: "One might really fancy that from an original paucity [shortage] of birds ... one species had been taken and modified for different ends." In other words, a pair of finches, or perhaps a small flock, had reached the Galápagos early on and hit the jackpot — plenty of food and few other birds to compete with them. They had adapted to eating different foods, and produced 13 different species.

Nobody took very much notice of Darwin's hint, because nobody realized what he was getting at: that *all* the species on Earth had appeared in the same way, by evolution — gradual development from other living species.

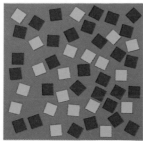

A simple board game
shows how a species evolves
through natural selection.

■ Equipped for flight

Darwin waited more than 20 years before he told the world of his idea. He was not the first person to think of it, but no one had believed the others. He wanted to collect as much evidence as he could, and he wanted to be sure that he could answer every criticism. His favorite motto was "It's dogged as does it," meaning that hard work and perseverance would reveal the truth. No one could have worked harder or been so critical of his own ideas.

He studied the fossils found in the rocks of different continents and found that the animals that lived there in the past were usually related to those living there now. Fossils also showed that life began with simple forms, and that

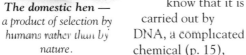

The domestic hen —
a product of selection by
humans rather than by
nature.

larger and more complex animals came only later. All this fitted with the idea of evolution.

The chances that an animal would be fossilized and the fossil then found were not very high. However, in some cases, there were enough fossils to show how one type had gradually developed from another. A whole series of fossils showed how horses had evolved from small doglike animals, how camels had evolved from much smaller ancestors, and how mammals had evolved from reptiles. During Darwin's lifetime, the "missing link" between reptiles and birds was discovered.

HMS Beagle
was the survey ship that carried
Charles Darwin on a five-year
voyage around the world.

■ *The Origin of Species*

Armed with this evidence, Darwin was convinced that evolution occurred. But to complete his theory, he needed an explanation of what made it happen. In the end he concluded that it took place through "natural selection" (p. 22). For natural selection to work, characteristics had to be passed on from parent to offspring in some way. Darwin did not know how this happened, but we now know that it is carried out by DNA, a complicated chemical (p. 15),

whose important role was discovered in the 1950s.

Darwin finally published his evidence and conclusions in *The Origin of Species*, which appeared in 1859. It caused considerable controversy. Darwin was very careful not to say much about human beings or how they originated, but it was clear that he thought they had evolved from the same ancestors as the apes. The Church attacked him vigorously, but in the end the sheer weight of his evidence won most people over.

■ Chemical evidence

In the twentieth century, more and more evidence has been found to support Darwin's theories. In particular, scientists have learned a lot from analyzing DNA. They have found that the DNA of all living things is basically the same, and it is translated into proteins by the same "genetic code." This shows beyond any doubt that all living things have evolved from a single common ancestor.

DNA can also be used to see how different animals and plants are related. This can be used to check family trees that have already been constructed by looking at other characteristics (p. 24). Except in a few rare cases, the DNA has produced the same family tree as that already formed by comparing anatomy (structural details). If Darwin were still alive today, he would have found it pleasing to be proved right so conclusively.

A tortoise
from the Galápagos — just one of
many species found there and
nowhere else.

Natural selection

A St. Bernard dog can weigh over 308 lb (140 kg), while a chihuahua often weighs less than 1 lb (0.5 kg). Yet both dogs — and the hundreds of recognized canine breeds — are descended from just *one* wild species, the gray wolf. All dog breeds were produced by humans. We repeatedly choose the "best" parents to produce puppies. Dogs are used for many different types of work, so "best" might mean long legs for speed or short legs for going down rabbit burrows (as in terriers).

Charles Darwin (pp. 20-21) was struck by the fact that artificial selection could change a wolf into a chihuahua. Could the same thing happen in nature, he wondered, but much more slowly? When Darwin read Malthus's ideas about population, he saw that it could.

■ DISCOVERY ■
Thomas Robert Malthus

The English clergyman and economist Thomas Robert Malthus (1766–1834) is best known for *An Essay on the Principle of Population* (1798). It argued that famine, disease, and war were necessary checks on the growth of population. Charles Darwin read the essay and saw that it applied to the whole living world, not just to humans. This meant that only a small number lived long enough to breed. In a flash of insight, Darwin saw how this led to "natural selection." The animals and plants that survived and had young would obviously be the ones best adapted to their way of life. In turn, they might pass on their winning characteristics to their young. This process could produce long legs in a horse and short legs in a weasel, in much the same way that dog breeders had produced long legs in an Afghan hound and short legs in a terrier.

■ You, the hunter

This board game shows, in a very simple way, how natural selection works. You are a predator hunting in a new area.

The small colored squares are your prey. All belong to the same species, but some have lighter coats (yellow squares), while others have darker coats (blue squares). You hunt at dusk, finding your prey by sight. You must make plenty of squares.

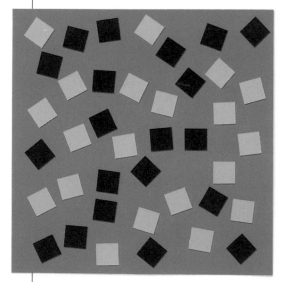

1 Because the prey have not been hunted by a predator like you before, the numbers with dark and light coats are roughly equal. Start with 20 of each. The lighter squares stand out more, so you always catch twice as many.

2 You begin to hunt, catching your prey at random, but always getting roughly twice as many light-coated (yellow) animals as dark-coated (blue) ones. The animals you have caught are taken off the board.

3 When the breeding season arrives, every pair of animals that is still alive will produce two young. Indicate this on the board by putting on two more blue squares for each pair of blue squares, and do the same for the yellow squares.

EXPERIMENT
The struggle for survival

Brine shrimps are small crustaceans whose eggs are used to feed aquarium fish. You can raise brine shrimps from their eggs and see what happens as they compete with each other for food in their miniature environment. Brine shrimp eggs can be bought from aquarium shops or pet stores.

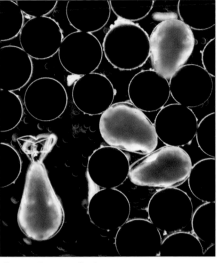

You Will Need
- *brine shrimp eggs* ● *sea salt*
- *tube of liquid fish food*

1 To start the culture, add 2 oz (50 g) of sea salt to 1 pt (500 ml) of warm water. Stir, cool, and add a few drops of fish food.

2 Sprinkle one level teaspoonful of eggs on the surface, and keep at a steady 70°F (21°C). The eggs should hatch in about two days.

A growing population
Using a hand lens, you will be able to see the young shrimps, called larvae (above), and then the adult shrimps as they appear. Once a day, stir the water, take out one teaspoonful, and estimate how many larvae or adult shrimps it contains. Do all the larvae grow into adults? What characteristics do you think would give a brine shrimp the best chance of surviving to lay eggs and produce young?

4 Again you move against your prey, catching more lighter-coated animals because of their high visibility. By now you, as the predator, are beginning to have some effect on your prey. What is happening to the lighter-coated animals?

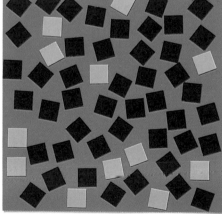

6 What has happened to the animals with lighter coats? Now try the game again, changing the rules each time. What happens if the survivors produce three young ones in each breeding season, for example, or even four?

5 Animals that have managed to survive reproduce again; add the blue and yellow squares. Notice that we are simplifying things by assuming that the young are all the same color as their parents. This is not always so (p. 48).

Classifying living things

IF YOU WATCH AND IDENTIFY BIRDS, you will know that there are distinct types, or species, with names like "house sparrow" and "common starling." Within a species, there are always small differences which natural selection (pp. 22-23) can work on. But on the whole, one male sparrow looks very like another.

When it comes to reproduction, the members of a species keep to themselves. You will never see a bird that is a cross between a sparrow and a starling, for example, because sparrows only mate with sparrows, and starlings with starlings. So, from a biological point of view, a species is a very important unit — in fact, it is the key to the way in which biologists classify the living world.

■ DISCOVERY ■
Carolus Linnaeus

Early naturalists tried to devise a system for naming species in a way that everyone could understand, regardless of their language. The scheme that biologists use today grew out of a system devised by the Swedish botanist Carolus Linnaeus (1707–1778). He used Latin names, and gave all animals and plants a two-part name, such as *Sturnus vulgaris* for the common starling. He used the two-part name for the same reason that people have surnames and first names: the surname shows what family they belong to, and the first name belongs to the individual. Scientific names for animals and plants work in the same way as the names of people, but the order is reversed, with the "surname" coming first. This surname covers a group of related species, known as a genus (the plural is genera). *Sturnus* is the genus to which all starlings belong, and *vulgaris* completes the name of one particular species in the genus — the common starling.

■ Classifying a tiger

When grouping related species, Linnaeus realized that a pattern kept repeating, with each group belonging to a larger group. He put related genera into families, families into orders, and orders into classes. A later scientist put classes into phyla, and phyla into kingdoms. This is the classification scheme for the tiger.

Kingdom — Animalia (Animals)	Many-celled organisms with no rigid cell walls, which cannot make their own food
Phylum — Chordata (Chordates)	Animals that have a single nerve cord at some time in their lives
Subphylum — Vertebrata (Vertebrates)	Chordates that have their nerve cord, encased within a backbone
Class — Mammalia (Mammals)	Vertebrates that suckle their young on milk and have a coat of fur or hair
Order — Carnivora (Carnivores)	Land mammals that have become specialized for hunting
Family — Felidae (Cats)	Carnivores with sharp front claws that can be retracted
Genus — Panthera	The five species of big cats — the lion, tiger, leopard, snow leopard, and jaguar
Species — Tigris (Tiger)	The tiger

Tiger
The diagram shows you how the classification scheme works for a single species — the tiger.

EXPERIMENT
Do-it-yourself classification

Imagine that Linnaeus had been more interested in do-it-yourself than in plants and animals. How would he have classified the objects shown here? You can try this experiment with any collection of everyday items: buttons, stamps, or pens and pencils. Arrange the objects into a "family tree" by deciding on characteristics that they have in common.

How to group the objects
All the objects here have first been grouped according to whether they are metal or plastic. The metal objects have then been divided into those with two parts and those with one, and then divided according to whether or not they have a screw thread. This scheme works, but it is only one way of classifying the objects. For example, how would you have classified a cup hook that had been partly covered in plastic?

Family trees in nature
There is only one right way to classify plants and animals, because they are actually all related. Correct classification reveals evolutionary relationships. This can be seen by comparing their DNA (pp. 14-15). The DNA of tigers is almost the same as that of lions (also in the genus Panthera), quite like that of other cats (family Felidae), similar to that of dogs and otters (order Carnivora), and so on.

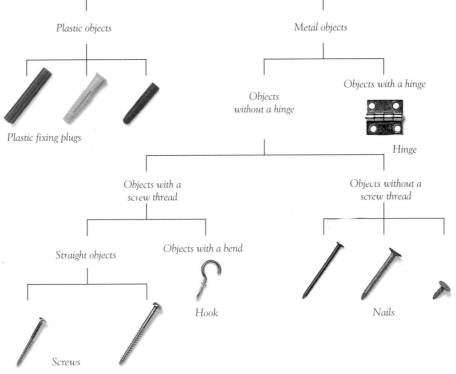

Plastic objects

Plastic fixing plugs

Metal objects

Objects without a hinge

Objects with a hinge

Hinge

Objects with a screw thread

Objects without a screw thread

Straight objects

Objects with a bend

Hook

Nails

Screws

■ Under the skin
You must look beyond the superficial when classifying, for animals that look the same may not be closely related. Dolphins have become streamlined like sharks, because swimming fast helps them catch prey. Their similar shapes are the result of "convergent evolution." Dolphins feed their young on milk, and breathe with lungs, telling us they are mammals. Sharks breathe with gills, showing they are fish.

Shark
A shark's fin may look very like a dolphin's flipper on the outside, but inside there are no bones, only long, stiff rods.

Dolphin
Inside a dolphin's flipper there are little bones arranged in rows, very much like your finger bones and those of all other mammals.

Bacteria, fungi, and plants

IT IS VERY EASY TO THINK of the living world as being made up of just two groups — plants and animals. But in fact, biologists think of it as being made up of at least five major groups, and perhaps as many as 20. These groups are known as "kingdoms" (p. 24). On the next four pages, you can find out something about these kingdoms of the natural world. You can also see where to look in this book to find out more about the living things that belong to each kingdom.

BACTERIAL KINGDOM
Bacteria

Bacteria are very tiny, single-celled organisms that are thought to be the most ancient forms of life on Earth. Their cells have a rigid cell wall, but are much simpler than those of plants and animals. Bacteria live in huge numbers in almost every habitat, including your body. Some are harmful, and can cause disease, but many others are useful to us.

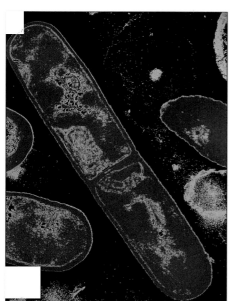

A dividing bacterium
The bacterium above has been photographed with an electron microscope, which can magnify many thousands of times. The bacterium is reproducing by splitting itself in two. In good conditions, it can do this every 20 minutes, so it soon becomes surrounded by enormous numbers of its offspring.

FUNGAL KINGDOM
Fungi

Fungi (pp. 64-69) live by absorbing food from other organisms that are alive, or from the remains of those that have died. Some look quite like plants, but they have a completely different way of life. Under a microscope, fungi look nothing like plants. They are made up of threads called hyphae, which have rigid walls. Like bacteria, fungi are very important in the natural world because they recycle the remains of other organisms.

Toadstools
Mushrooms and toadstools are the fruiting bodies that appear when some kinds of fungi reproduce.

Clump of fruiting bodies (toadstools)

Lichens
A lichen (p. 63) is a partnership between two organisms — a fungus and an alga.

Lichen growing on rock

PLANT KINGDOM
1: Nonvascular plants

All members of the plant kingdom can make their own food with the help of sunlight (pp. 38-43). They have complex cells, with rigid cell walls made up of cellulose.

The earliest plants evolved in water, and were "nonvascular." This means

Tough, leathery frond

Mound made up of many moss plants

Mosses
These are close relatives of the liverworts. There are 14,000 species of mosses. Many mosses (p. 63) form cushion-shaped clumps, and they often grow in damp places.

PLANT KINGDOM
2: Vascular plants

Vascular plants have true leaves and roots, and special channels in their stems that carry water and other substances through the plant. These channels allow a tree to absorb water through its roots, and send it up far above the ground to its leaves. The same system lets a potato plant make food in its leaves and store it in potato tubers underground. Of all the vascular plants, one group — the flowering plants — now dominates the Earth. Like many other animals, we rely on these for much of our food.

that they did not have special channels for carrying water or nutrients from one part of the plant to another. Most of their present-day relatives — which include algae, mosses, and liverworts — grow only where it is wet. Non-vascular plants do not have flowers.

Algae
Seaweeds (pp. 96-97) are the largest members of this group of about 25,000 species. Most grow on rocks; some drift in the sea. Other algae grow in ponds and lakes.

Rubbery, stemlike "stipe"

Liverworts
Some liverworts (p. 63) look very much like the first plants that adapted to life on land. There are about 9,000 species, and they grow only in damp places, such as the banks of streams.

Plant branches in two as it grows

Ferns
Ferns (pp. 62-63) have green fronds, which uncoil as they grow. Most of the 10,000 species of ferns alive today are low-growing, but some tropical ones form small trees.

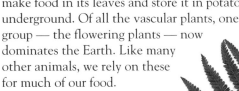

Frond divided into leaflets

Stem

Conifers
The distinctive trees whose seeds grow inside protective cones are called conifers (p. 51). Their leaves are usually tough, shaped like needles or flat scales. Unlike most ferns and horsetails, they are good at surviving if water is in short supply.

"Monocot" flowering plant
Grasses are all "monocots." Their seeds have one seed leaf, and their leaves have parallel veins.

Leaflets

Horsetails
At one time, the ancestors of the horsetails (p. 63) grew into stately trees. Today, horsetails are rarely more than 3 ft (1 m) tall. The best places to see them are patches of damp ground.

Hollow stem

Flowering plants
Flowers (pp. 46-49) have evolved into very many shapes, sizes, and colors. Botanists divide the 250,000 species of flowering plants into two major groups, the monocotyledons and dicotyledons — or "monocots" and "dicots," for short.

"Dicot" flowering plant
This cranesbill is a typical "dicot." Its seeds have two seed leaves (pp. 52-53), and its leaves have branched veins.

Leaves with branched veins

Leaves with parallel veins

Seed head

Protists and animals

PROTISTS ARE SINGLE-CELLED creatures that either eat particles of food or make food by using sunlight. In the past, some protists were classified as animals or plants. Today, most biologists put protists in their own kingdom.

True animals are made up of many cells. Their cells do not have rigid cases, like those of plants, and so they are free to change shape. This has enabled animals to evolve muscles, which they can use to move in search of food. However, not all animals move about. Some, such as corals and barnacles, sit still and wait for food to come to them.

PROTIST KINGDOM
Protists or single-celled organisms

Biologists use the protist kingdom as a "throwaway category" for everything that does not fit anywhere else. It contains any single-celled creature with a complex cell that is clearly not a yeast (p. 67) or an alga. Putting protists in kingdoms of their own would make classification very complicated.

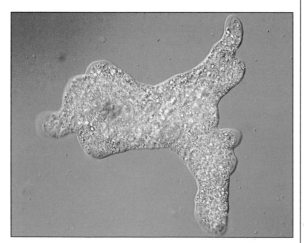

Forever changing
An amoeba is a protist that has no fixed shape. It can flow in any direction, and it uses its body to engulf its food. The amoeba's single cell is quite complex and has many organelles.

ANIMAL KINGDOM
1: Invertebrate animals

Most of the world's animals are "invertebrates," a word that means "without a backbone." Invertebrates range from very simple animals to agile and intelligent predators. There are over 30 phyla or groups of invertebrates. Here we show some animals from five of the phyla — cnidarians, arthropods, annelids, echinoderms, and mollusks.

Sea anemone

Annelids
There are nearly 9,000 species of annelids, or segmented worms, such as the earthworm (pp. 124-125). Annelids do not have a skeleton. They move by stretching and then contracting.

Garden snail

Cnidarians
This phylum includes the corals (pp. 94-95), jellyfish, and sea anemones (p. 93). There are about 9,000 species, all of which live in water. They all have a ring of tentacles around the mouth, armed with stinging cells.

Arthropods
The arthropods make up a huge phylum containing perhaps 10 million species. They live in water and on land. All have jointed limbs, and some — the insects — have wings. The insects make up the largest class of arthropods, followed by the arachnids and crustaceans.

Crustaceans, such as crabs and lobsters, have exoskeletons hardened by calcium carbonate. Wood lice are among the few crustaceans that live on land

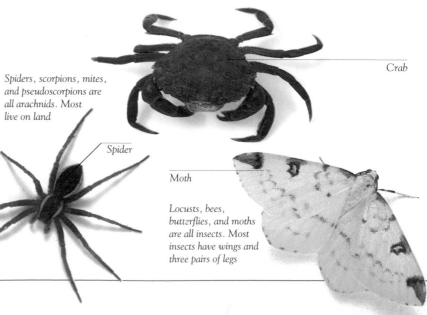

Spiders, scorpions, mites, and pseudoscorpions are all arachnids. Most live on land

Spider

Crab

Moth

Locusts, bees, butterflies, and moths are all insects. Most insects have wings and three pairs of legs

ANIMAL KINGDOM
2: Vertebrate animals

There are about 45,000 species of vertebrates, including humans. Unlike invertebrates, we have a backbone or vertebral column, and a skeleton that lies inside the body, rather than around it, as with insects and crustaceans. Vertebrates have keen senses and, in general, a large brain. This forms part of the well-developed nervous system that is needed to process information from the sense organs. Vertebrate groups include fish, amphibians, reptiles, birds, and mammals.

Earthworm

Fish
These divide into bony and cartilaginous groups. There are more species of bony fishes (pp. 82-83) than all other vertebrates put together.

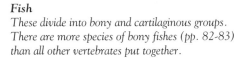

Yellow cichlid

Bony fish such as the yellow cichlid have evolved into a great variety of shapes and sizes. Their bodies are streamlined and covered with scales

Dogfish

Sharks, rays, and dogfish belong to an ancient group of vertebrates, each with a skeleton made up of rubbery cartilage rather than bone

Mollusks
Most mollusks (pp. 90-91) live in water, but some, such as snails (pp. 116-117), live on land. Many of the 110,000 species can be recognized by the hard shells that protect their bodies.

Amphibians
There are about 2,500 species of amphibians. This group includes frogs, toads (pp. 80-81), salamanders, and newts (pp. 78-79). They can live on land and in water. Their young are called tadpoles, and they change gradually into the adult shape.

Toad

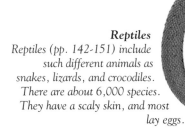

Echinoderms
This phylum includes starfish (p. 87) and sea urchins. These animals have a skeleton, or "test," made of calcium carbonate. Their bodies are sometimes made up of five identical parts.

Reptiles
Reptiles (pp. 142-151) include such different animals as snakes, lizards, and crocodiles. There are about 6,000 species. They have a scaly skin, and most lay eggs.

Tiger

Grass snake

Mammals
Mammals (pp. 152-179) are "warm-blooded" animals that feed their young on milk. Of the 4,000 species, all give birth to live young, except three species that lay eggs (p. 177).

Owl

Birds
All birds (pp. 126-141) have wings, and most of them can fly. All have feathers and a beak, but no teeth. There are over 8,500 species of birds.

Starfish

ECOLOGY

ECOLOGY IS THE STUDY of the complex interactions that make up our living planet. It is rapidly becoming one of the most important branches of biology, because only by understanding how plants and animals depend on each other and on their environment can we help them to survive in our changing world.

Tropical rain forest —
a spectacular example of a mature ecological "community."

In the 1950s, a rabbit disease called myxomatosis swept across Great Britain. As the number of rabbits plummeted, the grass that they had once nibbled short began to grow lush and tall. The ground's surface temperature fell — just slightly — because the tall grass screened more of the sunshine. This small drop in temperature was enough to create problems for a particular species of ant, one that relied on the warmth of the rabbit-nibbled turf. As time went by, the ant started to disappear. As it declined, so too did a particularly beautiful species of butterfly — the large blue. The large blue's caterpillar feeds not on leaves, but on the grubs of this one species of ant. It has come to look so much like an ant grub itself that the ants are tricked into carrying it into their nests, where it devours their offspring. Without the ants, the caterpillar cannot survive, so by the late 1970s the butterfly had become extinct in Great Britain.

This complex set of relationships, in which one organism is linked to another and then another, is an example of what ecology is all about. The term "ecology" was coined in 1869 by the German naturalist Ernst Haeckel (1834–1919). It is based on a Greek word for house, and Haeckel used it to mean the study of the "house," or position, of an organism in the complicated web of life.

Ernst Haeckel
realized the importance of studying the links between living things.

■ Biosphere, ecosystems, and habitats

The living world as a whole is known as the biosphere. Almost every part of the biosphere interacts, directly or indirectly, with every other. But the whole biosphere is so vast and complex that these interactions are impossible to study together. To make any sense of the living world, ecologists must divide it into smaller units with a particular set of plants and animals, such as lowland tropical rain forest, dry eucalyptus woodland, or northern pine-spruce forest. These they call ecosystems.

Even ecosystems are very large — in some parts of the world, for example, the same type of forest may stretch for hundreds of miles. To investigate what goes on in an ecosystem, ecologists look at the small part of it that is used by just a few dominant species. This is known as a habitat.

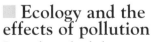

Tadpoles live
in water, frogs and toads mainly on land — an example of how a species can live in two different habitats.

■ The flow of food

The links between grass and rabbits and other animals — or any collection of organisms in an ecosystem — can be summed up by a food chain or food web (pp. 34-35). Working out food chains and webs is one of the first steps in studying an ecosystem.

Food chains show how energy (pp. 34-35) is passed from one living thing to another. But energy is only part of the story. Plants and animals also need nutrients such as nitrogen and phosphorus. These are passed from one organism to another as well. In the case of nitrogen, fresh supplies also come from the atmosphere. Nitrogen gas in the air is useless to plants and animals, but some bacteria can take this nitrogen and turn it into ammonia and then nitrates — nitrogen-containing chemicals that plants use for nourishment.

Interactions like this are far more important to us than you might think. Farmers depend on nitrates to grow their crops, and so it is vital for us to know what happens to such nutrients.

■ Ecology and the effects of pollution

By studying food chains, ecologists have been able to show exactly how pollution affects wildlife. For example, they have explained some of the puzzling effects of pollution in the sea. Mammals such as seals and dolphins have been found with very high levels of mercury and other poisons in their bodies, far higher than the other animals in the sea. We now know that this is the result of their being the "top predator" (p. 35), at the end of the food chain.

Ecologists have discovered that a warm-blooded animal uses up to 90 percent of its food on staying alive and moving about. Only 10 percent goes to fuel the animal's own growth. If a seal eats a fish containing a milligram of mercury, it retains most of that mercury because it cannot easily get rid of it. But the amount of weight it puts on is only a tenth of the fish's weight. So the mercury becomes far more concentrated in the seal than it was in the fish.

Unfortunately, this happens all along the food chain, so the fish eaten by the seal already contains a high level of mercury. This is called bioaccumulation, and it also occurs with some pesticides, such as DDT and dieldrin.

■ Ecological succession

Most farmland was originally forest. If it is abandoned, it gradually turns back into forest once again. First weeds cover the plowed fields, then grass takes over and grows very tall. Small bushes and young trees spring up in the grass, and in time they shade it out, causing it to die back. Eventually the growing trees shade out smaller bushes and establish

A quadrat enables you to make an ecological map of the plant life in a specific area.

Tracking animals is a way of seeing how they use the world around them.

themselves as a forest. This whole process is called ecological succession (p. 32). The point at which succession stops — in this case, forest — is called the climax vegetation.

Ecologists study succession in many different ecosystems, and it is easy to see it for yourself on a patch of bare ground or in a small lake. Over the years, water plants such as cattails grow well in the shallower parts of a lake, building up a great mass of roots under the water. Soil and silt get caught around these roots, and eventually fill the lake, which then becomes marshland. Water plants die out as young trees take over, and the marsh turns into swampy woodland.

In nature, succession occurs in lakes, or anywhere that new bare ground is created. Sometimes, it happens on a much larger scale. In 1980, the eruption of Mount St. Helens in Washington State wiped out plants and animals over hundreds of square miles. This created a huge natural laboratory in which ecologists are now able to study succession on a gigantic scale.

Lichens on a rock — a habitat that is perfect for some organisms can be useless for others.

■ Ecology and the forever–changing world

Human activities make it important for us to understand how plants and animals cope with changes in their environment. Bare land is

regularly created by farming, logging, and building. In most cases, succession produces the same sort of vegetation as before, but sometimes this does not happen. In these cases, ecologists try to find out why not.

When large areas of tropical rain forest are completely cleared, intricate relationships between plants and animals are destroyed and may never be reestablished. A great many rain-forest trees depend on fungi that live on and around their roots, supplying them with nutrients. Without the fungi, the trees cannot always grow in the same place again, and clear-cutting the forest may kill off these fungi.

Even where the forest is not clear-cut, animal life can suffer. In Southeast Asia, there are many fruit-eating birds and bats. Although these animals take many different kinds of fruit, figs are vital for their survival because they bear the heaviest crops. The largest fig plants use the tallest timber trees for support, and so logging, even if it is selective, reduces the number of figs, which in turn reduces the number of fruit-eaters. Since these animals are essential for dispersing the seeds of rain-forest plants, the whole forest suffers.

By discovering more about the ecology of tropical rain forests, ecologists can help conservation in partnership with the local inhabitants. They can work out methods of logging that do the minimum of damage and devise methods of replanting already-cleared areas.

A ring attached to a bird's leg lets scientists monitor the way a bird lives in its natural habitat.

Surveying the plant scene

THERE ARE MORE THAN half a million plant species in the world, and each is adapted to a particular set of environmental conditions. If you look at an individual habitat — such as a meadow, a coastal salt marsh, or a forest floor — you will see that it has its own characteristic kinds of plants. Plants that grow together in a habitat make up an ecological "community." Like animals, plants compete with each other to survive. If you watch a patch of newly cleared ground, you can see how the earliest plants to arrive are gradually "shaded out" by species that grow more slowly but eventually become taller. This process is known as succession.

Making a quadrat survey

A quadrat is a device that is used to mark out a patch of ground, so that you can map the plants growing on it very precisely. Botanical quadrats are usually about 3 ft (1 m) square. Smaller quadrats are more manageable, although they do not enclose so many plants.

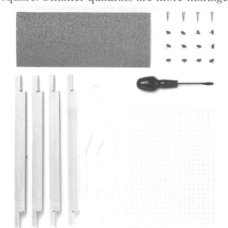

YOU WILL NEED
- *thumbtacks*
- *sandpaper*
- *screwdriver*
- *screws* • *string*
- *squared paper*
- *ruler* • *pencil*
- *4 identical pieces of wood, cut as shown*

Making a transect survey

A transect survey is a cross-section study. It enables you to record the different plants growing along a straight line marked out over the ground. Unlike a quadrat survey, which is limited to a small patch, a transect survey can cross many different types of ground. You can use it, for example, to see how the vegetation changes as you move from the damp ground around a lake to the shade of an adjoining wood.

Tightly stretched string marks transect line

Wooden pole driven into ground to hold string

YOU WILL NEED
- *2 wooden poles* • *strong string* • *squared paper* • *tape measure*

1 Assemble and screw the pieces of wood together to form a square frame. Using a ruler and pencil, divide each side into quarters.

2 Stretch pieces of string tightly across the frame at the quarter marks, and fix them with the thumbtacks, dividing the frame into 16 small squares.

3 Go to your chosen habitat, and throw the quadrat over your shoulder. Record the plants in each square, using the squared paper to make a quadrat map.

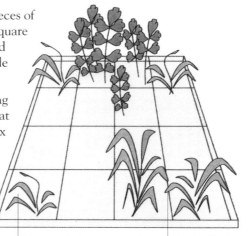

Map records the plants in each small square of the quadrat

Quadrat divides the plants into measured squares

Quadrat map
A plant map drawn with the aid of a quadrat will help you to appreciate the variety of plant life in one habitat. Try mapping a number of different habitats, and see which one has the most plant species.

1 Drive the poles firmly into the ground, and stretch the string between them, tying it securely. Make sure that the string is accessible all the way along.

2 Work your way along the string, recording the position and height of plants growing beneath it. You can then use the squared paper to make a record of the survey.

Transect map
Your finished survey will show how plants vary along the survey line, both in species and in height. If you carry out a transect survey in the same place at different times of the year, you can see how the plants grow upward as they compete with each other for light. The real competition begins in spring, when foliage appears that deprives smaller plants of light.

Height and position of plants beneath line is recorded

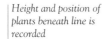

Height of transect string

Squares show position along string

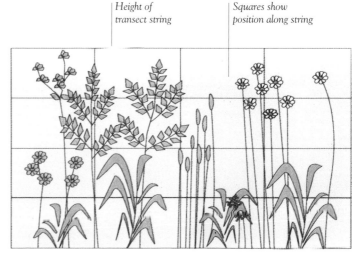

Food chains

IN ANY ECOSYSTEM —- from deserts to coral reefs — energy is constantly passed from organism to organism. Plants harness energy from the Sun (p. 40), and this energy supports the animals that eat the plants, as well as predators that feed on those animals. A "food chain" is a way of showing what eats what in a habitat, and therefore where the energy goes. Food chains can be thought of in layers. At the bottom are the "primary producers," the plants that make their own food. Plants feed "primary consumers," or plant-eating animals. These in turn feed predators, known as "secondary consumers." The dead remains of plants and animals provide food for "decomposers", organisms such as bacteria, fungi, and earthworms.

Leaves provide food for many small animals

Tree top community
A tree such as an oak forms the basis of a complex food web. Many of the organisms in the web are insects, as you can discover by using a beater tray.

Giving birth
This female aphid is giving birth to a live baby aphid — something you can see easily with the aid of a hand lens. In early summer, a female aphid can produce a baby every few hours, and soon becomes surrounded by her offspring. Aphids are "primary consumers", meaning that they feed directly on plants. Primary consumers are always more numerous than the animals that prey on them.

Making a beater tray

Most of the small animals that live on plants are difficult to spot. By using a beater tray, you can bring them into the open. The tray is made of white fabric stretched over a wooden frame.

YOU WILL NEED
● *wooden frame (pp. 32-33)* ● *square of white fabric* ● *thumbtacks* ● *stick*

1 THE FRAME USED HERE is the same as for the quadrat. Once you have assembled the frame, stretch the fabric tightly across and pin it in place.

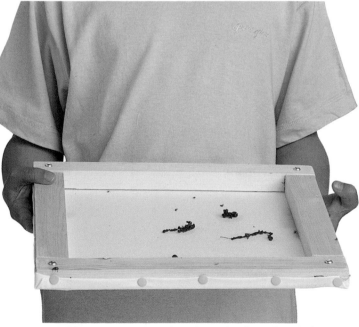

2 HOLD THE TRAY under a branch, then sharply hit the branch with a stick. Animal life comes tumbling out into the tray, and the frame stops any crawlers from escaping.

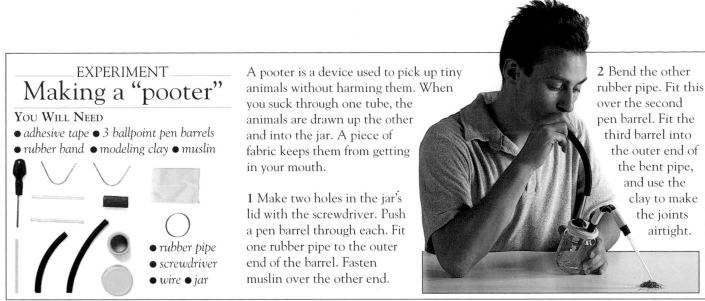

EXPERIMENT
Making a "pooter"

YOU WILL NEED
- adhesive tape ● 3 ballpoint pen barrels
- rubber band ● modeling clay ● muslin

- rubber pipe
- screwdriver
- wire ● jar

A pooter is a device used to pick up tiny animals without harming them. When you suck through one tube, the animals are drawn up the other and into the jar. A piece of fabric keeps them from getting in your mouth.

1 Make two holes in the jar's lid with the screwdriver. Push a pen barrel through each. Fit one rubber pipe to the outer end of the barrel. Fasten muslin over the other end.

2 Bend the other rubber pipe. Fit this over the second pen barrel. Fit the third barrel into the outer end of the bent pipe, and use the clay to make the joints airtight.

■ A forest food web

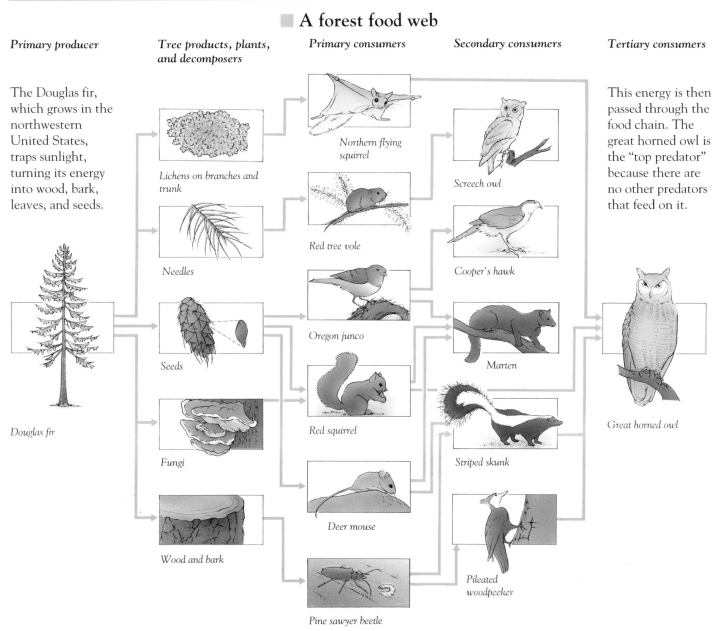

Primary producer

The Douglas fir, which grows in the northwestern United States, traps sunlight, turning its energy into wood, bark, leaves, and seeds.

Douglas fir

Tree products, plants, and decomposers

Lichens on branches and trunk

Needles

Seeds

Fungi

Wood and bark

Primary consumers

Northern flying squirrel

Red tree vole

Oregon junco

Red squirrel

Deer mouse

Pine sawyer beetle

Secondary consumers

Screech owl

Cooper's hawk

Marten

Striped skunk

Pileated woodpecker

Tertiary consumers

This energy is then passed through the food chain. The great horned owl is the "top predator" because there are no other predators that feed on it.

Great horned owl

The world of PLANTS and FUNGI

The beauty of plants and fungi
Much of the fascination of plants and fungi lies in their colors and shapes. These are all around us — for instance, in autumn leaves (above) as well as in rarer species, such as the strange fruiting body of the star stinkhorn (left), a fungus that lives on the remains of plants in Central America.

PLANTS ARE THE FOUNDATION STONE OF LIFE ON EARTH. They capture energy from our star — the Sun — and use it to build up leaves, stems, and roots, creating a green mantle that covers much of our planet. Plants are not the only living things that can use sunlight in this way, but they are by far the most successful. Without plants, many other living things, including humans, could not exist.

FLOWERING PLANTS

THE DOMINANT PLANTS on Earth today are the flowering plants. They first appeared over 100 million years ago, and since then have evolved hand-in-hand with the insects that carry their pollen from one flower to another. Flowering plants now have a bewildering variety of shapes, and live on almost every habitat on land, except where it is very cold.

People who care about the environment are often called "greens," or said to be part of the "green movement." This is because when we think of the living world, we automatically think of green, the color of almost all plants. The "chlorophyll movement" might not be such a catchy name, but it would do just as well, because the pigment that makes the plants green is chlorophyll. The "not-red-or-blue movement" is even less catchy, but that would be accurate too. Chlorophyll looks green to us because it absorbs blue light and red light, only reflecting the green parts of the color spectrum. (The spectrum is the total range of colors in the light coming from the sun — you can see them when a rainbow is formed.) Forests and meadows are green because this is the sort of light that plants make the least use of.

Boil a leaf
in alcohol — with adult supervision — and then test it for starch.

■ Living on light

All plants — including those with flowers and those without — use the red and blue parts of the spectrum to make their food. They do this in a process called photosynthesis (pp. 40-43). If you were a plant, and you felt hungry, you could stand in the Sun for a while, and, with water and carbon dioxide, your hunger would be completely satisfied.

The leaves of a plant are the main place where photosynthesis occurs.

They make sugars which are carried to the other parts, such as the roots, and flowers, in the sap, which is like a watery syrup. Sap flows through a plant rather like blood flowing through our bodies, except that there is no pump like the heart to push it along. Aphids feed on sap by tapping into the plant's "veins." They do not even need to suck, because the sap is under pressure inside the plant. When the aphid pierces a hole in the plant, the sap spurts into its mouth.

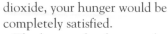

Cranebills
scatter their seeds by miniature catapults.

■ A successful group

Flowering plants are extraordinarily abundant — more so than you may realize, for many plants with inconspicuous flowers, such as grasses and broadleaved trees, actually belong to this highly successful group.

The tiniest flowering plant of all is a duckweed called *Wolffia arrhiza*. It floats on the surface of lakes, and each rounded, rootless plant is just about $1/100$ in (0.3 mm) across — only just big enough to be seen with the naked eye. Its flowers

Carnivorous
plants eat insects.

are even more minute, and develop in pockets on the surface of the plant.

Wolffia could hardly be more different from the 18,000 or so orchids that make up one of the largest families of flowering plants. Orchids are among the most highly evolved of all flowering plants, and often have flowers with bizarre, sculpted shapes. Some are tiny but strong-smelling; others are large with spectacular petals. Orchids have these forms in order to attract their pollinators. Many rely on just one species of insect for their survival, and their flowers have become elaborate lures to make sure that the right insect finds them. Botanists are still discovering new species of these extraordinary plants, and in many cases, the identity of their insect partners is still a mystery to us.

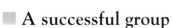

A plant's structure
helps to identify which family it belongs to.

■ How pollination has gradually evolved

The earliest flowers were large, simple structures, rather like those of the present-day tulip tree (p. 51), or of magnolias. The animals that pollinated these flowers were probably beetles. They landed on the flowers to eat their pollen, but in doing so, they also carried some of it from one flower to another. Later, flowers developed sugary nectar as a food for their pollinators, and they evolved partnerships with other insects that were more reliable pollinators than beetles. Among these were the ancestors of the bees, wasps, butterflies, and moths — insects that rely very heavily on nectar for their food. Some, particularly the bees, still feed on pollen as well, but they leave enough for the plant's own use.

■ Pollination

In the course of evolution, some flowering plants gave up their animal pollinators and found other means of pollination. Most of these use the wind to carry their pollen around, although a few pond plants, such as hornwort, rely on water. Wind-pollinated plants often have small green flowers — as you might expect, since they no longer need to catch the eye of passing insects. Grasses are the most common of these plants, but many trees are also wind-pollinated. Some produce their flowers in long dangling structures that are called catkins. When the wind blows, the catkins shake, and help to disperse the pollen.

Because wind pollination is a rather risky business, these plants have to produce a huge amount of pollen to ensure that some of it finds the right target. The pollen is also very light, which helps it become airborne. As a result, plants like these fill the air with their pollen during the flowering season, and there are large amounts in the air you inhale. If you are susceptible to hay fever, it is the wind-pollinated plants, such as grasses and ragwort in North America, that will make you

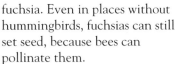

You can identify the food that plants make in their leaves by testing them with iodine.

Growing a seed in a glass lets you see how a flowering plant begins its life.

sneeze — one ragwort plant can release at least one billion pollen grains in an hour.

■ Birds and bees

A few flowering plants are pollinated by larger animals, mostly birds and bats. Such plants are only found in the tropics and subtropics, because there has to be a generous year-round supply of nectar to keep these heavyweight pollinators going. One group of bird-pollinated plants that you may see are the fuchsias, many of which will grow in quite cool climates. South America is their native land, and they are pollinated there by hummingbirds, which hover below the flowers and poke their beaks up into the bell-shaped center of the fuchsia. Even in places without hummingbirds, fuchsias can still set seed, because bees can pollinate them.

Most bird-pollinated flowers are orange, red, or yellow, although a few are other colors, including pink and blue. They have no scent, since few birds have a good sense of smell. Their flowers are large and often very tough, because birds' beaks and claws could easily damage them. Some flowers provide a perch for birds, but the ones that attract hummingbirds have no need to do this because the tiny hummingbirds can hover in front of the flower.

Making chromatograms lets you separate the pigments in leaves and flowers.

■ Pollination by other mammals

Bat-pollinated flowers rely on their large, pale petals, and their scent, to attract bats. But these are not the sort of scents that we use for perfume or soap. Bats seem to like musty or rank smells, and the flowers they feed at release some powerful and unpleasant odors. Bats tend to pollinate flowers on trees and large plants. This is because the flowers are usually prominently positioned, and bats can find them without having to fly among dense foliage, where they might damage their delicate wings.

Bat-pollinated rainforest trees often develop their flowers on the trunks. This means that the bats can fly through the forest below the level of leaves and branches. One rainforest creeper, growing among the branches, sends out its flowers on stalks up to 65 ft (20 m) long, so that they hang down among the tree trunks, just 5 ft (1.5 m) from the forest floor. The agave, a spiky desert plant, produces its blooms on long stems, so that they are held about 20 ft (6 m) above the ground, well away from rough-edged leaves.

Apart from bats, few other mammals act as regular pollinators. But in Australia, the honey possum feasts on the pollen and nectar of the large-flowered banksias. This tiny shrewlike marsupial, only 4 in (10 cm) long, has a tongue that can stick out as far as those of most humans, 1 in (2.5 cm) beyond its nose. Its long, slender tongue has a bristly tip, like that of a hummingbird.

You can grow plants from seeds found in the mud on your shoes.

A collection of plants can be grown from seeds that are found on a muddy path.

How plants make food 1

THE SUN BOMBARDS THE EARTH with energy. About 99 percent is absorbed by the oceans or land, or is reflected into space. The remaining 1 percent is absorbed by plant's leaves.

Plants are unique among living things in being able to make their own food. Their leaves act like solar panels. Using a chemical called chlorophyll, they gather the Sun's energy and set it to work in the process known as photosynthesis. This process uses light, water, and carbon dioxide to build up, or "synthesize," important substances for plant life. It is like the reverse of eating a meal. When you eat, you take in food and break it down to provide energy for your body. In photosynthesis, a plant takes in energy and uses it to make food. The food can be stored and then broken down to provide energy for growth.

A green mantle
The lush green color of this tropical rain forest is created by the chlorophyll in leaves. The combination of strong sunlight, warmth, and a damp atmosphere helps to provide ideal conditions for photosynthesis and growth.

EXPERIMENT
Plant pigments

Adult supervision is advised for this experiment

Make a series of chromatograms to see the many colored pigments in plants.

YOU WILL NEED
● *plants* ● *glasses* ● *acetone (nail varnish remover)* ● *scissors* ● *pencils* ● *stapler* ● *blotting paper* ● *pestle and mortar*

1 COLLECT SOME PLANTS. In a well-ventilated room, put them in a mortar and add 4 teaspoons (20 ml) of acetone. Grind the ingredients with the pestle until they become semi-liquid. Pour the mixture into a glass. Staple a strip of blotting paper around a pencil, and position it so that $1/_2$ in (1 cm) is in the acetone. Leave for one hour.

2 THE ACETONE, together with the various plant pigments, will be drawn up the blotting paper, forming a chromatogram. Remove the paper, and let it dry. Each pigment will have traveled a different distance, forming a separate band of color. Repeat the experiment with different plants.

EXPERIMENT
A gas from plants

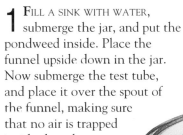

Adult supervision is advised for this experiment
When leaves carry out photosynthesis, they give off a gas. This gas usually passes unseen into the atmosphere. However, when underwater plants are placed in the light, the gas bubbles up from their leaves. You can collect and identify this gas.

YOU WILL NEED
● test tube ● jar
● wide-necked
funnel ● wooden
splints ● pondweed

1 FILL A SINK WITH WATER, submerge the jar, and put the pondweed inside. Place the funnel upside down in the jar. Now submerge the test tube, and place it over the spout of the funnel, making sure that no air is trapped inside the tube.

2 LET THE WATER out of the sink. Pour a little water out of the jar, and then place the assembled equipment on a sunny windowsill. The pondweed will start to photosynthesize, producing bubbles of gas which collect in the tube.

Gas produced by plant collects in tube

3 WHEN THE TUBE is half filled with gas, light a wooden splint and then blow it out. Pick up the tube, and insert the glowing end of the splint into it. The splint will suddenly burst into flame again, showing that the gas in the tube is pure oxygen. Now try the same test with a tube containing ordinary air, and compare the results.

How plants make food 2

DURING PHOTOSYNTHESIS, plants "fix" carbon from the carbon dioxide in air, meaning that they lock it up in energy-rich substances such as glucose and starch. Taken together, the Earth's living plants represent a huge store of carbon, which plant-eating animals use as a food source.

Carbon dioxide gets into a plant through tiny pores, called stomata, on the undersurface of the leaves. The other raw material needed for photosynthesis — water — travels up a plant's stem and across the leaves in tiny veins. The cells just under the surface of the leaf are packed with tiny green discs called chloroplasts. These are full of chlorophyll, and it is here that the first steps of photosynthesis are carried out.

EXPERIMENT
Testing a potato for starch

By means of photosynthesis in its leaves, a potato plant produces glucose (a sugar), which is converted into starch. Much of this starch is stored underground in swollen areas known as tubers. This experiment shows that a potato tuber is largely made up of starch.

YOU WILL NEED
● *iodine* ● *dropper* ● *potato*

Slice the potato in half, and put a few drops of iodine onto the cut surface. The iodine will change from orange-yellow to blue-black, showing that the potato contains starch. If you cut a thin slice off the potato and look at it under a microscope, the starch will show up as tiny oval grains.

■ Photosynthesis at work

Photosynthesis uses simple raw materials — carbon dioxide and water. It combines them to form glucose, and oxygen is given off as a by-product. This simple-sounding process is actually a complicated chain of many different chemical reactions. Only the first step uses chlorophyll, and has to take place in daylight. The reactions that use the energy captured by chlorophyll to build up glucose can take place in the dark.

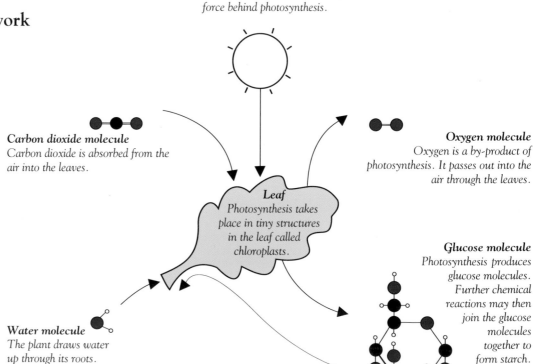

Sunlight
Energy from the Sun is the driving force behind photosynthesis.

Carbon dioxide molecule
Carbon dioxide is absorbed from the air into the leaves.

Oxygen molecule
Oxygen is a by-product of photosynthesis. It passes out into the air through the leaves.

Leaf
Photosynthesis takes place in tiny structures in the leaf called chloroplasts.

Glucose molecule
Photosynthesis produces glucose molecules. Further chemical reactions may then join the glucose molecules together to form starch.

Water molecule
The plant draws water up through its roots.

● Oxygen atom

● Carbon atom

○ Hydrogen atom

EXPERIMENT
Leaves in light and dark

Adult supervision is advised for this experiment
This experiment lets you compare the effects of keeping the leaves of a living plant in sunlight and in darkness.

Leaf wrapped in black plastic to exclude the light

YOU WILL NEED
- pan ● dropper
- heat-resistant beaker ● black plastic ● tape
- alcohol
- scissors ● petri dish ● tweezers

1 WRAP SOME OF A PLANT'S LEAVES in black plastic so that no light can get through. Now place the plant on a windowsill, and leave it for two days. When this time is up, pick two leaves — one that has been in the light, and one that has been covered — and carry out steps 2 and 3.

2 POUR ABOUT $3\frac{1}{2}$ FL OZ (100 ml) of alcohol into a heat-proof beaker. Stand this in a pan of water, and heat until the alcohol boils. Take the pan and beaker off the heat. With the tweezers, drop each leaf into the hot water for one minute, and then into the beaker. Leave until they are almost white.

3 PUT EACH LEAF into a petri dish or saucer, and add some iodine. The covered leaf does not contain starch, so the iodine will not change its color. The leaf that was exposed to light turns blue-black when iodine is added, showing that photosynthesis takes place (and produces starch) only in light.

Normal leaf
The green color is produced by the chlorophyll.

Leaf kept in dark
Iodine solution stains the leaf orange-yellow.

Leaf in light
Iodine solution stains the leaf blue-black.

Growth and movement

UNLIKE MOST ANIMALS, plants grow throughout their lives. Growth not only makes them bigger but it also allows them to move. Plants cannot shift from place to place, but they can react to the world around them. Their stems grow upward toward the light, and their roots grow downward into the ground. Some plants grow around others or catch hold of them, using slender leaves known as tendrils.

These special kinds of movement in response to outside conditions are called tropisms. They are caused when cells grow at different rates or when some cells rapidly swell up or collapse. If a plant grows in the open, for example, all the tips of its stems receive the same amount of light and grow at the same speed. But if one side of a stem is shaded, the stem has to bend toward the light. This bending movement is called phototropism.

Hanging on
You can test a plant's "sense of touch" by growing one that produces tendrils. Peas, cucumbers, and passion flowers are good plants to use. As the plant grows, its tendrils spread out until they come into contact with something solid.

The tip of the tendril winds around the object, and the rest of the tendril then coils up, pulling the plant toward the support. If you stroke a young tendril's tip with a pencil, you can see it start to bend. This response is called haptotropism.

■ Springing a trap

The Venus flytrap is a plant that can move fast to catch insects. The ends of its leaves are modified into pairs of pads that are joined at the base as if hinged, and are normally held apart. Each pad has a number of sensitive hairs. When an insect lands on one of the pads, it brushes against its hairs. The movement of the hairs makes cells in the "hinge" lose water and collapse. The pads then snap shut, just like a mousetrap, and the insect is imprisoned. Venus flytraps grow in the southeast United States, usually in swampy ground that is poor in minerals, and so lacks food for plants. By catching insects and digesting the soft parts of their bodies, they are able to survive in poor soil.

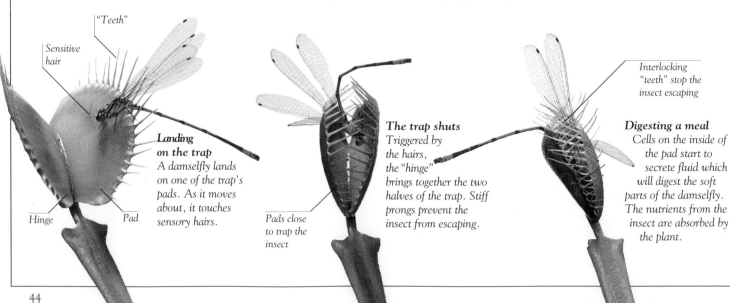

"Teeth"

Sensitive hair

Hinge   Pad

Landing on the trap
A damselfly lands on one of the trap's pads. As it moves about, it touches sensory hairs.

Pads close to trap the insect

The trap shuts
Triggered by the hairs, the "hinge" brings together the two halves of the trap. Stiff prongs prevent the insect from escaping.

Interlocking "teeth" stop the insect escaping

Digesting a meal
Cells on the inside of the pad start to secrete fluid which will digest the soft parts of the damselfly. The nutrients from the insect are absorbed by the plant.

EXPERIMENT
Searching for light

Most plants need light to live. They search it out just as tirelessly as animals search for their food. Light stimulates a plant to grow toward it — a process known as phototropism. You can see this at work by growing a bean in a shoebox, in which the source of light is masked by cardboard baffles. Using matt black paint minimizes the amount of reflected light inside the box.

YOU WILL NEED
● *adhesive tape* ● *beans* ● *matt black paint* ● *cardboard*
● *shoebox* ● *flowerpot* ● *potting compost* ● *paintbrush* ● *scissors*

1 Cut out two identical pieces of cardboard, as deep as the box and two-thirds as wide.

2 Cut a small hole in one end of the shoebox. Paint the inside of the box and the pieces of cardboard (the baffles) black.

3 Using the tape, attach the baffles to the inside of the box. Stand the box upright with the hole at the top.

4 Plant a bean in the flowerpot. Water it, and place it in the bottom of the box.

5 Fit the lid on the box, making sure that no light can get in around the edges.

6 Remove the lid once a day to watch the plant growing. How well can it find its way to the light? What happens if you plant another bean, and this time close the hole?

EXPERIMENT
Growing with gravity

Root is responding to gravity, and is growing downward

A plant's stem grows upward toward light, but its roots grow downward. They are responding not to darkness, but to gravity. To see this working, grow a bean in a jar with the jar on its side, then turn the jar upside down.

YOU WILL NEED
● *bean* ● *cork* ● *cotton wool* ● *glue* ● *jar with lid* ● *stiff wire*

1 Soak the bean in water for 24 hours. Glue the cork to the inside of the jar's lid. Push the piece of wire into the cork, and slide the bean halfway along the wire. Add some wet cotton wool to the jar.

2 Screw on the lid, with the bean attached. Lay the jar on its side. Let the seed grow until the root is $\frac{1}{2}$ in (1 cm) long. Now turn the jar so the root is pointing upward, and see what happens.

The structure of flowers

BRIGHTLY COLORED FLOWERS are living advertise-ments, promoting a sugary liquid called nectar. Insects, attracted by a flower's color and scent, land on it to feed. As an insect probes for nectar among the petals, it is dusted with tiny pollen grains — the flower's male reproductive cells. The insect carries the pollen to another flower, and here some of these male grains stick to the flower's female parts. Each grain grows a tube, and its sperm cells travel down it to join with an egg cell, or ovule. Fertilization is the result, causing a seed to form.

Petal

Stigma just visible

The complete flower
If a flower is brightly colored, if it has a strong smell, or both, this will tell you that it is pollinated by animals.

Sepals enclosing flower bud

■ The parts of a simple flower

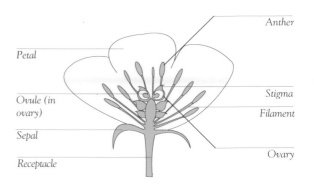

Petal

Ovule (in ovary)

Sepal

Receptacle

Anther

Stigma

Filament

Ovary

Most flowers contain male and female parts. The anthers are a flower's male parts, and they produce pollen. The female parts include the stigma, on which pollen settles, and the ovary, which protects the egg cell or ovule. In many flowers, the pollen and egg cells ripen at slightly different times, so the flower cannot fertilize itself.

The buttercup above has a simple circular plan, a few petals, and is pollinated by insects. Its male and female parts have evolved so that insect visitors cannot help brushing against them when they are in search of nectar. Not all flowers are pollinated by insects — pollen can also be carried by animals such as birds and bats, by the wind, and by water.

EXPERIMENT
Dissecting a flower

Adult supervision is advised for this experiment
Use a scalpel to dissect a simple flower — one that has just a few petals and a symmetrical shape. You can closely examine the flower's different parts by looking at them with a hand lens.

Inside a flower bud
Try slicing through a bud. You will be able to see all the parts of a flower packed inside.

YOU WILL NEED
● *flower* ● *scissors* ● *hand lens* ● *scalpel*
● *tweezers*

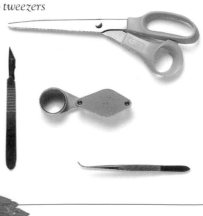

Receptacle

Ovary

Anthers

Stigma

Petals

■ Flower families

The flowers of related plants have similar basic shapes. Two of the world's largest plant families, the daisy family (Compositae) and the pea family (Leguminosae), produce very characteristic flowers. Daisy-family flowers are made up of a number of florets. The ray florets — those around the edge — have a single petal each, while the disc florets — those in the middle — have no petals, but produce pollen and egg cells. Pea-family flowers have an unusual shape. They have five petals, two of which are joined together. One petal, known as the "standard," forms a hood over the flower. Pea-family seeds are often produced in pods.

Individual flower

Disc florets

Ray florets

Flower of ox-eye daisy
(family Compositae)

Flower of tufted vetch
(family Leguminosae)

Seeds form in pods

Petals
Slice off the petals where they join the flower, and count them. Each different plant family has flowers with a characteristic number of petals. The flower shown here is a garden poppy. Like most other plants in the poppy family (Papaveraceae), it has four petals.

Stamens
Having removed the petals, you can see the parts of the plant that produce seeds. Carefully cut off the stamens — the male parts of the flower — and look at them through the hand lens. You should be able to see the pollen-producing anthers at the tip of each stamen.

Stigma

Ovary

Ovary
Pollen lands on the stigma and produces tubes which grow down to meet the egg cells or ovules, where they become the seeds. If you slice vertically through the stigma and ovaries, you will be able to see the ovules inside.

Seeds
If you can find a mature seed head, slicing through it will reveal the seeds.

Dry, empty seed head

Studying flowers

BY STUDYING A FLOWER, you can find out how it is pollinated, how its seeds are formed and spread, and what other plants it is related to. Over the years, botanists have collected and examined thousands of plant species. Many of these are preserved and kept in herbaria — special collections of plant specimens held in museums. By preserving flowers and leaves, you can make your own herbarium, and keep a permanent record of the characteristics of your favorite flowers. Pressing and drying are two ways of preserving them.

■ DISCOVERY ■
Gregor Mendel

Gregor Mendel (1822–1884), an Austrian monk, was the pioneer in genetics — the study of how characteristics are handed down from one generation to another. He carried out his researches with various plants, particularly peas. Mendel raised a number of different varieties of peas, and cross-pollinated their flowers. He was then able to collect the seeds, grow them, and see which characteristics were shown in the next generation. Through his research, we know that both parents' characteristics are inherited in the form of separate and distinct "genes."

EXPERIMENT
Transpiration

In many plants, water is constantly sucked up from the roots, through the stem, and into the leaves. This is called transpiration. When the water reaches the leaves, much of it evaporates through the stomata, the tiny pores in the leaf that the plant also uses for absorbing and releasing gases (p. 41). Water also travels up the stems of flowers and evaporates from petals. This experiment shows that the stream of water can carry other substances with it, and also that water in different parts of the stem is kept separate as it moves upward.

YOU WILL NEED
● 2 glasses ● food dye ● pale-colored flower
● sharp knife ● adhesive tape

1 Fill the glasses with water. Add some food dye to one of them, and stir well.

2 Slice the flower's stem in two, lengthways, stopping when you have reached the halfway point.

3 Fasten some tape around the end of the cut, to prevent the stem splitting further.

4 Put each half of the stem into a glass. Lean the flower against a window for support.

5 The food dye is drawn up the stem, and starts to color half the petals within one hour.

EXPERIMENT
Preserving flowers by drying

Adult supervision is advised for this experiment

One way to preserve flowers, and to keep their shape, is to dry them out. Colored silica gel crystals are blue when dry. After absorbing moisture, they become pink. Finely ground silica gel can cause health problems if they are inhaled.

YOU WILL NEED
● *flowers* ● *jar with lid* ● *silica gel, available from drugstores, chemical supply house, or hardware store*

1 POUR SOME lightly ground silica gel into the jar. Place the flowers upside down on the layer of crystals.

2 COVER THE FLOWERS with crystals. Put the lid on the jar, and leave it for at least a week to dry.

EXPERIMENT
Preserving flowers by pressing

Pressing is a method of preserving plants and flowers that is often used by botanists. You can buy flower presses, but heavy books or pieces of wood will work just as well. For this experiment, put the plants between two sheets of blotting paper before pressing. Pressing works best with plants that don't contain too much water.

YOU WILL NEED
● *flowers* ● *blotting paper sheets* ● *books, heavy wooden boards, or a plant press*

1 Arrange the flowers on the paper, not too close together. Lay a sheet of blotting paper on top.

2 Carefully add some books or another board. If you are using a press, screw it tight. Leave the flowers for about two weeks. Carefully lift the blotting paper and remove the pressed flowers.

Fruits and seed dispersal

BOTANISTS USE THE WORD "fruit" in a different way from other people. For example, a pea pod is a fruit, and so are a hazelnut and the seed head of a poppy. Because these all develop from the ovary of the flower, just as oranges or cherries do, they are all "fruit." Once a flower has been pollinated, it starts to change into a fruit. Its petals and anthers wither, then fall off, while other parts grow rapidly around the developing seeds, which are dispersed.

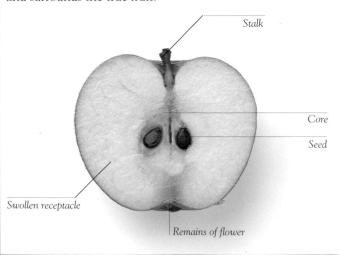

A protective case
The "fruit" of the sweet chestnut is the spiky case that protects the developing seeds. It opens up when the seeds are ripe.

■ Fruit investigations

By looking at any fruit, you should be able to spot a number of clues that will tell you how it was formed, and how its seeds are dispersed. If you can slice it open, you may see some remnants of the flower. A "true" fruit is made up only by the female parts (the ovary where the seeds are produced) of the flower, while "false" fruits (below) contain other parts as well. Anything fleshy or tasty is usually a sign that animals are involved in dispersing the seeds. Dry fruits disperse their seeds in a number of different ways (see opposite).

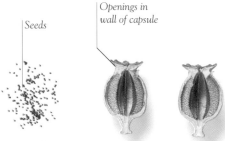

Seeds

Openings in wall of capsule

Poppy capsule
The seed head or capsule of a poppy is a dry "fruit" containing many seeds. While the seeds are still developing, they are safely sealed inside the seed head. As they ripen, the seed head dries out, and little openings, like windows, appear beneath the seed head's top. When the wind blows, the ripe seeds are scattered through these openings.

Armored seeds
Inside a cherry there is a single seed protected by a very hard shell — we call it the pit. The brightly colored fruit tempts the birds. If a bird swallows a cherry, the sweet flesh is digested, but the armored seed passes through the bird unharmed and is ready to grow in a new area.

Flesh

■ A false fruit

Apples and pears are not "true" fruits. In an apple, the fruit itself is the core. The juicy flesh of the apple develops from the receptacle (p. 46) of the apple flower, which swells up and surrounds the true fruit.

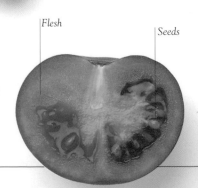

Stalk

Core

Seed

Swollen receptacle

Remains of flower

Flesh

Seeds

Vegetable fruits
Botanically speaking, a tomato is a fruit. Other fruit vegetables are egg plants, peppers, green beans, and avocados. The seeds are quite clearly seen, and we usually eat them.

■ Seed dispersal

If a young plant springs up right next to its parent, one or the other will lose out in the battle for light and moisture. Since plants cannot move about like animals, once a plant has grown, it has to scatter its seeds as far away as possible. Most plants produce many seeds so that some, at least, nearly always land on suitable ground. Some harness the wind or water to spread their seeds. Others use animals, while still others have special fruits that fling the seeds far away from the plant.

Water dispersal

A few plants use water to spread their seeds. The tulip tree of North America often grows by rivers, and its small, dry fruits float downstream. The coconut produces fruits that float — the "coconut matting" on the outside makes them buoyant, while inside there is a supply of fresh water for the young tree.

Floating and gliding

Seeds that are dispersed by the wind often develop in "fruits" that help them to get airborne. They may have fluffy hairs like a thistle, winglike flaps like a maple, or tiny parachutes like a dandelion, which help them to float away. In windy conditions, the seeds can be carried hundreds of kilometers away from the plant that produced them.

Cedar scale   Cedar seed

Conifer seeds

Conifers have no fruits. Instead, the seeds are produced in cones. If you look at a cone, you can often see the seeds, protected by hard, woody scales. These seeds are from a cedar tree. The cedar's cones slowly disintegrate on the tree, releasing the ripe seeds.

Large, simple flower of tulip tree

Cranesbill

Beaklike "fruit"

Animal dispersal

If you go for a walk on an overgrown path in late summer, you will probably pick up "burrs" that stick to your clothes by means of hooks and spines. When you knock them off, the seeds will fall and germinate given the right conditions. Other plants entice animals with seeds wrapped in a tasty fruit, or seeds that are themselves nutritious. Squirrels and other rodents eat these, but they often bury some for the winter, and forget to dig all of them up, so they grow.

Acorns are carried away and buried by squirrels

Mechanical dispersal

Many plants have do-it-yourself methods for dispersing their seeds. In some, the "fruits" dry out to form slings or catapults that eventually throw the seeds some distance from the plant. In the cranesbill (a type of geranium) each seed is flung from the plant by a tiny sling. Many seed-scattering devices burst open if touched. In some members of the cucumber family, the ripe fruit explodes and hurls the seeds across the ground.

Seeds and germination

SEEDS ARE PACKAGES of living matter. Each seed contains an embryo, which develops into a plant, and seed leaves, which supply the young plant with energy. They produce this energy from a store of food. Some seeds are immensely tough, and can stay dormant for months, years, or even centuries, but can suddenly be triggered into life by factors such as moisture, light, or warmth. In the process of germination, a seed's cells divide, its outer coat splits open, and a new plant is born.

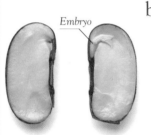

Inside a seed
Soak a bean in water for 24 hours, remove the seed coat, and open the seed leaves to reveal the embryo.

Embryo

EXPERIMENT
Different ways of growing

Why does grass always grow back, even after being cut by a lawnmower? You can find out about the growth points of plants by raising grass and cress seeds, and then trimming them with scissors.

YOU WILL NEED
- *potting compost* ● *cress seeds*
- *grass seeds* ● *scissors* ● *2 containers*

Grass after one week
The seeds have rapidly taken root, and have formed a dense mat of long, narrow leaves.

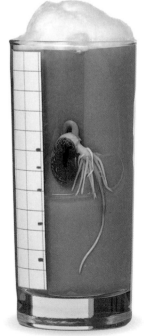

Grass one week after cutting
Because the growth point of grass is at ground level, the plants are still alive, and are continuing to grow.

EXPERIMENT
Germination and growth rates

Seeds normally germinate on or beneath the soil, making it difficult to see how they grow. By planting seeds in drinking glasses, you can clearly see their development. Different seeds germinate in different ways — this experiment uses bean, corn, and sunflower seeds. Line the inside of each drinking glass with blotting paper, then fill with cotton wool. Place the seed between the glass and the paper, and add water (but do not cover the seed). Put the glass in a dark place, and mark a scale on its outside to keep a daily record of the seed's progress. Add water every few days, to keep the paper moist.

YOU WILL NEED
- ● *bean, sunflower, and corn seeds*
- ● *glasses* ● *blotting paper* ● *squared paper* ● *scissors*
- ● *colored crayon*
- ● *cotton wool*
- ● *water*

Runner bean — day 1
Although nothing seems to be happening, the seed is absorbing water. Inside the seed coat, the seed is beginning to grow.

Runner bean — day 5
The root is growing quite rapidly, and a curved stem is starting to appear. The seed leaves are still inside the seed coat.

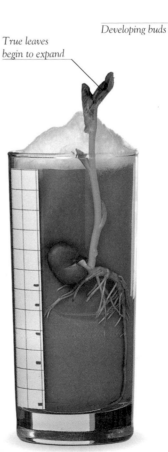

Stem grows at its tip

True leaves

Internode (length of stem between leaves)

Petiole (leaf stalk)

Developing buds

Cress after one week
Each cress plant contains a pair of green seed leaves, which are held up on a narrow stem.

Cress one week after cutting
These plants have stopped growing because their growth points, at the top of the stem, have been cut off.

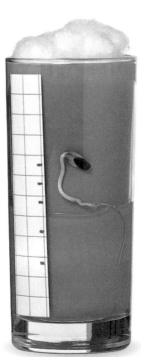

Leaves wrapped around tubular stem

True leaves begin to expand

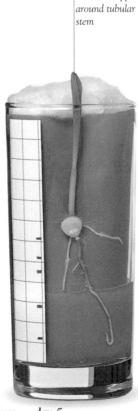

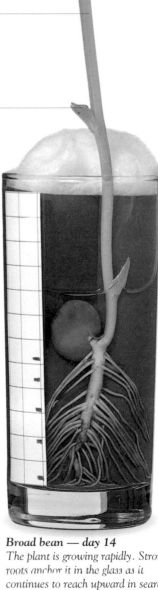

Sunflower — day 5
The sunflower seed has produced a long, thin root, and its stem is pulling the seed leaves out of the seed coat.

Corn — day 5
The corn seedling has produced a number of roots, and a tall, tubelike stem. The single seed leaf stays inside the seed.

Broad bean — day 8
The first true leaves have appeared. From this moment on, the plant can make its own food by the process of photosynthesis.

Broad bean — day 14
The plant is growing rapidly. Strong roots anchor it in the glass as it continues to reach upward in search of light.

53

TREES

TREES BELONG TO many different plant families. An oak tree and a pine tree are as distantly related as a bat and a bird. Yet, because they both have tall, woody trunks and look similar, we think of them as being alike. To a botanist, trees are a "mixed bag," a collection of plants that have used the same adaptation — height — to win a struggle for light.

A tree is just a very tall land plant — one that has evolved a specially strengthened stem, or trunk, so that it can tower above the plants around it to compete for light. Small plants have evolved into trees not once, but dozens of times, as evolution has hit on the same adaptation time and time again.

The scales of a cone
open in dry weather, to allow the seeds to fall out.

■ Ever upward

Over millions of years, natural selection (p. 22) has "stretched" trees until they are as tall as they can be. The tallest tree standing is a redwood in California over 368 ft (112 m) high — but this is not the tallest tree ever recorded. A eucalyptus felled in Victoria, Australia, in the 1800s was more than 430 ft (130 m), even though the top of the tree had already been lost. This tree may have been over 500 ft (150 m) tall in its prime. Several Douglas firs from British Columbia, Canada, and Washington State were once almost as tall as this, but such giants were felled by foresters long ago.

At the same time as trees evolved tall trunks for reaching toward the light, they also evolved strong roots for staying upright. Strong does not always mean deep. Most tree roots meet a rocky subsoil less than 3 ft (1 m) below the surface. This is difficult to penetrate, so the roots fan out across the surface, spreading the base as widely as possible. A large beech tree might have a circle of roots, called a "root plate," 16 ft (5 m) across.

Some rain-forest trees have "buttress" roots — solid extensions from the trunk, starting about 13 ft (4 m) above ground and widening out toward the surface. There may be four or more of these around the tree trunk. It had always been assumed that they helped to prop up the trees, which in a rain forest are very tall. Recently, however, some biologists decided to test this idea. They found that the trees with buttress roots did not seem to grow any taller than those without them, and they blew down just as often in storms. This does not completely disprove the idea that buttress roots make trees more stable than they would be without them, but it shows that, in the living

Many conifers
have an unbranched trunk that grows bolt upright. Cedars do not follow this rule.

The hard, oily leaves
of eucalyptuses have evolved to withstand scorching sun.

world, things are not always as simple as they seem.

Where water is in short supply, roots can reach great depths in their search for it. The deepest roots ever found were those of a wild fig. The roots penetrated a cavern more than 330 ft (100 m) below the surface of a semi-desert area of southern Africa, where the rock is very soft and sandy.

■ Tree types

There are five basic groups of trees on Earth today. The two most common are the conifers (such as the pines and firs) and the broadleaved trees (such as oaks, maples, eucalyptuses, and palm trees). The three rarest groups are tree ferns (pp. 62-63), the ginkgo, and cycads.

■ Conifers

Trees that produce cones as a protective covering for their seeds are called conifers. Apart from the "typical" conifers, such as pines and firs, this group of trees includes cypresses, redwoods, junipers, yellowwoods or podocarps, and yews.

Most conifers have leaves that are sharp and slender, like sewing needles, or flat and tough, like tiny strips of leather. With a few

Many broadleaved trees
produce large seeds, or nuts.

exceptions, they are evergreen and keep their leaves for three or four years. This means that the leaves must be tough enough to resist attack by insects. Chemicals known as resins, which give the leaves their strong "piny" scent, help keep insects at bay. Many conifers can be identified just by their smell — the great fir has leaves that smell like marmalade, and the western red cedar has an aroma of pineapples.

Not all conifers have hard, woody cones. In junipers, the cone is fleshy like a berry, and it attracts birds just like the berries of many flowering plants. This is an example of "convergent evolution," the process by which natural selection produces the same sort of structure in two quite different plants (or animals).

■ Broadleaved trees

All broadleaved trees are flowering plants. Cherry trees, for example, belong to the rose family, while acacias and wattles belong to the pea family.

The leaves of most of these trees are broad and thin, and for this reason, they are often called "broadleaved" trees, although not all of their leaves fit this description. Some broadleaved trees shed their leaves once a year. In the temperate regions, mainly in Europe and North America, they lose their leaves in autumn in preparation for the winter, which they pass in a state of suspended animation. Before the leaves fall, the trees take whatever useful material they can out of them, and during this process the leaves change their color to yellows, oranges, and reds. In parts of the tropics and

subtropics, where there is a dry season and a wet season (sometimes called a monsoon climate), the trees lose their leaves before the dry season begins.

Among the broadleaved trees, the type that is most strikingly different is the palm tree, which belongs to a subclass of flowering plants called the monocotyledons, a group that also includes grasses, orchids, lilies, and irises. Because of the special way they grow, these plants cannot easily form a tree shape. The "trunk" of a palm is quite different from the trunk of a pine, oak, or maple. It is made up of hardened leaf bases, packed together to form a hard trunklike structure. As the leaves fall, they leave their bases behind to help build up the trunk.

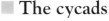

The rings on this pine tree trunk show even and quick growth.

■ The ginkgo

The ginkgo, or maidenhair tree, is a unique species. Although its nearest living relatives are conifers, it has neither needles nor cones. Ginkgos are now widely grown in parks and gardens, and from a distance look rather like large willows or elms. But if you get the chance to look more closely, you will see the strange triangular leaves, with veins that fan out from the base, that give the tree its English name.

California redwoods are the most massive living things on Earth.

Leaves like these cannot be found on any other living tree, but they can be seen in fossils 150 million years old, relics of a time when ginkgos were very common. Western botanists first saw living ginkgos in the 1700s, when they were discovered in Buddhist temples in China and Japan, where they had long been cultivated as sacred trees. It was thought that ginkgos had become extinct in the wild many millions of years ago, but during this century, they were found growing wild in a valley in China.

■ The cycads

These rare trees are distant relatives of conifers. They are found mainly in the tropics and subtropics. They look like rather short, fat palm trees, but they have massive cones, some even weighing as much as 80 lb (36 kg). These spectacular cones are bright red or yellow in some species. Like the ginkgo, the cycads have more primitive features than conifers and broadleaved trees, including pollen that releases male sex cells (sperm) that swim toward the female egg cells.

Sago, a nutritious form of starch, is a foodstuff produced from cycad stems and seeds. Sago contains poisons and must be cooked carefully.

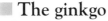

The water lost through a leaf can be calculated in a simple experiment.

A leaf skeleton — natural or "homemade" — reveals the tracery of veins used to move water and nutrients.

The structure of trees

TREES ARE THE LONGEST-LIVING of all plants. Their trunks have evolved to enable them to tower above other plants, and thus get plenty of light. If you look at trees in a forest and in the open, you will see that they are shaped partly by their surroundings. A tree in a forest is often hemmed in by its neighbors, and has to grow tall to reach the light. Often only its highest branches will bear leaves. A tree of the same species growing in the open will be quite different in shape. It does not have to struggle to reach the light, and instead of being tall and thin, it will usually be broad and round.

As there are many different types of trees, there are also many different types of wood. Balsa wood can be as little as a tenth as heavy as water, but black ironwood is 15 times heavier than balsa. If you were to throw a piece into water, it would sink.

Shaped by the surroundings
This hawthorn tree is growing on a windswept cliff top. The wind has shaped it by repeatedly drying out the buds on one side so they shriveled and died.

■ Looking at wood

The pattern of rings we see in wood is produced by the way in which trees grow — not only upward, but outward as well. Just beneath the bark is the cambium, or growth layer, in which cells divide. Growth in the cambium adds a layer of new wood annually, expanding the trunk.

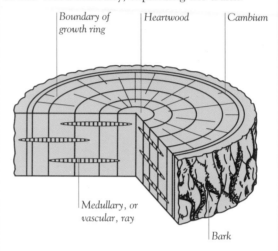

Boundary of growth ring   *Heartwood*   *Cambium*

Medullary, or vascular, ray

Bark

As the tree grows, older cells nearer the center of the trunk gradually become filled with a substance called lignin, and eventually die. Lignin is extremely tough, and these dead cells give the wood its strength. This central wood is called the heartwood, and it is usually darker. Channels called medullary, or vascular, rays connect the outer and inner layers of the trunk.

EXPERIMENT
Measuring the age of a tree

You can often estimate the age of a tree by measuring the circumference of its trunk. Most trees in temperate regions add an extra 1 in (2.5 cm) to their circumference every year. Dividing the total circumference by this amount will therefore give you the tree's age.

Not all trees follow this guide. North American redwoods, some firs, and eucalyptuses grow more than this in a year, while yews, limes, and horse chestnuts often don't grow as much. Palm trees often grow taller without growing fatter.

YOU WILL NEED
● *measuring tape*

1 Measure the circumference of the trunk at the standard height of 5 ft (about 1.5 m) above the ground.

2 Divide the circumference by 1 in (2.5 cm) to give the age.

◼ Growth rings

In most parts of the world, trees produce a burst of growth each spring, followed by slower growth in the summer. The summer wood is denser than the spring wood, and this shows up as a "growth ring." A wide ring shows that the tree grew well in a particular year, while a narrow ring usually means that the weather slowed growth. If a tree grows in the open, but out of the wind, the rings will be the same width all around. If the tree is shaded, or buffeted by the wind, the rings will be wider on the side toward the light, or away from the wind.

Bark

Heartwood

Knot produced by former branch

Branch

Region of growth

Sapwood

Unbalanced growth
The rings in this piece of oak are off-center and tightly packed. The left side of the trunk has grown faster than the right.

Balanced growth
This pine trunk shows even growth. Although it is the same size as the oak trunk, it has fewer rings because it has grown more quickly.

EXPERIMENT
Measuring the height of a tree

Here is a way of measuring the height of a tree without climbing it! It involves comparing a height that you can measure — that of a friend — with the tree.

YOU WILL NEED
● *measuring tape* ● *paper* ● *pencil* ● *stick*

Friend standing under tree

Stick held out at arm's length

1 Measure your friend's height, and write it down.

2 Ask him or her to stand at the base of the tree.

3 With a pencil in one hand, hold out the stick at arm's length in the other hand, lining up the top with your friend's head. With the pencil, make a mark on the stick that lines up with his or her feet.

4 Still standing at the same place, move the stick upward so that the top lines up with the tree top.

5 Make another mark on the stick, this time in line with the bottom of the tree.

6 You can work out the tree's height. The two marks on the stick show how much taller the tree is than your friend. Suppose it is 20 times as tall. If your friend is 4 ft 11 in (1.5 m), the tree must be 98 ft (30 m) tall.

Leaves and bark

LEAF TYPES HAVE EVOLVED to suit many different climates. Conifers have tough needles, which are well suited to the winter cold, bright sunshine, and high winds of mountainsides. The leaves of broadleafed trees are generally more delicate, especially in temperate regions. Since these leaves are replaced annually, they do not need so much protection from snow, sun, or wind. The leaves of evergreen broadleafed trees, such as eucalypts, are tough and leathery, enabling them to last for many years.

Bark, the skin around a tree's trunk and branches, can be thick and rugged, or thin and smooth. As a tree grows, its bark expands outward, producing a pattern of cracking or flaking in the outermost layer. The texture of the bark may change as a tree grows older, and sometimes the bark at the top of a tree is different from that near the bottom.

Bark rubbings
Making a bark rubbing is an easy way to compare different types of bark. Tape a sheet of strong paper to a tree trunk, and then rub it with a wax crayon. The ridges and furrows in the bark will become visible on the paper. You can use the same technique to record the shape of different leaves, but make sure the leaf is securely fixed to the paper.

EXPERIMENT
Leaf skeletons

Adult supervision is advised for this experiment
Strip away the soft parts of a leaf to see the stalk, midrib, and veins.

YOU WILL NEED
● *fallen leaves* ● *sal soda* ● *pan*
● *water*

1 FILL THE PAN WITH WATER, and add about 2 dessertspoons of sal soda per pint/40g of sal soda per liter. Heat the solution until it is nearly boiling. Take the pan off the heat. Place the leaves in the solution, and then leave them there for at least 30 minutes.

2 PUT THE PAN UNDER A FAUCET, and gently flush with cold water for a few minutes. Be careful not to splash yourself, as soda can harm the skin. The soft parts of the leaves will have fallen away, leaving skeletons which you can dry and keep.

Veins

Midrib

Stalk

EXPERIMENT
Water loss through a leaf

In this experiment, you can combine observation and mathematics to find out how much water passes through the leaves on a twig.

YOU WILL NEED
- *twig with leaves* ● *beaker* ● *cooking oil*
- *water* ● *squared paper* ● *crayon*

Living wood
The flow of water and nutrients in a tree occurs in the outer layers of the trunk and branches, just beneath the bark. The center of the tree is dead wood. Trees with hollow trunks show that only the outer layers of wood are essential for survival, which is why a tree dies if its bark is stripped off all the way around its trunk.

Leaf area can be estimated by adding up squares

Water is lost mainly through the underside of the leaf

1 DRAW AN OUTLINE of a leaf on the squared paper, and add up all the squares to give you the total area. To find out the amount of water lost (right), divide the water lost by the total leaf area to give the amount lost per unit area of leaf. Mark a scale on the outside of two beakers. Half-fill them with water, then add a layer of oil. Put the twig into one of the beakers.

2 NOTE THE WATER'S height on both beakers and put them in a light place. After eight hours, measure the amount of water that has disappeared in both beakers. The level of water and oil should have gone down in the beaker that had the twig in it. As water could not have evaporated through oil, it must have been lost through the leaves.

SIMPLE PLANTS

FLOWERING PLANTS ARE RELATIVE NEWCOMERS in the story of plant life on Earth. The conifers (p. 27) are a more ancient group, but oldest of all are the simple nonflowering plants such as liverworts and mosses. Together with the ferns and their relatives, these survivors from the past record the process through which plants have evolved.

Giant horsetails once grew into towering trees. Today few reach a height of 3 ft (1 m).

You may well have climbed up a tree or picked up an old flowerpot, only to find that your hands have become covered with a fine green dust. This green powder is a microscopic forest, countless cells of an organism called *Chlorella*, one of the simplest plants on Earth. Each plant is a single round cell, yet it is packed with the apparatus needed to harness energy from the Sun through photosynthesis (pp. 40-43).

Chlorella is an alga — a member of a group of simple but very varied plants over 25,000 species strong. It can live almost anywhere that is both light and damp — from a gatepost to a cliff face. In the tropical forests of South America, similar algae live in the fur of sloths, giving them a greenish tinge that improves their camouflage. Algae are of great importance to other forms of life. Vast numbers of them float in the sea, forming phytoplankton, which provides food for animals. Some live in association with other organisms — for example, inside lichens (pp. 62-63) or in the tissues of coral (p. 95) or giant clams, where they provide their hosts with food.

Tree ferns growing in the rain forest of northern Australia.

■ Living together

Not all algae consist of just one cell. Some, such as *Volvox*, are made up of individual cells living together in beautiful spherical colonies. Other algae are made up of many cells, just as higher plants are. The blanketweed *Spirogyra*, for example, is made up of long strings of cells, joined to form slender filaments.

The most complex algae of all are the seaweeds (pp. 96-97). They are made up of many types of cells, and their tough but rubbery bodies enable them to withstand the battering of the sea's waves.

■ Adapting to life on land

Although *Chlorella* lives on rocks and walls, it is not really thought of as a land plant because it can grow only when soaked with rain. As soon as it dries out, it goes into a state of suspended animation. Although it has survived on land for millions of years, its prospects are limited by its need for water.

The key to plant survival on land is to have roots that can draw water up from the soil and a waterproof covering to slow down evaporation from the leaves. Liverworts and mosses (pp. 62-63) are two groups of simple plants that show the first steps in this direction.

■ Liverworts

The most primitive land plants are the liverworts. The name "liverwort" is very old, dating from at least 1,000 years ago in Europe. The "wort" at the end of their name shows that these plants were used as an herbal medicine. It used to be thought that any plant shaped like a part of the body would cure disease in that part. Because the lobed shape of a liverwort resembles a liver, these plants were soaked in wine and used to treat liver complaints.

Liverworts have rudimentary roots, called rhizoids, but very little waterproofing. They are confined to damp places, such as springs and streamsides. One, called *Marchantia*, is common in flowerpots in greenhouses; it produces its spores in distinctive fruiting bodies that look like tiny open umbrellas.

A lichen is a living partnership between a fungus and an alga.

■ Mosses

Although mosses probably evolved from a simple ancestor that was similar to a liverwort, they are much better at withstanding dryness. Mosses are common in woodlands, under shade, or on branches where there is plenty of rainfall. Some mosses even live on roofs, where they become very dry in hot summers.

Mosses survive dry weather by using the same trick as *Chlorella* — going into a state of suspended animation, known as cryptobiosis. If you

Club mosses were among the first plants to become truly adapted to life on land.

find some clumps of dry moss, try keeping them indoors in dry, airtight jars. A year later, add rainwater to one and see if it revives. Try the next one after two years, and so on. How long do you think mosses might survive in this state?

One group of mosses, the *Sphagnum* species, soak up water as well as a sponge. If you pick up part of a *Sphagnum* clump, it feels heavy and wet. But if you wring it out with your hands, water pours out, leaving the moss plants light and fluffy. Dried *Sphagnum* is very absorbent, and its usefulness as a dressing for wounds was discovered in the 1880s. During World War I, the British army used a million *Sphagnum* dressings a month on their injured troops.

■ Ferns and their allies

Ferns, with their delicate lacy fronds, are familiar plants. (The term "fronds" is used instead of leaves, to distinguish them from the leaves of flowering plants.) Although many grow in damp, shady places as the mosses do, some thrive in much drier places, even on exposed, windswept hillsides — the best example being bracken.

The ferns took an important step forward in land plant evolution by developing proper roots and a far more effective waterproof covering for their fronds. They also have woodlike strengthening material in their stems, with special channels for conducting water up to the leaves. This allows the ferns to grow far taller than

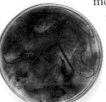

Spirogyra
clogs ditches with its filaments.

mosses. Because all plants need sunlight, growing tall is a passport to success — it enables a plant to shade out the competition. Mosses and liverworts have managed to survive in the more competitive plant world of today largely by making do with less light.

The tallest living members of this group today are the tree ferns that grow in some tropical and subtropical forests. These graceful giants look like slender palm trees, except that their fronds are divided into many fingers, like the fronds of an ordinary fern. Tree ferns are very small compared with other tropical rain-forest trees, and they only grow to about 60 ft (18 m) when standing alone. With other trees packed tightly around them, they can reach 80 ft (25 m).

■ Giants of the past

Ferns were slow to exploit the advantages of size, but their relatives — the club mosses and horsetails — once did so with great success.

About 350 million years ago, much of the Earth was covered by dense, swampy forest made up of giant club mosses and horsetails, 130 ft (40 m) or more tall. You cannot see such plants today — the remaining club mosses are just a few inches high, while horsetails are rarely more than 3 ft (1 m). When these giant trees reached a certain size, they became unstable in the swampy ground and

A fern frond
grows by unrolling like an unwinding spring.

fell over. There they rotted, or partially rotted, because decomposition is slow underwater. Over thousands of years, more and more trees fell, building up a massive layer of half-rotted tree trunks. These gradually became compacted and blackened with the weight of the new layers above. Those tree trunks are now coal.

■ Plants and pollution

Strange as it may sound, our lives today depend on the simple plants of long ago. When plants carry out photosynthesis, they turn carbon dioxide into sugars. The giant club mosses and horsetails did this too, taking carbon dioxide from the air and locking it up in their trunks. Because those trunks turned to coal, the carbon has been locked up ever since.

When we burn coal or other "fossil fuels," such as oil, we are turning that carbon back into carbon dioxide gas. This makes the Earth's atmosphere hotter because carbon dioxide acts like a blanket, keeping in heat that would otherwise escape into space. This is known as the "greenhouse effect," and it may lead to a change in the world's climate.

Modern farming and fishing, and many other aspects of human life, depend heavily on fossil fuels and the maintenance of weather patterns. Burning the remains of simple plants may therefore both help and harm us.

Lichens
are important indicators of air pollution.

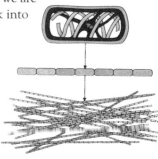

The cells of the alga
Spirogyra *link up to form long filaments.*

Damp places
are where mosses are most often found.

Plants without flowers

THE SIMPLEST LAND PLANTS all produce spores. These are microscopic specks of living material enclosed by a tough protective wall. A fern spore that falls in a good spot can grow into a new plant, but the spore does not grow into a new fern as you might expect. Instead, it grows into a small green disc, often heart-shaped, called a prothallus. This tiny, short-lived blob of life needs wet soil to grow. Its function is sexual reproduction. Egg and sperm cells develop on it, and the sperm cells fertilize the eggs, which grow into sporophytes, or new fern plants.

Having two separate stages to the life cycle is normal in simple plants. In mosses, the two stages are joined together, and the moss plant itself is the prothallus. Its brown or red spikes are the other stage in the cycle — they are the sporophytes, which produce the spores.

■ The life cycle of a fern

The two stages have special names. The fern plant is called the sporophyte (because it produces spores), and the other stage is called the prothallus or gametophyte (because it produces eggs and sperm, known as gametes).

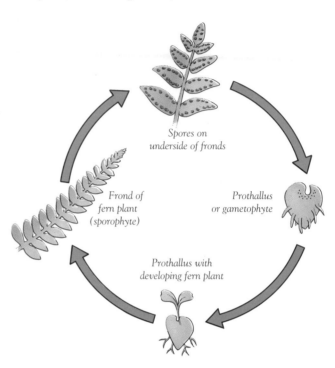

Spores on underside of fronds

Prothallus or gametophyte

Prothallus with developing fern plant

Frond of fern plant (sporophyte)

■ Ferns and fronds

Most ferns have divided fronds, cut into tiny fingerlike leaflets. The male fern and the polypody fern on the left both have divided fronds. A few, such as the hart's tongue ferns, have undivided, straplike fronds. One feature of fronds is that they emerge from the ground tightly rolled like a snail's shell and gradually unfurl themselves. All ferns produce their spores on the undersides of the fronds, in structures called sporangia.

Male fern

Polypody

Hart's tongue fern

Club moss
Selaginella (resurrection plant) is a club moss, a relative of the ferns. Club mosses now grow mostly in the tropics and the subtropics, and all are small plants, unlike their giant relatives whose forests built up the earth's coal seams hundreds of millions of years ago (p. 61).

EXPERIMENT
Growing ferns from spores

By growing your own fern plants from spores, you can clearly see the two different kinds of plant that make up a fern's life cycle. The best time to do this experiment is in the late spring and summer. When looking for a fern leaf, look in damp woods, in hedgerows, and on shady walls and rocks. The spores are only ripe at certain times of the year, so check the underside of the fern before you pick it. They look rather like cocoa when the leaf is shaken. Put the frond in a plastic bag to transport it safely.

YOU WILL NEED
- *fertile fern frond* • *petri dish*
- *soil or sand/peat mixture*

1 PICK A FERTILE FROND — one that has brown spore-producing bodies on the underside — from any kind of fern. Put it in a warm, dry place for a few hours to make sure that its spores are ready to be shed.

2 FILL A PETRI DISH with soil, or a mixture of sand and peat, and add enough water to make it damp. Hold the frond over the dish, underside downward, and tap it. Do not cover the spores with soil.

3 PUT THE DISH in a warm, damp place. The spores will germinate into tiny prothalli (above), which will wither when the ferns appear. Transfer the potted ferns to stronger light.

Moss
Most mosses need damp growing conditions, but a few can withstand dryness. This moss is growing on a rock from beside a stream.

Horsetail
A very ancient group of plants, horsetails (scouring rush) are seen mainly in damp places. However, their roots penetrate deep into the subsoil and survive for years, so they can spring up anywhere if the ground is cleared.

Lichen
Fungi with algal cells trapped inside them (p. 65) are called lichens. The algae feed the fungus by means of photosynthesis. This duo is highly successful, and is resilient to great cold and dryness.

Liverwort
Mosses and liverworts are closely related. This is a liverwort's prothallus, or gametophyte. The eggs and sperm are produced in little cups on its surface.

Lichen on trees
Many species of lichens are killed by acid rain. The number of lichens on trees is usually a good indicator of the extent of pollution in the air.

Yellow lichen	Gray lichen

FUNGI

THERE ARE MILLIONS of tiny spores in the air you breathe. Most of these are the "seeds" produced by fungi, some of the most successful living things on Earth. Fungi take their food from dead and decaying material, or they live as parasites on the bodies of living things. By producing so many spores, fungi can be ready to grow wherever the chance arises.

When a piece of stale bread or some old fruit gets moldy, fungi are at work. When a tree dies, and its dead trunk starts to crumble away, fungi are the cause. And if a tiny nematode (roundworm) suddenly finds itself caught in a minute ring-shaped trap, a fungus is its killer.

Fungi make their living in a number of different ways. The ones that make food get moldy, and feed on other dead remains of plants and animals, are known as saprobes. Although they can be a nuisance in the kitchen, they play a very important role in the environment, because they remove the leftovers of the living world.

Parasitic fungi feed on things that are still alive. Fortunately for us, relatively few infect humans, apart from the ones that cause athlete's foot and an infection called thrush.

Predatory fungi are those that attack living animals smaller than themselves. These fungi live on tiny creatures such as nematodes, rotifers, and those with just a single cell, including amoebae (p. 28).

Winter fungus
attacks tree trunks with
devastating results.

■ Toadstools and feeding threads

The smallest of the fungi are the yeasts, single-celled saprobes that feast on fallen fruit, and that we use to make wine, beer, and bread. Mushrooms and toadstools are at the other extreme — they are the most spectacular fungi.

Mushrooms and toadstools are deceptive because they are not the main part of the fungus, but only their "fruiting bodies." They are the part responsible for producing spores and dispersing them. The real fungus is hidden from view in the soil, within a cow pat, or deep inside the wood of a tree. Here the fungus extends slender feeding branches, called hyphae, just as a bread mold does within a single crust. When it has built up its strength, and the time is right, it will push up toadstools to shoot out spores into the air.

■ Are fungi really plants?

Modern biologists place all the different forms of fungi in a kingdom of their own — the fungal kingdom. Fungi are neither animals nor plants, but a separate group entirely. It is traditional to include fungi in books about plants, but the only real resemblance between a fungus and a plant is that the fungus is rooted to the spot, not moving around as most animals do.

If you examine the hyphae of a fungus under a microscope, they will look like a mass of tangled cotton. The walls of the hyphae are rigid, but unlike those of plant cells, they

Porcelain fungus.

are not made of cellulose. The liquid inside the hypha flows like a stream from one end of the hypha to another, something that never happens in plants. Also, there is no central stem and no roots; the hyphae absorb both water and nutrients.

Higher fungi — the kinds that produce mushrooms and toadstools — are slightly more elaborate, but follow the same basic plan. Although a toadstool looks solid like a plant, it is actually made up of a mass of hyphal threads that are packed tightly together.

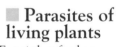

The large threads
of honey fungus
under bark.

■ Parasites of living plants

Fungi that feed on living plants cause a great deal of damage to farmers' crops. Among the fungal diseases that affect crops are powdery mildew, downy mildew, and rust. They get their names from the tiny fruiting bodies that break out on the leaves and disperse the spores. As with toadstools, the "real" fungus is hidden from view within the leaves of the plant. Here, the hyphae squeeze themselves into the gaps between the plant cells and soak up its nutrients.

One fungal disease affects the flowers of grasses, including cereal crops, and

An immature
puffball.

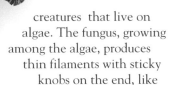

produces a hard black fruiting body in place of the seed. This body is called an ergot, and it contains toxins that cause serious illness if eaten. In the Middle Ages, several epidemics of ergot poisoning occurred in Germany and France. However, the active constituents of ergots, when purified and used in small amounts, are useful drugs for the treatment of migraine. Another fungal product with medical uses is penicillin (p. 67).

Fungi that infect plants penetrate their cells by breaking down cellulose. However, fewer fungi can break down lignin, the substance that makes tree trunks woody and plant stems rigid. In the course of evolution, lignin has developed into the chemical equivalent of a thief-proof lock. A lignin molecule is so complex that few enzymes (pp. 18-19) can break it up, or "unlock" it. However, there are some fungi that can overcome lignin, and these can attack tree trunks. A crop of toadstools sprouting from the trunk of a living tree is often the first sign that it is fatally infected.

▪ Fungi that live on animals

Fungi that parasitize animals are rarer than those that attack plants. This is because most animals have a battery of defenses, called an immune system, that can easily defeat them. In humans, fungal diseases do not often become a serious problem unless the immune system is not working properly. This can happen in some diseases, such as AIDS. It can also occur after transplant surgery,

when patients are given drugs to curb the effects of their immune system.

Some fungi have become specialized parasites of animals such as insects and fish. They sometimes change the behavior of their victims in a remarkable way. One species of ant, which lives in the tropical rain forest, climbs high into the trees when a particular fungus infects it. When the ant finally dies, the hyphae of the fungus ensure that its dead body sticks to a leaf. At the same time, the fungi send out their fruiting bodies. Because the ant is high up, the fungal spores are dispersed more widely than they would be in the still air near the forest floor.

A spore print
is created by spores falling onto a card.

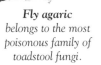

Fly agaric
belongs to the most poisonous family of toadstool fungi.

▪ Predatory fungi

Even more extraordinary than these parasites are the fungi that can feed as predators. Some live in pond mud, where they trap amoebae, using sticky hyphae. Once the amoeba is stuck fast, the fungus sends hyphae into its cell to absorb the contents.

The fungi that trap nematodes live in the soil. Their fast-moving victims are caught in tight rings that branch off the hyphae. As a worm wriggles through one of these rings, the ring swells up, catching the worm.

A completely different but equally successful approach to capturing prey is found in a pond-dwelling fungus that "fishes" for rotifers. These are microscopic

Many bracket fungi
show growth rings, like those on trees.

Mushrooms
and toadstools form their spores in basidia.

creatures that live on algae. The fungus, growing among the algae, produces thin filaments with sticky knobs on the end, like baited fishing lines. A rotifer, mistaking one of these knobs for a blob of algae, grasps it with its mouth. The knob holds the rotifer and digests it, soaking up the body contents.

▪ Fungi that form associations with plants

Not all fungi are so aggressive and predatory. Many form long-standing associations with plants, growing around their roots and channeling nutrients to them from the decaying material in the soil. In return, the plants' roots supply the fungus with a little sugar for energy. The symbiotic association between plant roots and fungi is known as mycorrhiza. Some plants, such as orchids, cannot survive without fungi.

Lichens (pp. 60-63) are another association, this time involving fungi and single-celled algae. The algae grow within the tight embrace of the fungal hyphae, but receive enough light to photosynthesize. They supply the fungus with some of the sugar that they make. Exactly what benefit the alga receives is not clear, since most can grow quite well on their own without the fungus. The algae may be "captives" of the lichen fungus — an unusual situation in which one organism is parasitizing another smaller than itself. With fungi, however, almost anything seems possible, for they are among the strangest living things on Earth.

The fruiting bodies
of the honey fungus bursting through the bark of a tree.

The structure of fungi

FUNGI HAVE ALWAYS BEEN a source of myth and legend, partly because their fruiting bodies often appear magically almost overnight, and partly because many of them are mildly poisonous, and a few of them are deadly. Fungi grow in a bewildering variety of shapes and sizes. The fruiting body of a giant puffball can reach a diameter of more than 5 ft (1.5 m), while yeasts are single cells, each too small to see. Despite these differences, all fungi form spores, and it is the way these are produced that helps biologists to classify fungi into groups. Yeasts, for example, are offshoots of a group called the sac fungi, or ascomycetes. Mushrooms and toadstools are basidiomycetes. A third group, often called "lower fungi," produce spores in simpler fruiting bodies, such as those of pin molds (right).

EXPERIMENT
Growing a pin mold

YOU WILL NEED
● *bread* ● *petri dish*

Fruiting bodies of bread mold

Put some bread in a petri dish. Scatter dust on it to infect it with spores. Add a few drops of water, and cover. Within two days, mold should fill the dish. If you touch it, be sure to wash your hands afterward.

Sporangium releasing black spores

Maturing sporangium

Immature sporangium

Fungal threads (hyphae)

Morel
The tasty morel produces spores in dimples on its wrinkled surface. Like the bladder cup (below right), it is a sac fungus, or ascomycete.

Honey fungus
This fungus attacks wood. It is a club fungus, or basidiomycete. This is the most familiar group of fungi, in which spores develop at the tips of tiny clubs, or basidia, on the gills under the cap.

Bracket fungus
Bracket fungi form horizontal shelves on the sides of tree trunks and fallen logs. These can last long after the spores have been shed.

Woody bracket (basidiocarp) expands outward, building up concentric layers like the rings of a tree trunk

Bladder cup
This fungus, the bladder cup, is an ascomycete, or sac fungus. In this group, the spores are usually produced by microscopic sacs that lie on the inner surface of the cup.

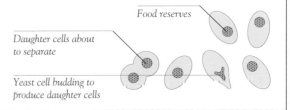

Porcelain fungus
This is one of the many species that grow on dead wood. Soon after shedding its spores, it disintegrates.

Slime mold
This jellylike object is the fruiting body of a slime mold, one of a group of very unusual organisms. Slime molds spend much of their lives creeping over the ground and engulfing bacteria. Some form large, thin sheets that constantly change their shape, while others live as many separate cells. To reproduce, the sheets develop fruiting bodies such as the one shown here. Slime molds with separate cells are able to reproduce themselves when the cells join together into a crawling, sluglike mass, which eventually produces spores.

■ DISCOVERY ■
Alexander Fleming

In 1928, Sir Alexander Fleming (1881-1955), who was a Scottish bacteriologist, made a chance discovery about a fungus that revolutionized the treatment of infections. He was growing bacteria in a petri dish when he noticed that a mold had contaminated the dish. Much more important, he saw that it had killed the bacteria near it. The chemical produced by the mold, penicillin, became available for medical use in 1942. In 1945, Fleming won the Nobel Prize for medicine, with Howard Florey and Ernst Chain, who had purified and tested the drug.

Penicillin
This important drug is produced from the fungus Penicillium notatum *and its close relatives. Other fungi also produce antibiotics which have been isolated and are used in medicine.*

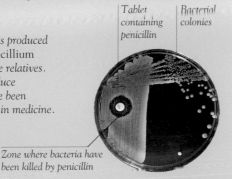

Tablet containing penicillin

Bacterial colonies

Zone where bacteria have been killed by penicillin

EXPERIMENT
The products of fermentation

Put a spoonful of sugar in a glass of water, and add a little yeast. Stir and cover with a lid. Wait a day until bubbles have appeared. Lift the lid, and quickly hold a lighted splint over the surface. The splint will go out, because the glass is full of carbon dioxide, produced by the yeast as it feeds on sugar.

YOU WILL NEED
- *yeast*
- *cardboard*
- *glass*
- *splint*
- *sugar*

Bubbles of carbon dioxide on the surface

Lighted splint

Glass containing water, sugar, and yeast

■ The role of yeast

Fermentation is the breakdown of a food substance in the absence of oxygen. During this process, the single cells that make up yeast feed on sugars, turning them to carbon dioxide and alcohol in the absence of air. Each cell divides rapidly as it feeds.

Food reserves

Daughter cells about to separate

Yeast cell budding to produce daughter cells

How toadstools reproduce

TOADSTOOLS HAVE JUST ONE FUNCTION — to produce spores on a massive scale. In one hour, an ordinary edible mushroom can liberate 30 million of these tiny grains, scattering them into the wind which carries them far and wide.

If you pick a toadstool and turn it upside down, you will see the structures that produce and disperse its spores. In some toadstools — for example, the mushroom — the spores are produced on the surface of downward-pointing gills. The gills are packed under the cap so that the spores can fall out easily. Some toadstools have no gills; instead their spores are shed from vertical tubes.

Hyphae
The feeding threads of the honey fungus are unusually long.

■ The development of a toadstool

Mushrooms and toadstools are made up of a mass of hyphae, or feeding threads, which live in soil or decaying wood. It is from these that a mushroom or toadstool springs. First, a mass of threads forms a "button" — a budlike structure that is often hidden underground. This expands upward, and its outer skin tears to reveal a stalk, topped by a cap. While the stalk grows, the cap begins to expand. Its skin tears to uncover the gills, which begin to release the spores. In some species, growth from button to mature toadstool can take just a few hours, because the hidden mass of hyphae only has to absorb water to expand to its full size.

Cap and stalk develop

Skin splits to reveal gills

Outer skin splits

Button elongates

Button

■ How a fairy ring forms

Fairy rings are circles of toadstools that you can sometimes see on lawns. Several species of fungi form these rings.

1 A FUNGAL SPORE LANDS on the ground and develops into an underground network of feeding threads (hyphae). Toadstools may appear on the surface and die away, but the threads continue growing underground.

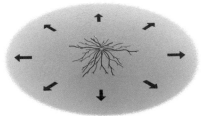

2 THE THREADS GRADUALLY USE UP the nutrients in the soil and have to spread out in search of fresh supplies. The oldest threads die away, leaving a ring of younger ones.

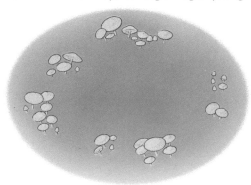

3 THE YOUNG THREADS continue to grow outward. When they produce toadstools, the result is a "fairy ring."

Dissolving toadstools
Ink caps are common fungi of gardens and fields. Almost as soon as an ink cap toadstool matures, its spores are released into the breeze to be dispersed, and the gills begin to dissolve into a black liquid.

Gills beginning to dissolve

Cap shrinks as the gills turn to liquid

Toadstools can be poisonous
Some toadstools are poisonous, and so you should not put them in your mouth.

Convex cap with scales

Stalk

Developing toadstool

Ring formed by torn skin

Fly agaric
The brightly colored fly agaric is a typical gilled fungus. Some of the gills run from the stalk to the rim of the cap, while shorter gills are slotted in between. The cap protects the gills from rain, while the stalk holds the gills high enough above the ground for the falling spores to catch the breeze. Fly agaric and its close relatives are found throughout the Northern Hemisphere.

Puffball
These fungi do not have gills. Instead, their spores develop inside a structure that dries out to become like a paper bag. If the puffball is touched — by a passing animal, for example — spores pour out of a central hole. Some puffballs roll in the wind to scatter the spores.

EXPERIMENT
Making a spore print

Fungal spores have distinctive colors, from white or yellow to jet black. You can see this by making a "print."

You Will Need
● *toadstool caps* ● *colored card* ● *plastic bowl* ● *artist's fixative spray*

3 In a well-ventilated room, spray the print with fixative to keep the spores from being rubbed off.

1 Place a toadstool cap on the card. Put the bowl over it for protection.

2 A day later, carefully lift the cap from the card. The spores should now have formed a print. Be careful not to touch the spore print, or it will smudge.

4 Collect other prints, using colored cards to contrast with the spores.

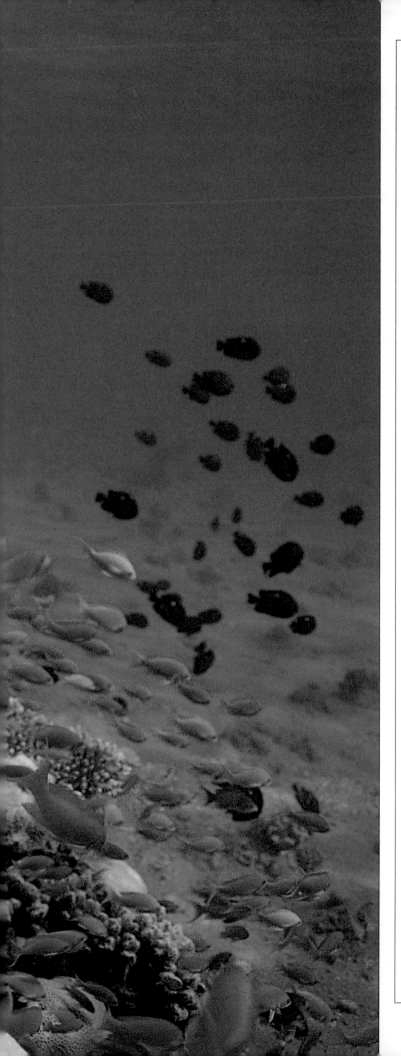

Life in WATER

Spectacular specimens
The creatures and plants found in watery habitats, and particularly in marine haunts, are some of the living world's most exotic. This eye-catching Nautilus scrobiculatus shell (above) lives in the sea, like the shoal of bright fish (left) swimming past a coral cliff on Australia's Great Barrier Reef.

LIFE ON EARTH BEGAN IN WATER and only slowly moved from there onto the land. Today, water is still the home of an astounding variety of living things. From the sea's darkest depths to its sunlit surface, different species take part in a struggle for survival that has lasted for billions of years. On land, many plants and animals have adapted to life in another watery environment — the freshwater world that includes rivers, streams, lakes, ponds, and puddles.

FRESHWATER LIFE

WATER IS ESSENTIAL TO LIFE ON EARTH. It covers nearly three-quarters of the surface of our planet, and the seas and oceans contain a total volume of just under 350 million cubic miles (1.5 billion km³). Lakes and rivers hold just a tiny fraction of that amount, but their fresh water is an important habitat for wildlife, which is easy to investigate.

If you have tried the experiment with the potato on p.17, you will have seen how a concentrated sugar solution can draw water through the membranes of cells by osmosis. Dissolved substances such as sugars and salts — or their absence — play an important part in the biology of everything that lives in water.

■ Keeping water out

Freshwater shrimp
are among the animals that can be attracted to a light trap.

All organisms have dissolved salts inside their cells. The concentration of these salts is about 35 parts per thousand — — the same as that of seawater. This is a reminder that life evolved in the sea. Even the relative amounts of the individual salts in the mixture are roughly the same as those in seawater. An animal that lives in the sea is as "salty" as the water around it, and, as a result, water is drawn neither into its cells nor out of them.

But for animals living in a lake, things are very different. The fluid inside their cells is much more salty than their surroundings, and so osmosis tends to draw water into the cells. Without any special measures to protect them, these animals would swell up and explode.

All freshwater animals have evolved ways to deal with this problem. Many single-celled animals get

The backswimmer
is one of the animals to be found at the water's surface.

rid of water in the same way as someone using a bucket to bail out a leaking boat. As fast as water is drawn in, organs called contractile vacuoles pump it out again. Larger animals are protected by a waterproof skin. Freshwater fish, for example, are often covered by a layer of waterproof mucus, while insects (p. 74) rely on external skeletons for protection.

Animals, such as eels (p. 82) and the inhabitants of rockpools (p. 92), can adapt to different levels of salt. For most water animals, moving from salt water to fresh water, or vice versa, is impossible and will kill them.

■ The hydrological cycle

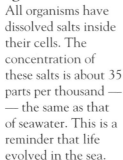

Freshwater fish
kept in captivity are fed special fish food.

Rivers and lakes are constantly replenished through the "hydrological cycle." The Sun evaporates water from the sea, the vapor forms clouds as it blows over the land, and then it finally falls as rain. This flows into the rivers and lakes, and much of it eventually runs into the sea again. Seawater contains salts, but when it evaporates, the salts are left behind. This is why rain is made up of salt-free, or "fresh," water. When rain falls and begins its

journey to the sea, it completes the last link in the cycle. How long it takes to reach the sea depends on where it falls, and this also affects the life that is found in it.

Tubifex worms
are a food for goldfish.

■ The biology of flowing water

If rain lands on the steep slopes of a mountain, the beginning of the journey is very rapid, as the rainwater joins a stream and tumbles quickly downhill to meet a river. Cold, fast-flowing water has both advantages and disadvantages for wildife. As it splashes against rocks, the water dissolves oxygen from the air around it. Oxygen-rich water is ideal for fish such as trout, but a strong current makes life difficult. It quickly dislodges anything that is not stuck fast, or — like the trout — strong enough to hold its own by swimming against it. Most smaller animals in fast-flowing streams have evolved ways to hang on to rocks and stones.

By the time the stream or river reaches lower ground, much of the force of the initial descent has been spent. The water flows more sluggishly, offering plenty of opportunities for wildife. Plants, such as floating algae, reeds, and rushes, thrive. Animals, such as water snails, ducks, and fish, feed

The toad's feeding technique
relies on speed and surprise.

on the plants, and they support predators, including larger fish, terrapins, and otters. The water may spend days or weeks in the lower reaches of a river until eventually it meets the open sea.

Sometimes, the journey to the sea can take far longer. Not all the rain that falls flows into surface streams and rivers. In some places, it sinks through the soil and rock to become "groundwater," part of the network of natural rivers and reservoirs that exist in porous rocks. Many parts of the world — even dry ones such as the Sahara Desert — contain huge stores of this underground water. Groundwater flows very slowly — sometimes just a yard or so every year — so it can be thousands of years old. Shut off from the Sun's energy, it is usually devoid of life.

Fascinating lake habitats

A large amount of the Earth's fresh water is held in lakes, which are one of the most fascinating habitats that you can study. Lakes have many permanent inhabitants, but they are also the home of many animals that live in water only when they are young. These include the tadpoles of amphibians (pp. 78-81) and the larvae of insects (p. 75). By having an adaptable life, they are able to make use of more than

Minute bloodworms
live in water with little oxygen.

A young toad
about to move from life in water to life on land.

one kind of habitat and source of food.

No two lakes have exactly the same kind of water, and small differences in the chemical balance of the water can make a large difference to wildlife. Lowland lakes are often very rich in tiny plants and animals — as you can see if you collect some of the water and view a few drops under a microscope. If the water is rich in nutrients, small algae (p. 27) grow very rapidly, and the water becomes like a green soup. This can cause problems for other organisms, particularly when the algae die and rot.

By contrast, the water of a lake high in a mountain can be quite different — sparklingly clear, but home to far fewer organisms.

Hidden boundaries underwater

If you have gone swimming in a lake in summer, you may have noticed that the water feels much cooler if you let your legs trail beneath you. What you are feeling is the "thermocline," the meeting point of the surface water, which has been heated by the Sun, and the cooler, heavier water beneath it.

Biologists have found that seasonal changes in water temperature are very important to life in lakes. Throughout the summer, the

Fish are well adapted
to life in water with streamlined bodies and fins for steering.

These salamanders,
like many amphibians, lay their eggs in water.

warm water floats over the cool water below, dividing the lake into two layers.

Floating algae grow rapidly near the surface, sometimes undergoing population explosions known as "blooms." The algae stay near the surface either by beating tiny whiplike growths called flagella or by using gas-filled floats inside their cells. As the season progresses, different species of algae dominate the surface waters in succession. As each uses up the water's nutrients, it begins to die off and decay.

In the fall, the surface water begins to lose its heat, and eventually it becomes as cold as the water beneath it. The two layers merge, and water from all levels of the lake can mix. This mixing is important, as it brings nutrients back to the surface where they can be reused.

There is another invisible barrier that has an important effect on the life of lakes. Water plants can live only where there is enough light for them to carry out photosynthesis. Below a certain depth — the "compensation level" — the light energy they would receive is less than the energy they need to live. So plants can grow only to a certain depth. In murky water, they must be much nearer the surface than in clear water.

Tiny crustaceans,
such as this Cyclops, live in salt water and fresh water. These species are the most common multicellular animals in the world.

Animals of lakes and streams

FRESHWATER HABITATS are found across all the world's land masses, in dry areas as well as wet ones. Where rain falls only occasionally, freshwater animals have to battle against the clock in order to survive — sometimes they have only a few days in which to reproduce before their water dries up. Where rainfall is more frequent, lakes and streams are permanent habitats. Lake life nearly always includes tiny, single-celled creatures, such as amoebae, as well as flatworms, snails, and insects. Many of these animals use lakes as nurseries. The larvae develop underwater, and change into adults that live on land.

Ramshorn snail

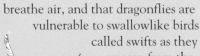

■ Freshwater inhabitants

The pictures here show just some of the animals that are to be found in lakes and streams. You can see all these animals with the naked eye, though a hand lens can be useful when you look at *Daphnia* or *Cyclops*. Fresh water also teems with much smaller animals and plants. You will need to use a microscope to see these.

Mosquito larvae
These hang from the water's surface and sink quickly to escape danger.

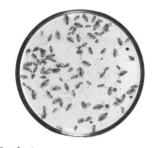

Daphnia
Also known as "water fleas," Daphnia build up to vast numbers.

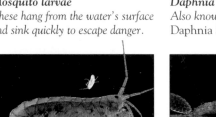

Freshwater shrimp
This lives among rocks and gravel, feeding on decayed remains.

Cyclops
Small enough to fit in a drop of water, they feed on tiny animals.

Water boatman
This is a predator that swims upside down and stabs its prey.

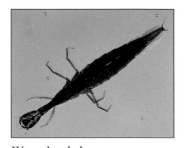

Water beetle larva
This is a fierce hunter that consumes small fish and tadpoles.

Dragonfly larva
This insect larva, or nymph, lurks in muddy vegetation in lakes.

Great pond snail
Pond snails scrape away at their food with sandpaperlike tongues.

■ DISCOVERY ■
Mysteries of Water Life

The English naturalist, Rev. Gilbert White (1720–1793) is best known as the author of *The Natural History and Antiquities of Selborne* (1789). He was one of the many people who have made important discoveries about plants and animals by hours of patient observation. He found that fish could move their eyes (people at the time thought they could not), and that they were responsive to movements they could see above water. He also found that newts breathe air, and that dragonflies are vulnerable to swallowlike birds called swifts as they emerge from the water to begin their life as adults.

EXPERIMENT
Trapping underwater nightlife

If you shine a light on a lake at night, you should be able to see a host of small animals near the surface. These may include tiny crustaceans, such as water fleas, and also young fish, which are known as "fry." By feeding at night, these animals run less risk of being caught by predators. To get a closer look at the nightlife of lakes, you can make this special trap. It works rather like a lobster pot. Small animals are attracted by the light of a flashlight. They swim into the trap through the spout of a funnel, and then cannot find their way out. Don't forget to pour the animals back into the lake when you have finished examining them.

YOU WILL NEED
- waterproof adhesive tape ● black plastic ● rubber bands ● funnel
- glass jar or bottle with lid ● string ● small flashlight ● wide plastic piping, 1 ft (about 30 cm) long

1 Tape the funnel to one end of the pipe, with the narrow end of the funnel pointing into the pipe.

2 Tie the string around both ends of the pipe, but leave the string slack in the middle to make a carrying handle.

3 Switch on the flashlight, and put it in the jar, so that the light shines through the bottom. Screw the lid on tightly.

4 Put the jar into the pipe, with the light shining out of the funnel. Fix the plastic to the pipe's open end with rubber bands.

5 Lower the trap into the water, and try not to disturb the bottom of the lake too much. Leave overnight.

6 Lift the trap, remove black plastic, and pour the water into a bucket or bowl. You can now examine your catch.

Making a pond

A GARDEN POND can be a powerful magnet for wildlife.
There are three main ways to make a pond — shaping
one out of concrete, using a preformed plastic liner, or
laying down a flexible liner. Plastic ponds often look
artificial, concrete ponds are liable to crack, whereas
flexible liners make natural-looking, durable ponds. It is
best to dig a shelved hole as shown below, line it with
sand or newspapers to cover sharp
stones, and then put in the flexible
liner (preferably heavy-gauge
butyl rubber, which does not
degrade in sunlight). If the
water you use to fill the
pond comes from a faucet,
leave it for at least a week
before adding animals, so
that the chlorine used in
the water treatment can
evaporate.

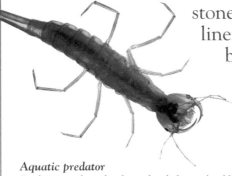

Aquatic predator
*Predators such as this diving beetle larva should
not be put in a freshwater aquarium, as they will
quickly reduce the numbers of other animals.*

■ Looking through a pond

A wildlife pond should have at least two levels — a shelf about 8 in (20 cm) deep,
where water's edge plants can be grown, and a deep area, with at least 18 in (45 cm)
of water. The deep water allows animals enough room to escape from their predators,
and, in all but the coldest climates, keeps the pond from freezing solid in winter.

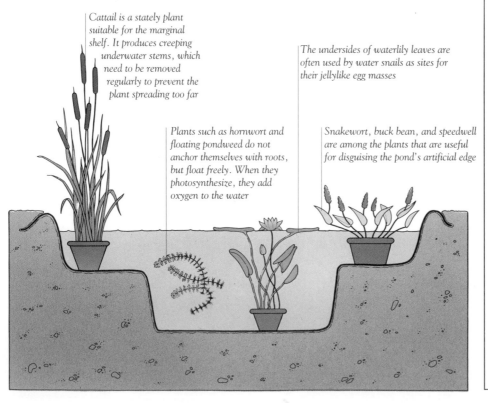

*Cattail is a stately plant
suitable for the marginal
shelf. It produces creeping
underwater stems, which
need to be removed
regularly to prevent the
plant spreading too far*

*Plants such as hornwort and
floating pondweed do not
anchor themselves with roots,
but float freely. When they
photosynthesize, they add
oxygen to the water*

*The undersides of waterlily leaves are
often used by water snails as sites for
their jellylike egg masses*

*Snakewort, buck bean, and speedwell
are among the plants that are useful
for disguising the pond's artificial edge*

EXPERIMENT
Making an aquarium

By creating an indoor aquarium, you
can study animals underwater without
disturbing them.

A freshwater aquarium is a closed
ecosystem. All it needs to work is light
energy from the Sun. To be a long-term
success, it must have the right balance
of nutrients, plants, and animals. If the
water has a high mineral content, tiny
algae will flourish, taking up most of
the dissolved oxygen and turning the
water murky. To avoid this, use clean
gravel and scrub any objects, such as
rocks. Slightly soluble rock, such as
chalk or limestone, should not be used.

YOU WILL NEED
● *tank* ● *gravel* ● *water plants* ● *water
animals* ● *rocks or dead wood* ● *pond water
or rainwater*

1 FILL THE BASE OF THE TANK with
aquarium gravel that has been well
rinsed to discourage algae.

2 USE ROCKS AND PIECES of dead wood
to create an underwater landscape,
and surfaces for snails to feed on.

3 ADD ENOUGH WATER to fill the tank to about half its depth. Overfilling the tank may reduce the amount of oxygen that is dissolved in the water.

4 ADD ROOTED PLANTS in pots, or plant them in the gravel. Essential oxygenating plants, such as floating pondweed, can be left to float freely.

5 YOU CAN NOW STOCK THE TANK with animals. Adding a small amount of pond water will introduce tiny animals such as daphnia (water fleas, p. 74).

Floating on the surface
In this tank, tiny duckweed plants are spreading across the surface of the water. Duckweed has to be kept under control, or it will prevent light from reaching plants below it.

6 PLACE THE TANK IN BRIGHT LIGHT (but not in direct sunlight). The plants in the tank will grow and provide the food needed by the animals.

If you plan to raise tadpoles in the tank, exposed surfaces are essential to give the young frogs or toads somewhere to sit

Dead matter may eventually build up on the gravel, and this will have to be removed to keep the water clean. You can do this without emptying the tank, by siphoning off the debris using a tube

Aquatic snails feed on encrusting algae by rasping them away with their rough tongues

Finely divided leaves give off oxygen, which dissolves in the water

Amphibians

FROGS, TOADS, AND NEWTS all live in
watery habitats. The name amphibian
means "having two lives," a reference to
the fact that these animals are able to live
on land or in water. Many species spend
most of the year on land — in trees,
bushes, or long grass — returning to water
to lay their eggs. The powerful back legs
that enable them to hop when on land
become transformed into paddles for
swimming. Frogs and toads have no tails,
but the tails of newts and other
salamanders are long and distinctive.

Peter Pan amphibian
*The axolotl is a salamander that,
like Peter Pan, never grows up. It
becomes a giant tadpole, complete
with pink external gills. Axolotls do
mature and lose their gills if iodine
is added to the water. Like*
*humans, they need iodine to
produce a growth hormone. Unlike
normal tadpoles, axolotls can mate
and lay eggs. This ability is called
"neoteny," and is found in some
other amphibians as well.*

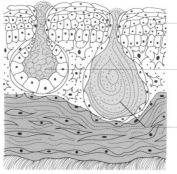

*Thin skin of the surface cells
allows oxygen to pass into
the blood*

*Mucous
glands help to
prevent skin
drying out*

*Poison glands
deter predators*

Section of skin of spotted salamander
*The salamander's skin helps to protect it
from danger and dehydration, and allows
it to breathe.*

■ Warning coloration

These spotted salamanders have poison glands in
their skin, which make predators reluctant to eat
them. Their striking color — yellow markings on a
black background, just like a wasp — is a classic
warning signal. As long as their
"protective clothing" works, spotted
salamanders enjoy a long life. They have
survived in captivity for 25 years — a
remarkable time for such a small animal.

*Four fingers on
fore limbs*

*Bright spots warn that
animal is poisonous*

*Five toes on
hind limbs*

"Swimming" on land
*The way that a salamander
moves on land is more like
swimming than walking.*

*The body bends from
side to side, helping
the short legs to
move forward*

Thin, rubbery skin

■ Newts

For about half the year, newts (a type of small salamander) live in ponds and slow-moving streams. For the rest of the time they can be found on land, usually concealed in damp undergrowth. In an elaborate courtship ritual, the male dances and displays to the female. Newt eggs hatch into tadpoles with external gills, but these external gills are lost as the newt grows up.

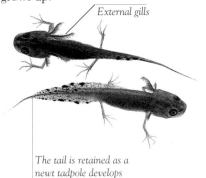

External gills

The tail is retained as a newt tadpole develops into an adult

■ Frogs and toads

There are roughly 3,500 species of frog and toad, compared with just 360 species of salamander and newt. Their powerful back legs are probably one reason why these amphibians are so successful. Some species can jump 10 ft (3 m) — 60 times the body length of the record-holder, the South American sharp-nosed frog. If kangaroos could perform such a feat, they would leap the length of a football field with a single jump.

Powerful jumping enables frogs and toads to travel at high speed. A few species of frog can hop across the surface of a pond without sinking.

EXPERIMENT
Feeding a toad

Adult frogs and toads all feed on animals. Toads often move quite sluggishly, but their tongues can catch small animals with lightning speed. You can see this technique in action by putting food in front of a toad. Beetle larvae, such as mealworms, are a favorite food. You can find out if the toad reacts to movement by chilling the larvae in a refrigerator (the cold will keep the larvae still). What is the greatest distance from which the toad can catch the prey?

YOU WILL NEED
● *toad* ● *beetle larvae*

Ear

Front feet have four fingers

Mealworm

Webbed back feet

Spotting the prey
Most toads have a slow, crawling gait when they are searching for food. When a likely meal is *spotted, the toad watches it carefully while gauging its distance.*

Powerful hind legs

On the attack
The tongues of most toads are attached to the front of their mouths. The toad leans forward, *and the sticky tongue flicks out, catching the prey in a sudden moment.*

A successful catch
The tongue flicks back with the prey. Frogs and toads will eat almost anything small enough to *swallow, sometimes pushing food into their mouths with their front feet.*

From tadpole to toad

AMPHIBIANS UNDERGO METAMORPHOSIS — fascinating changes in body shape — as they grow up. As a tadpole develops, it changes from being a purely aquatic animal to one that can also live on land.

Except in the tropics and in dry habitats, frogs and toads breed at a set time. For common toads, breeding time is early spring. Males usually arrive at a pond first and announce their presence by croaking loudly, especially in the evening. The female toads are attracted by the croaking, and arrive at the pond, their bodies large and swollen with eggs. The males grasp the females in a tight grip, known as amplexus. After a day or so, with the male still holding on tightly, the female lays her eggs. As she does so, the male releases sperm and fertilizes them.

■ The developing egg

The egg of a frog or toad starts as a single cell (1). It has a gray crescent-shaped area at one side, and experiments show that this controls its development. If an egg is cut in two, and both halves contain some of the gray crescent, then two normal tadpoles result. But if one half has none of the gray crescent, it grows into an abnormal mass of cells. Thirty minutes after it has been laid, the egg cell divides to give two cells (2). After another thirty minutes it divides again to give four cells (3), then again to give eight cells (4). At first the cells all divide in step with each other (5 and 6), but after six hours the divisions speed up (7), and each cell goes at its own pace.

1
2
3
4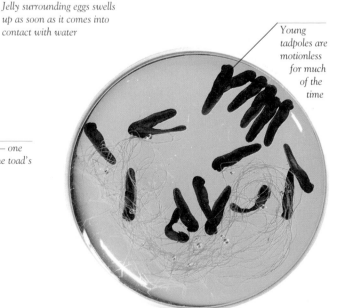
5
6
7

Toad spawn

The common toad lays its eggs in rows which are joined to form a long, twisted string, bound around the stems of water plants. The eggs are held together by a thick coat of jelly. A single female toad can produce thousands of eggs. If you look at toad spawn with a hand lens, you can see the cells dividing to form an embryo.

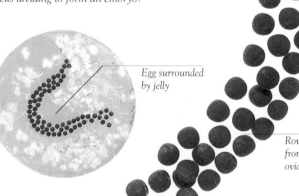

Egg surrounded by jelly

Rows of eggs — one from each of the toad's oviducts

Each egg has divided into a number of cells

Young toad tadpoles

For a day or two after hatching, the tadpoles hang on to the jelly that surrounded their eggs. They may eat some of the jelly, or the algae growing on it. They only move away if they are disturbed. The gills are very tiny at this stage, but they can just be seen as tiny flaps.

Jelly surrounding eggs swells up as soon as it comes into contact with water

Young tadpoles are motionless for much of the time

Early development

The speed at which tadpoles develop depends on the temperature of the water. Early in their growth, the gills grow large and feathery, to extract oxygen from the water. Gills link amphibians with their ancestors — fishlike animals which emerged from lakes and rivers about 380 million years ago, and which also had gills.

Gills take in oxygen from the water

Hidden changes

Inside the tadpole, lungs have started to develop. When they are able to breathe air with these lungs, the tadpoles lose their gills. The gills do not drop off, but are absorbed by the body. The nutrients contained in them are saved and recycled into new body parts.

An invisible line (the lateral line) of sensory organs runs along each side of the tadpole's body

Tadpoles gradually change from eating plants to eating animal food

Preparing for life on land

A tadpole's back legs develop gradually alongside the tail. Within the tadpole's fat, round body, the front legs are also taking shape, but they are hidden under flaps of skin. They pop through suddenly, fully formed. Often one of the tadpole's front limbs comes out before the other, so the tadpole is three-legged for some time. This presents no real problem, as the tadpole is still a totally aquatic creature.

The young toad

Once the tadpole has developed all four legs, its tail begins to shrink. This is absorbed by the tadpole's body, and recycled just as the gills were. The tadpole is almost a toad now, and it begins to emerge from the water for longer and longer periods. Once its tail has gone completely, the young toad will leave the pond altogether. It will only return to the pond to breed, many years later.

Fish

IN THE MAJORITY OF WATERY HABITATS, fish are the most successful and abundant of the larger animals. Their fins and scales superbly equip them for an aquatic life. The sideways movement of the tail fin propels them forward, and the other fins provide stability and steering, while a smooth coat of scales gives a tough yet flexible surface to minimize water resistance. Some species can make their way on dry land too. At night, eels can slither from stream to stream through damp grass, while the mudskippers of mangrove swamps forage at low tide. Like most other fish, eels and mudskippers cannot breathe air, so on land they extract oxygen from a reservoir of water around their gills.

■ The migration of eels

Fish live in either salt or fresh water, but a small minority move from one habitat to the other. The common eels of Europe and North America live in streams and rivers, but apparently return to the Sargasso Sea to breed. They lay eggs and die, leaving the larvae to make the journey back.

Migration of European eel

Migration of North American eel

Europe

North America

Breeding area in Sargasso Sea

Eel larvae
Swept along by the currents and then guided by instinct, these leaf-shaped larvae make their way toward land.

Adult eels
Although no one has ever actually found a live eel making the journey, scientists believe that all adult common eels swim back to the Sargasso Sea to breed.

Dogfish
This is one of the smallest cartilaginous fish.

■ The two types of fish

Fish divide into cartilaginous and bony types. The bony fish are more numerous. Their skeletons are white and hard like ours, and you can see the typical bones if you eat cod. In the cartilaginous fish — sharks, rays, and skates — only the teeth are calcified. The rest of the skeleton is made of cartilage (pp. 158-159). Press the end of your nose to feel what cartilage is like.

Angelfish
This bony fish has an unusual body shape, allowing it to feed on the polyps of a coral reef.

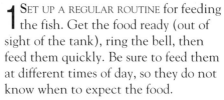

1 SET UP A REGULAR ROUTINE for feeding the fish. Get the food ready (out of sight of the tank), ring the bell, then feed them quickly. Be sure to feed them at different times of day, so they do not know when to expect the food.

2 AFTER TWO WEEKS, get someone to help you test the responses of the fish. Hide and watch when your helper rings the bell. How do the fish respond?

■ Inside a bony fish

All bony fish have a balloonlike organ inside them known as a swim bladder. It contains gas, which gives the fish extra buoyancy. The amount of gas can be increased or decreased whenever the fish needs to change its depth. In the earliest ancestors of the bony fish, this organ started out as a lung. These fish had gills as well, and could probably switch from using gills to lungs when they needed to breathe air — if the water they were in became stagnant and low in oxygen, for example. Lungfish, which live in swamps in tropical Africa and South America, can still do this.

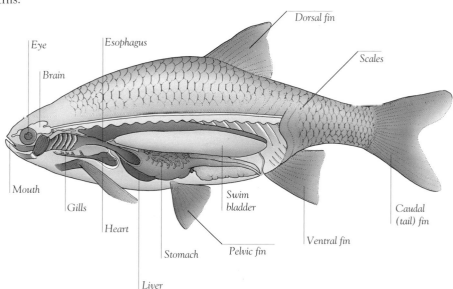

Eye
Esophagus
Brain
Dorsal fin
Scales
Mouth
Gills
Heart
Stomach
Liver
Pelvic fin
Swim bladder
Ventral fin
Caudal (tail) fin

LIFE ON THE SEASHORE

THE SEASHORE IS A PLACE of constant change, a habitat where land and sea battle for supremacy, and where life has to cope with the daily rise and fall of the tide. If you explore the shore, you will soon discover that many different plants and animals have managed to adapt to these changing conditions with remarkable success.

Starfish glide
along on tiny "tube-feet." Some starfish use their feet to prise open the shells of mollusks.

Unlike other habitats, the seashore is always on the move. As waves pound against the land, they break it up, and eventually currents carry the debris away. In places such as southern California, the sea can advance as much as 30 ft (10 m) a year as it eats into the crumbling cliffs. Houses that were once safely inland perch precariously on the cliff tops, where a storm may one day send them crashing onto the beach.

However, the contest between land and sea is not entirely one-way. As the sea cuts away one part of a coast, it adds to the shoreline in another. The ancient English town of Winchelsea, for example, was once a thriving port. Today, it is well inland, and every year the former shore retreats even further behind a growing bank of shingle.

■ Tides and built-in clocks

The battering of the waves is not the only problem for seashore life. Twice a day, the tide rises up the shore, submerging plants and animals, and then falls back again, leaving them high and dry.

Thousands of years ago, people noticed that tides were related to the positions of the Sun and Moon, and we now know that it is the gravitational pull of the Sun and Moon that makes tides

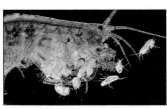

An amphipod with its young
— amphipods are crustaceans found in salt and fresh water.

occur. Compared to the force of the Earth's gravity, this pull is quite weak. But the world's seawater has an enormous mass, and so the force that acts on it is considerable. When the Sun and Moon line up with the Earth — as they do every two weeks — the effect of their gravity combines. The result is a "spring" tide — one that is higher than normal. When the Sun and Moon are at right angles to the Earth, the result is a "neap" tide — one with a much smaller range.

The rise and fall of the tide follows a very regular pattern, and many shore animals have their own biological "clock" that causes their behavior to fit in with it. Fiddler crabs, for example, live in burrows in mangrove swamps, and emerge at low tide to feed. If a fiddler crab is kept in a tank with constant light and no tides, it will still appear promptly at "low tide" time, and disappear underground again as the nonexistent tide rises once more.

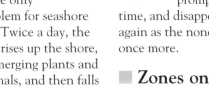

The hard skeleton
produced by a free-living coral animal, or polyp.

■ Zones on the shore

Tides have a great influence on seashore life. A plant or animal that cannot survive out of water lives only below the low-tide mark of spring tides. One that needs to be out of the water all the

time has to be above the high-tide mark of spring tides. Between these levels are plants and animals that can cope with a mixture of conditions — sometimes submerged, and sometimes exposed to the air. Each has adapted to the particular conditions on one part of the shore. This is known as zonation (p. 88), and you can see it most clearly when the tide is out. As you walk down the shore toward the sea, you will notice that the species of plants and animals change as you get nearer the water. These different species tend not to compete for food, staying within their zone.

A seaweed's frond,
buoyed up by gas-filled bladders that act as floats.

The width of these different zones depends on the average rise and fall of the tides, and this in turn depends on where you are in the world. The highest tides are found in narrow bays facing the open ocean. Here, the coast acts as a funnel and the water piles up as the tide surges toward land. In the Bay of Fundy on the east coast of Canada, which has the largest tides in the world, the difference between the high- and low-water levels can be as much as 48 ft (14.5 m). In the Mediterranean, the tidal range is small. Where the tidal range is great, the zones of shore life are wide. Where the range is narrow, they are squeezed together.

A worm shell
spirals at random, as it grows.

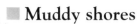

■ Getting a grip

Shores made of hard rock abound with life because they offer plants and animals something that other shores do not — a firm anchorage. Here you can see limpets and barnacles, two animals that are perfectly adapted to facing the fury of the waves. Limpets are mollusks that wander over the rock, scraping off small plants with their hard tongues. Each limpet has a "home," a small depression in the rock that it returns to after feeding. The shell fits against the rock so tightly that neither waves nor hungry seabirds can dislodge it.

At one time, biologists thought that barnacles were mollusks. However, by looking at their larvae, it was found that these small armored animals are actually crustaceans. After spending its early life as a larva floating in the water, a barnacle glues its back to the rock and then secretes a shell which protects it not only from the waves but also from the Sun and wind at low tide. When submerged, the barnacle opens a "door" on the top of its shell and then uses its legs to collect tiny particles of food from the water. In some places, it is not unusual to find barnacles covering rock in huge numbers, as many as 9,000 per square foot (100,000 barnacles per square meter).

Making a special viewer *gives you a chance to have a close look at life in rockpools.*

■ Survival in a shifting habitat

When part of the land, such as a rocky cliff, collapses into the sea after a storm, the sea begins to grind it up into smaller fragments. Over a process that takes hundreds of thousands of years, the rock becomes boulders, the boulders become pebbles, and the pebbles are finally ground into grains of sand.

A pebble beach is a difficult place for plants and animals to survive. The sea constantly smashes the pebbles together, and any animal larvae or plants that settle on the pebbles are soon crushed. The only place where plants and animals can survive is well above the high-tide mark, and here lack of moisture is a problem. You may find small animals living in the flotsam (odds and ends thrown up by the tide), but otherwise there is often very little wildlife to be seen.

Sand is an altogether kinder habitat. Although the upper layers of sand swirl around at high tide, beneath them animals can burrow in safety. Here, there is no danger of drying out, and the only problem is to find food. Some sand-dwellers need only the sand itself, but most live by collecting food from the water. Some sieve the water through tiny filters, pumping it into and then out of their burrows. They can be spotted by tiny air holes in the sand. Others trap food in long tentacles, or pick it up off the surface. Larger animals, such as crabs, can live in these different habitats where they scavenge for their food. The coral crab, for example, frequents coral reefs, and rocky-bottomed shores, as well as sandy areas.

A beautiful shell *or "test," made of calcium carbonate, lies beneath a sea urchin's spines.*

Tough shells protect the bodies *of winkles and other mollusks from the force of the waves.*

■ Muddy shores

Rivers bring silt down to the sea, and muddy shores are created. As a river nears the sea, it gradually slows down, and the silt that it carries settles out of the water. The tide then shapes this silt into soft banks that are often treacherous places for us to walk on. Plants are rare in muddy water because not enough light can penetrate the water for photosynthesis (pp. 40-43) to occur.

At first, mud may not seem like a very promising place for wildlife, but it is actually full of nutrients. Not many species have adapted to this salty habitat, but the ones that have reach huge numbers. If you could somehow remove the mud from a muddy shore, and leave behind the organisms that it holds, you would see a vast mass of life. Some of these animals — which include crustaceans, delicate fanworms, and mollusks with beautifully sculpted shells — collect edible particles from the seawater, while others burrow through the mud, eating leftovers and other animals. In a study of just 11 square feet (one square meter) of mud on the coast of Denmark, biologists counted approximately 60,000 tiny snails feeding on the surface. Because muddy shores teem with life, they are favorite feeding areas for wading birds such as oyster catchers.

Crab larvae *are among the many tiny organisms floating in the sea.*

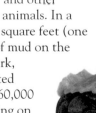

A shore crab *shelters inside the shell of a scallop.*

Seashore types

To a naturalist, all types of shore — even muddy ones — are fascinating places to explore. If the coastline near you is tidal, the period just before low tide is the best time to investigate shore life. During a spring tide (p. 84), just before the sea reaches low water, you will be able to see many plants and animals that are normally submerged. Local newspapers often publish "tide tables," which will enable you to plan a visit so you arrive at the best time.

Forest at the sea's edge
On muddy shores in the tropics, trees called mangroves grow out into the shallow water, forming swamps that are almost impossible to clamber through. Their tangled root system traps mud that eventually builds up into dry land. Unlike most other trees, mangroves can survive in very salty conditions. They have special breathing roots called pneumatophores, which grow upward into the air.

■ Shingle shore

The pebbles on a shingle beach are easily moved by the waves, making it a difficult place for plants and animals to survive. You can discover this for yourself by marking some pebbles with colored paint. As the tide rises and the waves reach the pebbles, you can see them being thrown about by the sea. Because pebbles don't fit snugly together, there are often large gaps between them. Water rapidly drains through these gaps, dragging any animals with it. Life is safer above the high-tide mark. Here, plants and lichens can grow beyond reach of the waves, and birds such as plovers can use the shingle banks to lay their eggs.

Part of an oyster shell

Egg case of a dogfish

Skeleton of a heart urchin, which lives in a burrow in mud

Part of a cockle shell

Razorshell (razor clam), a long bivalve mollusk

Dark color of sand is due to mud carried down by a river

Fragments of shell are gradually worn away to form sand

■ Sand and mud

As long as you wear boots and are equipped with a shovel, investigating wildlife in sand and mud can be an enjoyable experience. Most of the animals on sandy and muddy shores live below the surface, but many have burrows which you can spot at low tide by small holes on the surface. These animals are sensitive to the vibrations created by approaching feet, and will retreat deep into their burrows unless you walk softly. If you dig rapidly near a burrow, you should be able to uncover segmented worms and filter-feeding or predatory mollusks. (Remember to put them back afterward.) At low tide, muddy shores attract birds, known as "waders," which probe for these animals with their long beaks.

Boulder beach

Fixed rocks offer the most secure places for plants and animals. Once the sea breaks off a piece of rock, the boulders that it produces may still be large enough to stay in one place as the sea rages around them, and they can offer a safe site for animals such as barnacles. Once they become broken down into smaller rocks, anything living on them is quickly crushed as the rocks are ground together and carried away by the sea.

Large boulders worn down by the sea

Pebbles worn smooth by the waves

Barnacles on the shell of a mussel

Claw of a crab, dropped by a feeding gull

Cuttlebone — the internal shell of a cuttlefish

Arms that grow back

Starfish are slow-moving marine invertebrates that mostly live near the shore. Many starfish, such as the Crown of Thorns, are poisonous. Most starfish have five arms, and if you turn one over, you will be able to see that each one has rows of tiny, suckerlike feet. It uses these feet to move, and also to prize apart the shells of its prey. If a starfish loses an arm, it gradually regenerates (grows back).

1 STARFISH OFTEN LOSE ARMS when the movement of the sea rolls rocks on top of them. Some species also shed arms if they are attacked, as a way of escaping from the predator.

2 THE ARM SEALS ITSELF OFF at the break, and cells inside the stump start to divide quickly.

3 WITHIN A FEW WEEKS, the arm is well on its way to recovery. The other arms are used for feeding and moving.

4 AS LONG AS THE CENTRAL DISC is undamaged, some starfish can recover even after losing four out of their five arms.

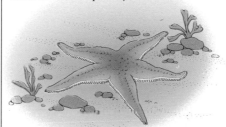

Life on rocky shores

ROCKY SHORES ARE very demanding habitats. The animals and plants that live on them must withstand being pounded by the waves, and also being submerged or exposed as the tide (pp. 84-85) rises and falls. If you examine the rocks, you will see that life between the highest and lowest tides is organized into zones. On many rocky shores, closely related species live in different zones, so they do not compete for food or living space.

Hidden in a shell
Crabs escape the force of the waves by retreating into crevices. This one is secure in a scallop shell.

■ Growing in the open sea

Many of the animals that live on the rocky shore breed by releasing their eggs or young into the water. The shore crab is a good example. Female shore crabs carry their eggs in clusters on their undersides. The eggs produce tiny larvae, called zoeae, which float away in the water, becoming part of the "plankton" — the mass of tiny plants and animals that float freely in the open sea. Later the zoeae turn into crabs. By reproducing in this way, crustaceans, mollusks, and many other animals can disperse their young over a wide area.

■ Sharing the rocky shore

This zonation diagram shows where similar species live in zones created by the tide. Where the tidal range is small, the zones are squeezed together. Where the tide rises and falls much farther, the zones are more spread out.

EHWS
Extreme high-water level of spring tides — the shore above this point is always out of the water

MHWS
Mean high-water level of spring tides — the zone below this point is fully or partly submerged by the highest tides

MHWN
Mean high-water level of neap tides — the zone below this point is fully or partly submerged by least extreme tides

MSL
Mean sea level — the average height of the sea as it rises and falls

MLWN
Mean low-water level of neap tides — the zone above this point is fully or partly exposed by least extreme tides

MLWS
Mean low-water level of spring tides — the zone above this point can be fully or partly exposed, but only by the most extreme tides

ELWS
Extreme low-water level of spring tides — the shore below this point is always underwater

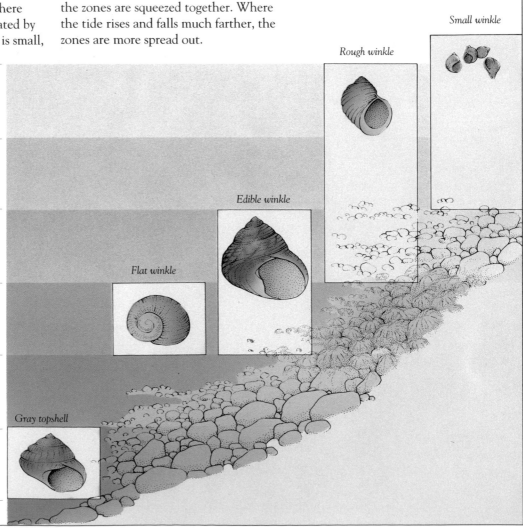

Small winkle

Rough winkle

Edible winkle

Flat winkle

Gray topshell

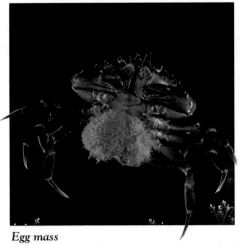

Egg mass
A female shore crab carries a mass of eggs under her body. She flaps her abdomen to wash fresh, oxygen-rich water over them.

Ready to hatch
The eggs are joined together by filaments, rather like grapes in a bunch. Here, the black eyes of the larvae can be seen in each egg.

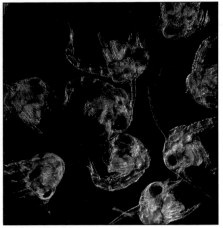

A floating life
Zoeae live in open water. They change into megalopa larvae, which walk on the sea bed, and then into mature crabs.

EXPERIMENT
Making a rocky shore aquarium

You can watch the behavior of animals such as crabs and prawns by setting up an aquarium that imitates a rocky shore. A filter containing ceramic tubes provides a surface on which algae and bacteria can grow. Bacteria keep the water clean by removing animal waste products.

You Will Need
● *rocks* ● *shell sand* ● *seawater* ● *shore animals such as mussels, prawns, sea anemones, and shore crabs* ● *tank* ● *filter unit with ceramic tubes*

1 ADD THE SHELL SAND to the bottom of the tank. The calcium it contains will help crabs and mollusks to grow strong, healthy shells.

2 POSITION SMALL ROCKS and stones. These will provide a refuge for crabs, and an anchorage for mollusks and sea anemones. Add the seawater.

3 BE GENTLE with the shore animals when you put them in the tank. Feed crabs, prawns, and sea anemones on small pieces of meat. Mussels require finely ground fish food (available from pet shops).

Shells

A SHELL IS A MOBILE HOME and a suit of armor rolled into one. All the shells here belong to mollusks — soft-bodied animals that produce hard shells to protect themselves. Their shells are made chiefly of calcium carbonate, the substance we know as chalk. This is secreted by a layer of living tissue called the mantle. As a mollusk grows, the edges of the shell grow too.

Inside a nautilus
This nautilus shell has been cut in half to show the spiral growth that is a feature of many mollusk shells. The animal lives only in the largest chamber, which is open to the sea. As it grows, the nautilus seals off the shell behind it, creating a gallery of buoyancy chambers.

Thread of tissue connecting the chambers

Paired valves
The shells of sunset siliquas and scallops are paired when the mollusks are alive, but are often found separated after their owners have died.

Lamellose wentletrap
This shell's name comes from the German word Wendeltrappe, meaning "spiral staircase."

Scallop

Sunset siliqua

Chiton (sea cradle)
The chiton shell is made up of eight plates. It is attached to a soft-bodied animal that lives on rocks and other shells.

Green tusk shells
The animals that make tusk shells are called scaphopods. They live buried in sand, with the tips of their shells showing.

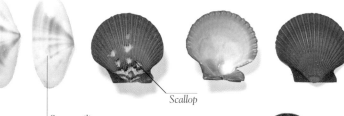

Seeing inside a shell

The spiral shells of gastropods are some of the most fascinating shapes produced by living organisms. If you look at a shell closely, you will see lines, rather like rings on a tree trunk, which are produced as the shell grows.

YOU WILL NEED
● *shell* ● *coarse sandpaper*

1 GRIP THE SHELL TIGHTLY, and rub it vigorously against the sandpaper. Be careful not to scratch your hands.

2 AS THE SHELL begins to wear away, look closely to see the lines that are produced as a shell grows.

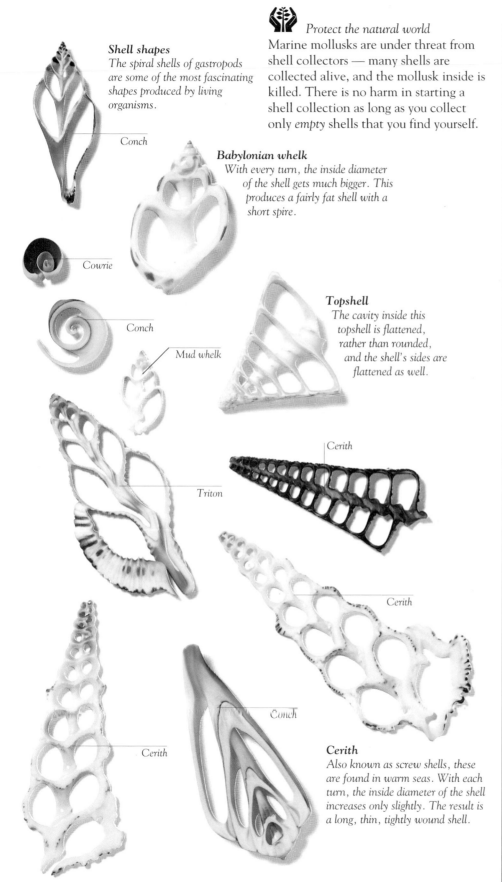

Shell shapes
The spiral shells of gastropods are some of the most fascinating shapes produced by living organisms.

Conch

Protect the natural world
Marine mollusks are under threat from shell collectors — many shells are collected alive, and the mollusk inside is killed. There is no harm in starting a shell collection as long as you collect only *empty* shells that you find yourself.

Babylonian whelk
With every turn, the inside diameter of the shell gets much bigger. This produces a fairly fat shell with a short spire.

Cowrie

Conch

Mud whelk

Topshell
The cavity inside this topshell is flattened, rather than rounded, and the shell's sides are flattened as well.

Cerith

Triton

Cerith

Conch

Cerith

Cerith
Also known as screw shells, these are found in warm seas. With each turn, the inside diameter of the shell increases only slightly. The result is a long, thin, tightly wound shell.

Mollusks

The vast majority of mollusks belong to three groups — the cephalopods, bivalves, and gastropods. Slugs and snails — the only mollusks that live on land — belong to the gastropods.

Cephalopod with external shell
All cephalopods have tentacles, big eyes, and large brains, but only the nautilus has a true external shell.

Cephalopod with internal shell
Some cephalopods, such as squids and cuttlefish, have internal shells. They swim by squirting water backward through a funnel.

Bivalve
The shell is made of two halves held together by a hinge. Bivalves feed by filtering tiny food particles from the water around them.

Gastropod
Most gastropods have a right-handed spiral shell. Whelks appear in all the oceans, and can be found at low tide.

Rockpools

UNLIKE PUDDLES LEFT AFTER A STORM, most coastal rockpools are permanent habitats. They have their own distinctive plant and animal life, which includes seaweeds and other algae, together with invertebrate animals such as limpets, sea anemones, and prawns. All these species are adapted to conditions that are much more variable than in the open sea. When a rockpool is cut off by the falling tide on a sunny day, its water begins to heat up and evaporate. As the volume of water falls, the remaining water becomes more saline, until the pool is like a hot, salty bath. Then, some hours later, seawater pours in once more, and the temperature and salinity suddenly change back again.

Starfish
Most starfish and sea urchins have five-sided symmetry, unique in the animal kingdom.

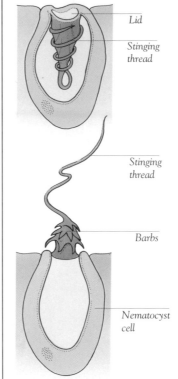

Lid

Stinging thread

Stinging thread

Barbs

Nematocyst cell

■ A sea anemone's stinging cell

Nematocyst before discharge
The stinging thread is coiled up inside the cell, and kept in place by a lid.

Animals such as sea anemones, jellyfish, and corals are called cnidarians, and they all have special stinging cells called nematocysts. In large sea anemones these are poisonous enough to kill a fish.

Discharged nematocyst
The stinging cell is triggered by touch. When the anemone touches a predator, the lid springs open and the threadlike filament whips outward, turning inside out and injecting the poison.

EXPERIMENT
Making a rockpool viewer

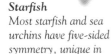 *Adult supervision is advised for this experiment*
One of the problems with looking at rockpool life is that the water's surface reflects light from above, making it difficult to see through. Polarized sunglasses will help, but this easily made device guarantees a clear view.

YOU WILL NEED
● *large-diameter plastic pipe, 1 ft (30 cm) long* ● *clear hard plastic sheet* ● *waterproof tape* ● *scissors* ● *saw* ● *felt-tip pen*

Place one end of the pipe on the clear hard plastic, and draw round it with a felt-tip pen. Ask an adult to cut out the circle of clear plastic with a saw. Tape this to the pipe, taking care not to leave any gaps where water could get in.

Wartlet anemone

Sagartia anemone

Stinging cells

■ How sea anemones feed

The waving tentacles of sea anemones sometimes make them look like plants, but in fact they are carnivorous animals. They live on smaller animals that venture too close to their stinging tentacles. Sea anemones have no eyes, and detect their food entirely by the chemicals that the food releases into seawater. You can see a sea anemone's reaction to food by holding a piece of meat near the tentacles. (Wear rubber gloves; an anemone's sting can cause allergic reactions.) Sensory cells pass messages to the anemone's simple nervous system, and muscles contract to make the tentacles stretch toward the food. The tentacles make contact, trap the food, and maneuver it toward the anemone's mouth, which is connected to a simple cavity in which the prey is digested and absorbed. Remains are orally excreted.

Rockpool neighbors
These sea anemones on the Australian coast are sharing a rockpool with a starfish. The sea anemones are permanent residents, while the starfish is a short-term visitor.

Open arms
Underwater, the tentacles of these sea anemones are fully extended. If anemones are exposed at low tide, they withdraw their tentacles and become round, jellylike blobs.

Each tentacle is covered with a battery of stinging cells

Young sea anemones are formed by eggs ejected from the parent's mouth

Mussel encrusted with barnacles

Coral reefs

DESPITE THEIR PLANTLIKE APPEARANCE, corals are animals. They are close relatives of sea anemones (p. 93), and, like them, they catch their prey with stinging tentacles. Each coral animal has a soft body, known as a polyp, which secretes a limestone casing as it matures. The polyp then reproduces itself by splitting in two, and the new polyp grows its own casing. In this way a coral reef is made up of millions of coral polyps that live in colonies and slowly build up the reef year by year.

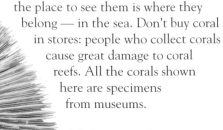

Red coral
This colorful red coral has slender branches that can grow up to 6 ft (2 m) high. The polyps are arranged around a rod of chalky material that contains a bright red pigment. Once the coral dies, it loses its bright color.

Brain coral
Easily recognized by its chainlike appearance, the brain coral is made up of many polyps that have reproduced but have not completely split off.

🌱 *Protect the natural world*
Corals are beautiful to look at, and the place to see them is where they belong — in the sea. Don't buy coral in stores: people who collect corals cause great damage to coral reefs. All the corals shown here are specimens from museums.

Mushroom coral
This skeleton of the mushroom coral Fungia *was created by a single large polyp. Unlike most other corals, mature mushroom corals can move about. They are able to pull themselves the right way up if another animal turns them over.*

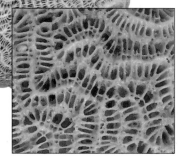

Close-up of brain coral
The polyps of brain coral lie in long lines. Each polyp is clearly connected to its neighbors, and they often share one long collection of tentacles. A brain coral's rounded shape can withstand the battering of waves.

■ Coral reefs
There are three main types of coral reef — barrier reefs, fringing reefs, and atolls. Atolls are really a special type of circular barrier reef surrounding a lagoon. Charles Darwin (pp. 20-21) investigated atolls while traveling on the Pacific Ocean. He thought that they formed around small volcanic islands, which then gradually sank beneath the sea under the weight of the reef. This theory is now widely accepted.

Most coral reefs grow in the warm waters of the tropics, and the greatest number of reef-building species are found in the seas off Australia and southeast Asia. Reefs can grow only where the water is clear.

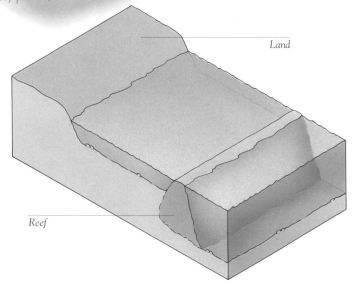

Land

Reef

Barrier reef
A barrier reef runs parallel to the coast, but is separated from it by a channel. The seaward side of the reef forms a cliff that rises up from the sea floor — the waves supplying food and oxygen to help it grow. Sediment settles on the landward side and breaks down the coral.

The Great Barrier Reef
Over 1,250 miles (2,000 km) long and up to 330 ft (100 m) deep, this giant reef off the coast of Australia is the largest existing single structure ever made by living things. A poisonous and predatory starfish, known as the Crown of Thorns, is currently destroying part of the reef.

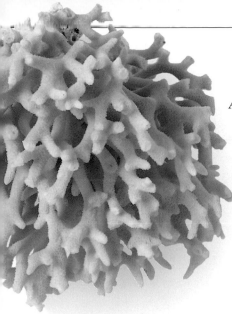

A coral skeleton
This branched skeleton of the staghorn coral was formed by thousands of polyps. A skeleton like this is built up slowly — just a few centimeters are added every year.

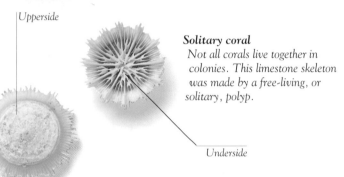

Upperside

Solitary coral
Not all corals live together in colonies. This limestone skeleton was made by a free-living, or solitary, polyp.

Underside

Coral polyps

A coral polyp feeds on small animals, which it catches with its stinging tentacles and pulls toward its mouth. Some corals have single-celled algae living in their cells. The algae gain protection by being within the coral's body, while the coral receives nutrients from the algae. As it grows, a coral polyp builds up a limestone casing beneath it, and it is this that forms a reef. Coral polyps are not the only organisms that help to build reefs — in some places, sponges lay down more limestone than the corals.

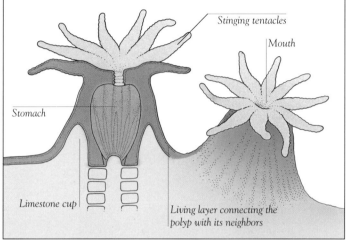

Stinging tentacles

Mouth

Stomach

Limestone cup

Living layer connecting the polyp with its neighbors

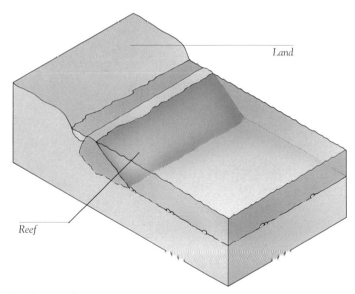

Land

Reef

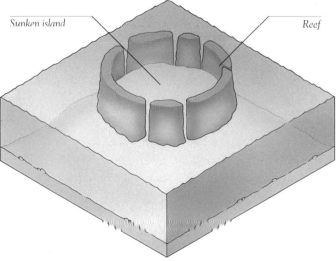

Sunken island

Reef

Fringing reef
This reef is in an early stage in reef development. It hugs the coastline, with little or no space between it and the shore. The reef does not form near the mouths of rivers, because these carry silt, which makes the water cloudy and unsuitable for reef-building corals. The most far-flung reefs are found to the east of major landmasses — off Florida and Japan, for example — where currents carry warm water northward from the tropics.

Atoll
Usually ring-shaped, an atoll looks like the classic "desert island." Atolls are common in the Pacific Ocean, where many of them are topped with sand, allowing plants such as the coconut palm to take root. The water in the center of the atoll is called a lagoon. The lagoon is quite shallow, but the outside of the reef often faces water that is many thousands of meters deep.

Seaweeds

IMAGINE A PLANT that can grow 1 ft (30 cm) in a day, and can reach a length of over 160 ft (50 m) in the first year of its life. This is the California giant kelp, the largest seaweed and the fastest-growing plant on Earth. Like all other seaweeds, the giant kelp is an alga. It has no flowers, and reproduces by spores. In place of a stem, it has a rubbery "stipe," and instead of true leaves, it has pointed fronds, often buoyed up in the water by a gas-filled bladder.

If you walk across a weed-covered shore at low tide, you will probably see many brown seaweeds with stipes and fronds like the giant kelp. But in rockpools and at the water's edge, you may find delicate green seaweeds, which are much simpler in structure, or red seaweeds, some of which have hard, chalky shells.

Beauty underwater
At low tide, seaweeds sprawl over the rocks in an untidy, slippery mass, but when they are submerged, their true shape becomes apparent.

■ Seaweed lookalikes

Not all "seaweeds" are quite what they seem. These tiny creatures that resemble seaweeds are called bryozoans or moss animals. They do not move about, but live together in a colony.

Thin filaments

Colony anchored to a stone

Individual bryozoans filter food from seawater

Flat folds

Gas-filled bladder

Fronds with floats
"Wracks" are brown seaweeds whose fronds often float upright in the sea on gas-filled bladders. A wrack can become so buoyant that it lifts up the rock on which it is growing.

Red seaweed
Although red seaweeds do contain green chlorophyll (p. 40), it is masked by red pigments called phycobilins. These pigments make the best use of the weak light in deep water, allowing red seaweeds to grow at greater depths than green or brown seaweeds.

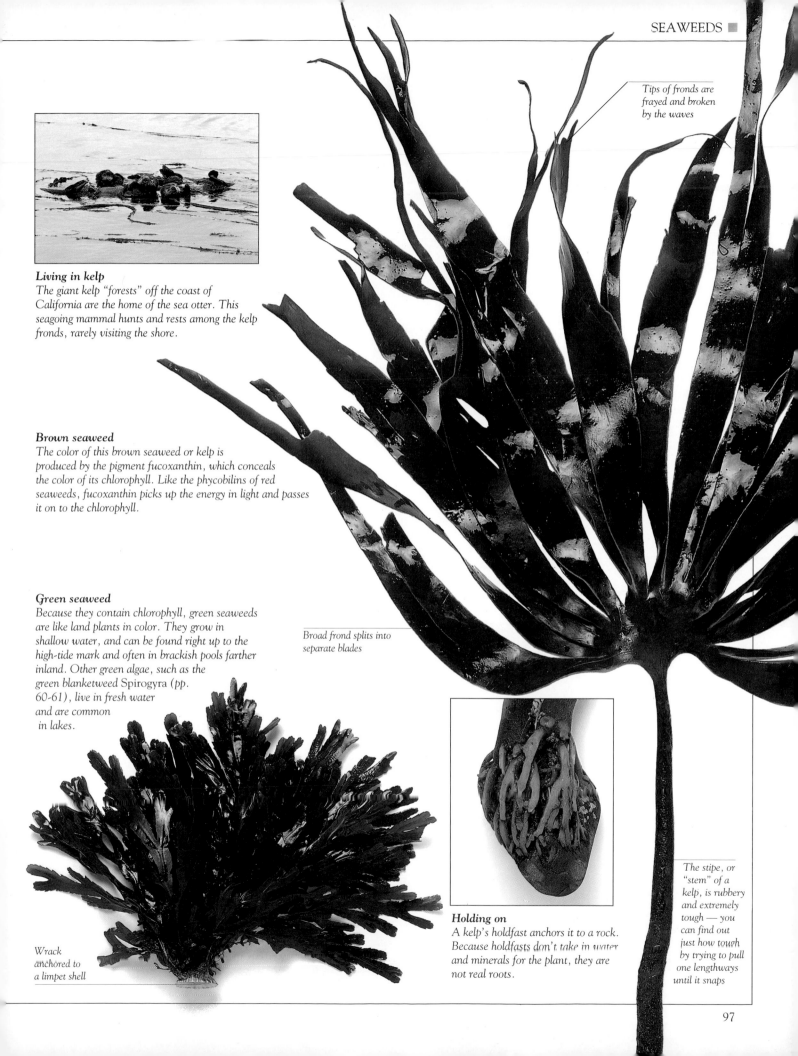

Tips of fronds are frayed and broken by the waves

Living in kelp
The giant kelp "forests" off the coast of California are the home of the sea otter. This seagoing mammal hunts and rests among the kelp fronds, rarely visiting the shore.

Brown seaweed
The color of this brown seaweed or kelp is produced by the pigment fucoxanthin, which conceals the color of its chlorophyll. Like the phycobilins of red seaweeds, fucoxanthin picks up the energy in light and passes it on to the chlorophyll.

Green seaweed
Because they contain chlorophyll, green seaweeds are like land plants in color. They grow in shallow water, and can be found right up to the high-tide mark and often in brackish pools farther inland. Other green algae, such as the green blanketweed Spirogyra (pp. 60-61), live in fresh water and are common in lakes.

Broad frond splits into separate blades

Wrack anchored to a limpet shell

Holding on
A kelp's holdfast anchors it to a rock. Because holdfasts don't take in water and minerals for the plant, they are not real roots.

The stipe, or "stem" of a kelp, is rubbery and extremely tough — you can find out just how tough by trying to pull one lengthways until it snaps

97

INSECTS
and other
INVERTEBRATES

Small-scale wonders
Although the invertebrate group includes some diminutive creatures, they tend to be good at looking after themselves. This garden snail (above) carries its home on its back, while a South American bird-eating spider (left) creeps over a rotting log, feeling its way with its feet.

THERE ARE SO MANY INSECT SPECIES ON EARTH that the total is still a matter of guesswork. So far, about a million species have been described and named by scientists, but ten times that number may still be awaiting discovery. Together with creatures as different as spiders and earthworms, insects make up the invertebrates — a huge and fascinating array of animal life.

THE WORLD OF INVERTEBRATES

To many people, all insects and other creepy crawlies are "bugs." But to a biologist, a bug is a particular type of animal — an insect that has a flattened body and a beaklike mouth that it uses for piercing plants or the skin of animals. Bugs are just one collection of species among a vast number that make up the fascinating world of invertebrate life.

Biologists divide the animal kingdom into two groups — the vertebrates (animals with backbones) and the invertebrates (those without). Because humans have backbones, it is easy to imagine that vertebrates are the most important or the most successful animals. We even call people "spineless" when we mean that they are weak or timid. But in the animal kingdom, there is nothing particularly special about having a backbone, and many animals do very well without one.

In fact, vertebrates are very much in the minority among animals. They make up only three percent of species found today. All the rest, from corals and sponges to spiders and butterflies, are invertebrates.

Dragonflies *are airborne predators that seize their prey on the wing.*

on the Earth for hundreds of millions of years without becoming very numerous or evolving into larger or more complex forms. All of these small invertebrates need to live in water of some kind — living on dry land is difficult for these simple animals, and only the insects have made a real success of it. Many of the world's smallest invertebrate animals live in the sea, or in lakes. Others live in the thin layer of water that covers soil particles (p. 122). A few make use of places that are wet some of the time, such as ditches, puddles, gutters, and the leaves of moisture-loving plants such as mosses. The best known of these are the rotifers, tiny animals with vase-shaped bodies that look as if they have a plume of large feathers on their heads. In fact, this is called a corona, and it looks feathery because it is covered with tiny hairs, or cilia, which beat rhythmically to draw a stream of water toward the rotifer. By filtering this water, the rotifer extracts particles of food.

When their ditch or puddle dries up, rotifers can shrivel and go into a state of suspended animation, coming to life again when they next get wet.

One place that is always wet is inside a living animal, and many of the smallest invertebrates are parasitic. They feed simply by absorbing food from the fluid around them inside the other animal's body.

Most people think of animals as creatures that move about, but

Flowers provide food *for bees, and the bees spread the flowers' pollen.*

many of the invertebrates are sessile — in other words, they sit in the same place, day in, day out. Some, such as the sea anemones, can move about if they need to, while others, such as sponges, are permanently fixed to one spot. Many sessile animals find food by filtering edible particles, including smaller plants and animals, from the water around them. Because they do not move around, they have no need for keen senses, and most have no obvious head or eyes. It is easy to mistake them for plants unless you look at them closely.

A sweep net *enables you to catch and examine insects without harming them.*

■ Small invertebrates

The smallest invertebrate animals are so tiny that you can see them only with a microscope. They belong to dozens of different animal groups, and they are often difficult to identify. Because they are noticed only by biologists, they have no common names, only scientific ones, such as gastrotrichs or kinorhynchs. Many of the smaller invertebrate animal groups are evolutionary "dead ends" — they have been

Marking snails *helps you to investigate their behavior.*

■ Large invertebrates

The world's largest invertebrate — the giant squid — is about 500,000 times longer than the smallest rotifer. It also lives in water, but it is so elusive that scientists have never seen it in its

The female *glowworm's light attracts a mate.*

Bright colors warn *that the wasp is dangerous.*

natural habitat. Giant squid have occasionally been washed up on the shore, but they are usually injured, ill, or already dead. A large specimen can measure 60 ft (18 m) long. The giant squid is an enormous relative of octopuses and cuttlefish. Its beaklike mouth is surrounded by a ring of tentacles, equipped with suckers. Two of these tentacles are much longer than the other tentacles — up to 40 ft (13 m) in the biggest animals — and the squid uses them to grab hold of its prey and pull it toward its mouth. The squid can shoot backward through the water by "jet propulsion," as it forces water through a nozzle behind its head.

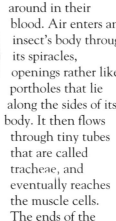

Butterflies undergo "complete metamorphosis" as they grow up.

Between these two extremes of size — from the rotifers to the giant squid — is an amazing variety of animal life. Yet most of us see only a few major groups, animals such as the insects, the spiders, the earthworms, and the crustaceans (such as crabs and shrimps). The most familiar group of invertebrates — the one that has been outstandingly successful on land — is the insects.

■ Species of insects

If you look at a wasp, you can see a narrow "neck" behind the head, and a slender "waist" after the wings. These divide the wasp's body into three parts: the head, the thorax, and the abdomen. Such a body structure is typical of insects, but even more characteristic are the wasp's wings. Of all of the invertebrates, only the insects have the ability to fly.

The most primitive insects, such as silverfish (thysanuran), have no wings, but all other insects either have wings or have evolved from insects that once had them. Like other arthropods (p. 28), insects have an external skeleton which has to be shed to allow them to grow.

There are more species of insect on Earth than all of the other animals combined. Just one group of them, the beetles, contains nearly 400,000 species. Some experts think that there may be over 10 million species of insects in the world today. When biologists recently studied an area of rain forest in Peru, four-fifths of the insects that they found were new to science. Apart from polar ice, the only habitat that insects have not managed to conquer is the sea, which was successfully colonized by crustaceans before the insects could move in.

Locusts undergo "incomplete metamorphosis" as they develop.

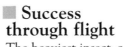

■ Success through flight

The heaviest insect, a beetle, is only 6 in (15 cm) long, and most insects are much smaller than this. Their size allows insects to grow on a small

Leaflike camouflage *protects this katydid from its enemies.*

amount of food. They live on and in anything that is edible, from live and dead animals to rotting wood, soap, and even crude oil. Some insects have powerful jaws that can chew through bark, while others have sharp beaks that pierce plant stems or the skin of an animal.

Wings for flight give insects great advantages because with them, they can cover large distances. The wings of a bee or wasp beat about 200 times in a single second, creating the distinctive humming sound which tells us that they are nearby. The high-pitched whine of an approaching mosquito is produced by wings that beat faster still — up to 500 beats per second.

Because insects' bodies are usually quite small, their muscles can get all of the oxygen they need directly from the air, and they don't have to carry it around in their blood. Air enters an insect's body through its spiracles, openings rather like portholes that lie along the sides of its body. It then flows through tiny tubes that are called tracheae, and eventually reaches the muscle cells. The ends of the tracheae are so tiny that some of them actually reach right inside the muscle cells. This means that they can carry oxygen directly to where it is needed the most, and take away the carbon dioxide waste.

Jean-Henri Fabre (1823–1915), one of the most famous entomologists (insect specialists).

Heat and light *drive tiny animals out of the soil.*

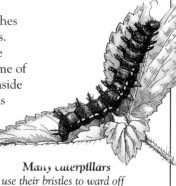

Many caterpillars *use their bristles to ward off attack by birds.*

Rearing insects

KEEPING AND STUDYING INSECTS is fascinating. In the next six pages, you can find out how to construct and use a cage suitable for rearing two very different types of insect — locusts and butterflies. Young locusts look quite like their parents, and you can watch them gradually develop as they grow up. Caterpillars look completely unlike their butterfly parents, and if you are lucky, you will see the sudden and dramatic change in shape as they become adults.

Before starting to build the cage, remember that young locusts, in particular, are active animals, and will escape if they can. As you work, make sure that all the cage's parts fit together tightly. Once the insects are in the cage, remember that they will depend on you for their survival. They will need a daily check to make sure that they are healthy and have enough food.

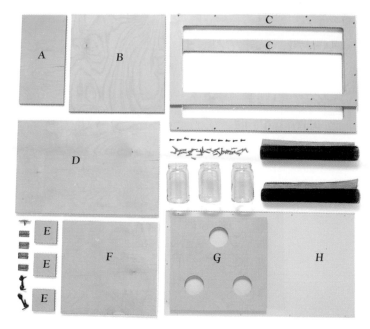

EXPERIMENT

Making an insect breeding cage

Adult supervision is advised for this experiment
The cage is made of plywood, which is light and strong. The hard, clear plastic front allows you to watch the insects closely, while metal mesh sides ensure good ventilation. A hinged lid allows access to the breeding area, while a rear door gives access to the jars. When the cage is in use, put it somewhere light and airy, but away from draughts.

YOU WILL NEED
$^1/_2$ *in (15 mm) softwood ply:* **A** *rear door 6 in x 12 in (14.5 cm x 30 cm)* **B** *top 12$^1/_2$ in x 13 in (30.5 cm x 33 cm)* **C** *2 sides 24 in x 12 in (60 cm x 30 cm)* **D** *back 18 in x 12 in (45 cm x 30 cm)* **E** *3 jar supports 2$^1/_2$ in x 2$^1/_2$ in (6 cm x 6 cm)* **F** *floor 11$^1/_2$ in x 12 in (29 cm x 30 cm)* **G** *false floor 11$^1/_2$ in x 12 in (29 cm x 30 cm)* **H** *hard, clear plastic 24 in x 13 in (60 cm x 33 cm)* ● *4 hinges* ● *2 hook-and-eye catches* ● *swiveling door catch* ● *3 jars, to fit into holes about 2$^1/_2$ in (6 cm) in diameter* ● *2 pieces of fine metal mesh 24 in x 12 in (60 cm x 30 cm)* ● *screws* ● *glue* ● *electric drill* ● *drill bits* ● *countersink bit* ● *electric jigsaw* ● *measuring tape* ● *pencil* ● *tri-square* ● *fine-toothed saw* ● *screwdriver* ● *sandpaper*

1 Cut the plywood as shown. Cut out the centers of the sides (C), leaving two frames 1 $^1/_2$ in (4 cm) wide. Cut three circular holes in the false floor (G), the same diameter as the jars. Sand down all cut edges.

2 Pre-drill screw holes around the edges of the sides (C) and the hard, clear plastic (H).

3 Glue the pieces of metal mesh on to the two sides (C).

4 Screw the back (D), floor (F), and false floor (G) to one of the sides (C), then screw on the other side (C).

5 Screw the plastic (H) to the sides (C) and floor (F).

6 Attach two hinges to the rear door (A) and two to the top (B). Attach both to the back (D). Fit the eyes to the sides (C) through the plastic (H), and fix the swivelling door catch to one side (C) so that it fastens the rear door.

7 Install the jars, pushing them up into the holes in the false floor (G) from below, using the wooden jar supports (E) to keep them in place.

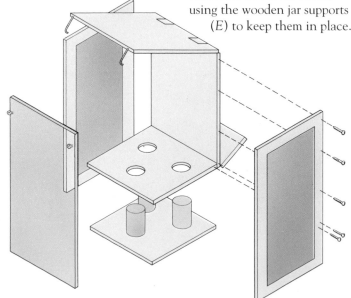

Raising butterflies

When you are raising butterflies (pp. 106-107), the jars are used as vases to hold the caterpillars' supply of leaves. Fill the jars with water, and insert each one beneath a hole in the false floor, supporting it with its square of wood. Finally, cut out three cardboard rings, and place one over each jar. The hole in each ring should be just large enough for a plant stem. The rings will prevent the caterpillars walking down the stems, into the water.

Jars for caterpillars' food plants

Cardboard ring

Installing the jars

When the cage is in use, there must be no gap between the mouths of the jars and the holes above them. This is to prevent insects getting into the bottom of the cage.

Top folds back on hinges

Mesh sides allow ventilation

Jars filled with sand

Raising locusts

Locusts need sand in which to lay their eggs, and you can provide this for them in the jars. Although locusts can survive in quite cool temperatures, they need a certain amount of warmth to breed. If the temperature around the cage is not high enough, you can provide artificial heat (p. 105).

Locusts and grasshoppers

AS THEIR NAME SUGGESTS, grasshoppers use their powerful hindlegs to hop from place to place, although, like locusts, most can fly if alarmed. Grasshoppers and locusts are found in warm, dry places all over the world. They belong to a group of insects called Orthoptera, which means "straight wings." Most grasshoppers live singly, but locusts can form huge swarms when they are short of food. Such a swarm can contain five billion insects and can ruin a field of crops in minutes.

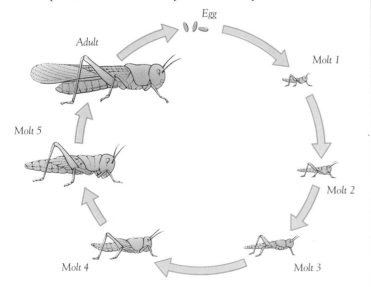

Face to face
Two brilliantly colored grasshoppers confront each other on a leaf. Many species use their legs to make sounds, by rubbing them against their hard forewings — a process called "stridulation."

■ The life cycle of a locust

Locusts lay their eggs in sand. The eggs hatch after about ten days, and the young locusts, or nymphs, scrabble their way to the surface. They have large heads and no wings, but otherwise look like adults. As they grow, they shed their skins, and after the fifth molt they are mature, with fully formed wings and sexual organs. Locusts develop their adult form gradually, without any sudden change in body shape. This kind of development is called "incomplete metamorphosis."

Egg

Adult

Molt 1

Molt 5

Molt 2

Molt 4

Molt 3

■ How a locust sheds its skin

Like all other insects, a locust has to shed its hard outer skeleton, or skin, in order to grow. Here, a developing locust is shedding its skin for the fifth and final time as it becomes an adult. The adult's body is already fully formed inside the skin of the immature locust. Once the skin has been shed, the wings can expand to their full length.

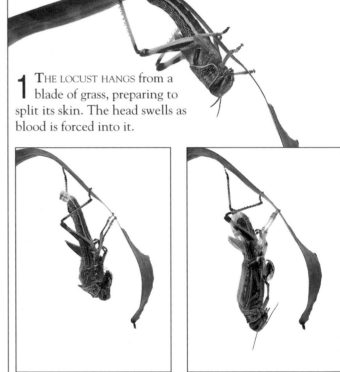

1 THE LOCUST HANGS from a blade of grass, preparing to split its skin. The head swells as blood is forced into it.

2 THE OUTER SKIN breaks along a line of weakness. The head begins to emerge.

3 THE ADULT struggles free. The skin of the hind legs clings to the leaf.

4 MOST OF THE OLD SKIN has been shed, as well as the inner surface of the mouth.

5 THE LOCUST KICKS its legs as the old skin works itself loose.

6 WITH A SUDDEN EFFORT, the locust arches toward the leaf and grabs it.

7 GRIPPING THE LEAF, the locust pulls itself free from its old skin.

8 THE WINGS are now starting to expand. The locust sits so that they point downward, letting gravity help the process.

9 BLOOD PUMPS into the wings as they grow longer. They must have room to spread, or they will be permanently damaged.

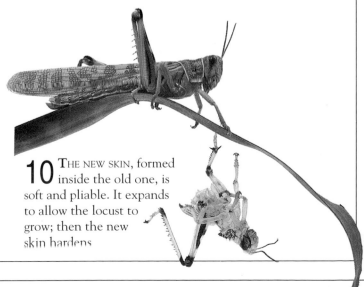

10 THE NEW SKIN, formed inside the old one, is soft and pliable. It expands to allow the locust to grow; then the new skin hardens

Looking after locusts

YOU WILL NEED
● *breeding cage adapted for locusts (p. 103)* ● *light bulb*
● *light bulb holder*
● *electrical cord*

Locusts are easy insects to raise in captivity. Their natural habitat is in the tropics and subtropics, and so they need to be kept at a high temperature — 95°F (35°C) — if they are to breed. In cold climates, a light bulb will provide them with enough warmth to breed. If you give the locusts food, warmth, and some sand to lay their eggs in, you should be able to observe them at every stage of their fascinating life cycle.

Put fresh green leaves in the jars for the locusts to eat

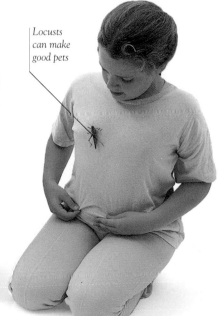

Locusts can make good pets

Breeding butterflies

FEW SIGHTS IN THE natural world are as dramatic as the moment when a butterfly emerges from its chrysalis (right). The chrysalis's case splits open, and the adult butterfly is slowly revealed. At first, its wings are soft and crumpled, but as blood is pumped into them they extend and stiffen. Within an hour or two, the butterfly is ready to take to the air. Butterflies and moths are members of the insect order Lepidoptera, meaning "scale-covered wings." On becoming adult, they undergo complete metamorphosis, changing both their body shape and their way of life. You can watch this process at close quarters by collecting the eggs of common butterflies to raise in captivity.

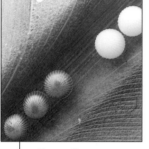

Butterfly eggs
Some butterflies lay their eggs in large batches, and, when young, their caterpillars often live and feed together.

■ The life cycle of a butterfly

Most butterfly eggs hatch into caterpillars (larvae), which shed their skins several times as they grow. The mature caterpillar forms a chrysalis (pupa), in which the adult's body develops. The adults emerge and mate, and the females then lay eggs.

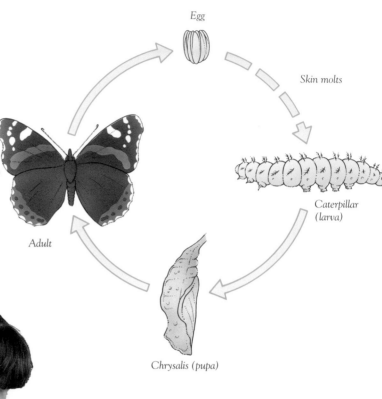

Egg

Skin molts

Caterpillar (larva)

Chrysalis (pupa)

Adult

EXPERIMENT
Raising butterflies

YOU WILL NEED
● *breeding cage (p. 103), adapted for butterflies*

The breeding cage enables you to raise caterpillars and watch them turn into adults. Caterpillars have large appetites, so it is essential to provide them with a supply of fresh leaves. Always pick stems from the plants on which you found the caterpillars or butterfly eggs. Any other plants may be unsuitable.

1 THE RED ADMIRAL (the species shown in this experiment) lays its eggs singly on the leaves of nettles, and its caterpillars live on their own.

Water supply
Add water to the breeding cage jars to maintain the foliage that caterpillars feed on, and place them securely under the false floor.

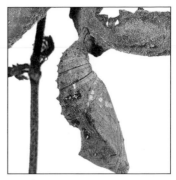

2 FROM THE MOMENT they hatch, caterpillars feed voraciously. For some, their first meal is the shell of their egg. Many caterpillars have spines along the body to protect them from predators.

3 MATURE CATERPILLARS form chrysalises, on their foodplants, on the ground, or underground, depending on the species. The red admiral forms its chrysalis beneath a nettle leaf.

4 INSIDE THE CHRYSALIS, which is often known as the "resting stage," most of the tissues of the caterpillar's body are broken down. New organs and tissues develop to form the butterfly.

5 AFTER ABOUT TWO WEEKS, the transformation of a red admiral caterpillar inside a chrysalis is almost complete. The wings can be seen through the translucent skin of the chrysalis.

6 THE BUTTERFLY forces open the skin of the chrysalis and emerges, holding tightly to a leaf. Blood flows into veins in the wings, making them rigid and ready for the first flight.

Skin of chrysalis

Wings expand and harden

Antenna used for detecting scent

7 ALTHOUGH SOME BUTTERFLIES live for years, many survive for only days or weeks — just long enough to mate and lay eggs. Adult butterflies have long, coiled tongues and feed mainly on flower nectar.

Moths

THERE ARE FAR MORE MOTHS than butterflies in the world, but because many moths are nocturnal, they often go unnoticed. Atlas moths are the largest type of moth — their wingspan can be up to 10 in (25 cm). Pygmy moths are the smallest — their wingspan is only $\frac{1}{4}$ in (5 mm). They are so minute that their caterpillars can live between the upper and lower surfaces of leaves, where they excavate wiggly "mines" as they feed. Body shape is one of the most convenient ways of telling a moth from a butterfly. Unlike butterflies, moths usually have heavy, furry bodies, and hold their wings flat when they settle.

Angle shades moth
There are over 25,000 species of noctuid (night owl) moths. Many are camouflaged, like this angle shades moth, which merges well with dead leaves or wood.

Pink-barred sallow moth
This moth derives its name from its foodplant, a species of willow. The sallow moth's body hairs help to keep it warm, by retaining the heat produced by its muscles.

Potato pest hawkmoth
Long forewings make these hawkmoths large, powerful fliers. Their caterpillars feed on sweet potatoes.

Roseate emperor moth
Emperors are large moths with eyespots on their wings. The roseate emperor is commonly found in southern Africa.

■ Picking up the scent

Many female moths attract mates by releasing scent chemicals, called pheromones, into the air. Like the pheromones used by social insects (p. 110), these trigger a particular pattern of behavior. When the male senses the pheromone, he flies in a zigzag path upwind, to where the scent is strongest. This eventually leads him to the female.

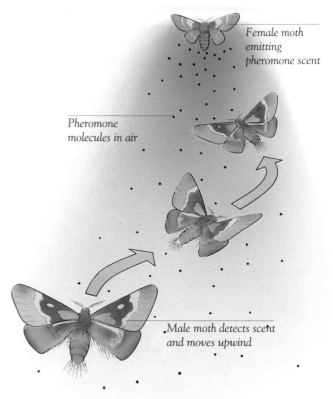

Female moth emitting pheromone scent

Pheromone molecules in air

Male moth detects scent and moves upwind

■ Finding a pheromone

Many moths have large, feathery antennae. Male moths' antennae are particularly well developed to detect females' pheromones. They are so sensitive that they can detect a single molecule of female scent.

Slender filaments give the antennae a large surface area. This increases the chance of detecting pheromones

Making a moth trap

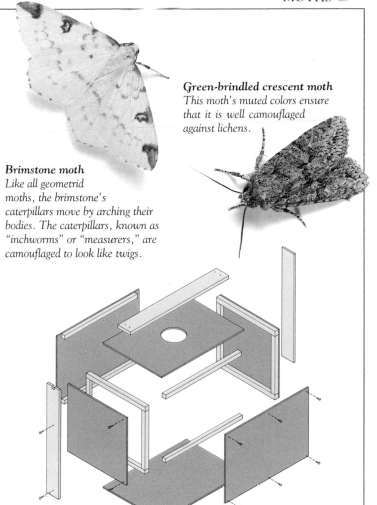

Brimstone moth
*Like all geometrid
moths, the brimstone's
caterpillars move by arching their
bodies. The caterpillars, known as
"inchworms" or "measurers," are
camouflaged to look like twigs.*

Green-brindled crescent moth
*This moth's muted colors ensure
that it is well camouflaged
against lichens.*

Adult supervision is advised for this experiment
Moths are attracted to light. When they fly toward this light
bulb, they fall down a funnel and settle on an egg-tray perch.

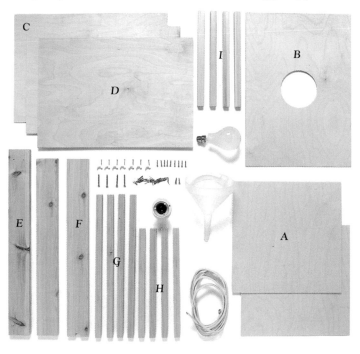

You Will Need

$^1/_4$ in (5 mm) plywood: **A** *2 side panels 14 in x 14 in (36 cm x
36 cm)* **B** *top panel 20 in x 13 in (50.75 cm x 35.25 cm) central
hole: 4 in (12 cm) in diameter* **C** *panels for front and back
20 in x 14 in (50.75 cm x 36 cm)* **D** *base panel 20 in x 13 in
(50.75 cm x 35.25 cm)* ● $^3/_4$ *in x 2 in (2 cm x 6 cm) timber:*
E *top bar 24 in (60 cm) long* **F** *2 side bars 22 in (57 cm) long*

● $^3/_4$ *in square (2 cm square) timber:* **G** *4 cross battens 18 in
(46 cm) long* **H** *4 horizontal side battens 13 in (35.25 cm) long*
I *4 vertical side battens 12 in (31.5 cm) long*
● *cable clips* ● *egg tray or cardboard* ● *electrical cord* ● *large plastic
funnel* ● *light bulb holder* ● *light bulb* ● *panel pins* ● *screws*

1 Connect the light bulb holder to the electrical cord, and
screw it to the center of the top bar (E). Attach the cord to the
bar with cable clips. Cut a small notch on one of the side bars
(F), just big enough for the cord to pass through.

2 Screw the side battens (H and I) to the side panels (A). Fix
the cross battens (G) to the front and back panels (C). Leave a
$^1/_4$ in (5 mm) gap between the battens and the panels' edge.

3 Assemble the side, front, back, and base panels (A, C, D) so
that they form a rigid box. Put the egg tray or cardboard inside.
Screw on the side bars, and attach the top bar to them.

4 Cut a $4^3/_4$ in (12 cm) diameter hole in the top panel, and
place it on top of the box. Do not fix it into position.

5 Trim the bottom of the funnel, so that it is at least $1^1/_2$ in
(4 cm) wide. Sit the funnel in the hole in the top panel. Fit the
bulb, and the trap is complete. Put the trap somewhere dry and
dark, switch on the light, and wait for the moths to arrive.

*Take care when
removing the light bulb*

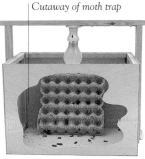

Cutaway of moth trap

Inspecting your catch
*Switch off the light, and wait
for the bulb to cool down.
Remove the bulb and funnel,
and then carefully lift out the
egg tray. If you work quickly,
you should be able to count
the moths and identify some
of the larger ones before they
fly away.*

Ants and termites

MANY ANIMALS GATHER in groups, often to feed or for defense. But for some, being part of a group has become a highly specialized way of life. This is particularly true of the "social insects" — ants, wasps, and bees (which form a group called the Hymenoptera) — and also of termites. Ants and termites are not close relatives, but they have similar life styles. They tend to make underground nests, often resemble each other, and behave in the same way — an example of convergent evolution (p. 25).

Social insects divide up the work needed to keep their community alive. Usually only one individual — the queen — produces young. Tasks such as finding food, tending the young, and standing guard are carried out by others, working instinctively in response to pheromones, or chemical messages, from the queen.

Egg machine
The bloated, maggotlike creature in the center of this picture is a queen termite. Entombed in a cell beneath the termite mound, she produces a steady supply of eggs. Termites are thought to be the first insects to have evolved a social way of life.

EXPERIMENT
Making a formicarium

Adult supervision is advised for this experiment
To study the behavior of a colony of ants, you can make a formicarium.

YOU WILL NEED
● *black fabric* ● *earth* ● *jar* ● *jug* ● *modeling clay* ● *plaster of Paris* ● *screwdriver* ● *screws*
● *seeds* ● *spoon* ● *wide-diameter pipe* ● *ants (including a queen)* ● *hard clear plastic* ● *tape*

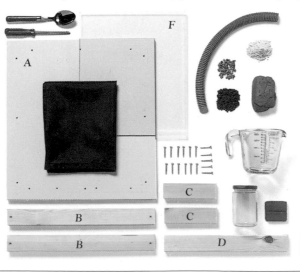

A *plywood mold base 17¹/₂ in x 16 in (44 cm x 41 cm)*
1¹/₂ in x ³/₄ in (4 cm x 2 cm) cross-section timber:
B *2 mold sides 16 in (41 cm) long*
C *2 mold sides 6 in (15 cm) long*
D *mold side 13¹/₂ in (34 cm)*
E *entrance strip 10 in (25 cm)*
F *hard clear plastic 13¹/₂ in x 12 in (35 cm x 30 cm)*

1 SCREW THE SIDES to the base. Put in the clear plastic and add the entrance strip. Shape the modeling clay.

2 FIT THE PIPE, using the modeling clay. Mix the plaster of Paris, and pour into the mold, leveling the surface.

3 LEAVE FOR AT LEAST ONE DAY before carefully easing out of the mold. Fill the formicarium with soil.

Ant alert!
Be sure to take great care when you collect your ants, because some can inflict a nasty bite. Wear thick gloves to protect your hands, then quickly scoop the ants into a jar.

Resting and nesting
Many ants nest under flat rocks, and this is a good place to find them.

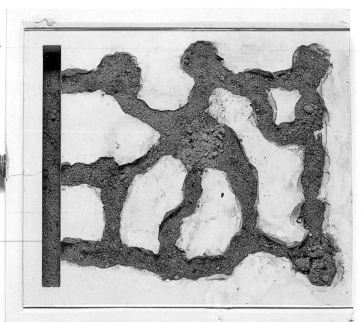

Formicarium covered by clear plastic lid

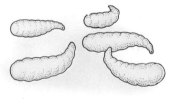

Food inside jar

4 CUT A HOLE IN THE LID of the jar, and fix the pipe into it with modeling clay. Add some mixed seeds to the jar and screw the jar to the lid. Now carefully pour in the ants. After fitting the clear plastic lid, watch out for escape attempts: you may have to seal the lid with tape if there are any gaps. Cover the plastic lid with the black fabric, and wait for your ants to settle into their new home.

■ Development and body shapes
Adult ants grow from eggs that are laid by the queen. The eggs develop into grublike larvae, then into pupae, and finally into adults. In many ant colonies, the adults have different shapes according to the work they carry out. In some species, soldier ants, which guard the colony, can be 50 times heavier than worker ants.

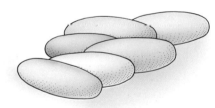

Eggs
After the queen has laid them, the eggs are carried away by workers. The eggs are then incubated together in chambers.

Larvae
The eggs hatch into wingless larvae. These form oval pupae, which are often mistakenly known as "ants' eggs."

Soldier ant
Soldier ants have large jaws to attack intruders. These can include other ants, which plunder nests, forcing workers to forage for them.

Winged ant
Winged male and female ants fly out from the nest to mate. The males soon die, and the females create new colonies.

Worker ant
The workers in a colony of ants can number from a few hundred to more than 20 million in some tropical species.

Bees and wasps

ALTHOUGH ANTS AND TERMITES (pp. 110-111) are gregarious and live in colonies, the many species of bees and wasps live in a variety of different ways. Some are completely solitary. In these species, the female lays a number of eggs, but they develop into adults and fly away without forming a colony. At the other end of the social scale is the honeybee, which forms colonies up to 80,000 strong. Between these two extremes are countless species of bees and wasps that form colonies of different sizes. Most bees live on plant matter, but many wasps also eat insects.

Floral food
A bumblebee gathers nectar and pollen from a dandelion flower.

■ Life in a honeybee colony

In many ways, a colony of honeybees is like a single animal. Each bee operates as a cell within a body, and chemical messages from the queen act like nerves and hormones to ensure that the colony's work is carried out in a coordinated way. Bees store food and raise their young in hexagonal cells that they make out of wax.

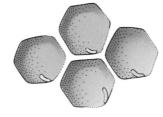

Eggs
Each egg has its own cell. The queen can control whether eggs are fertilized or not. Fertilized eggs develop into workers or queens, while unfertilized eggs develop into drones.

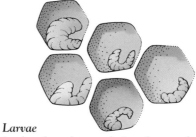

Larvae
It takes about three weeks for a larva to develop into an adult bee. Larvae that are destined to become queens are fed entirely on a rich substance called "royal jelly."

Queen
A queen mates just once, after flying away from the colony in which she was born. The rest of her life is spent laying eggs, while being groomed and fed by the worker bees.

Worker
Workers are female bees. Each one carries out different tasks as it becomes older, first inside the colony, and only venturing out to collect food for the last two weeks of its two-month life.

Drone
Drones are male bees that mate with young queen bees. Each colony contains only a few drones, and in fact these die soon after mating, having served their purpose.

Dig a hollow in the ground deep enough for the flowerpot to fit into. Put a small pile of sawdust or wood shavings at the bottom. Put the upturned flowerpot in the hole, and place the lid over the top of it, supporting it with the corks. A bee may crawl in through the hole and make its nest.

Wasp nests

Most social wasps make their nests by chewing away pieces of dead wood and mixing them with saliva to form a paste. The queen wasp molds the paste to begin a nest, in which she lays a few eggs. These hatch into workers who take over nest building.

The nest is made up of concentric shells

The cells are hidden inside layers of shells

When the nest is in use, the entrance hole is heavily guarded

Rapid repairs
Wasp nests are quite fragile. This nest has been damaged, and the cells inside can be seen. The wasps are setting about the task of repairing it with wood pulp.

"Bee" careful!
Bees and wasps use their stings as a last resort. When watching them, move slowly. Never stand close to the entrance of a hive or nest.

Wasps eat both animal and plant food, and love sugary fruit

Wasps in winter

In countries with cold winters, most wasps are killed by the first frosts. Queen wasps hibernate in sheltered, dry places, wings tucked under their legs. In spring, they wake and search for a nest site.

How bees find food

HONEYBEES NEED FOOD to stay alive and to feed their young. From dawn to dusk, a constant stream of bees leaves the hive to gather sugar-rich nectar and pollen. During their brief lives, worker bees make thousands of these visits. They drink nectar with their tubular tongues, and pollen sticks to the hairs on their bodies. The bees scrape it off into structures called pollen baskets on their hind legs. Once they return to the hive, they can turn the nectar and pollen into honey, a food store that will sustain them through cold weather. Worker bees do not search for food at random. As you can find out for yourself in a fascinating experiment, they have a marvelous communication system that enables one bee to tell many others where food can be found. After the first bee finds food, it returns to its hive and performs a special dance. The bees around it are able to understand the dance's hidden message, and they take to the air, flying in exactly the right direction. Within minutes, the food source is surrounded with jostling bees.

Secret senses
Bees are sensitive to ultraviolet light, which we cannot detect. This flower, photographed with ultraviolet-sensitive film under ultraviolet light, shows "honey guides" — markings that guide bees to where the nectar is located.

EXPERIMENT
Training honeybees

In this first experiment, you can train honeybees to come to an artifical "flower" made out of cardboard. At the center of the flower is a small pool of sugary water on which the bees can feed. Once your bees are trained, you can do more experiments to find out how they tell others where the "flower" is.

YOU WILL NEED
● *colored cardboard* ● *5 watch glasses or identical bottletops* ● *sugar* ● *water*

Sweet discovery
Dissolve the sugar in the water. Cut the card into colored "flowers," and place them on a table outside. Place a watch glass in the center of each flower, and add sugary water to one. Eventually, a bee will discover it, and tell others where it is.

EXPERIMENT
Testing position and color

Having trained your bees to come to a certain color, you can test how they find food. First, remove the watch glasses from all the flowers. Then try putting the sugar water on a "flower" of the same color, some distance away. Do the bees fly to the new flower? Move the sugar water to a nearby "flower" of another color. Does the difference in color put the bees off?

This flower holds no food, and the bees are ignoring it

A bee drops in to see if the yellow flower contains food

Knee-deep in nectar

If you slowly approach the feeding bees, you can watch them drinking. Feeding bees are very preoccupied, and are unlikely to fly away unless frightened by a sudden movement. The sugar solution in the watch glass is easy for the bees to reach, and they drink it by lapping with their tongues. In some flowers, nectar is produced inside long tubes, and the honeybees have to extend their tongues fully to reach it.

Tubular tongue

Body hairs to catch pollen

Finding the food

Once a bee has found the food source, it fetches other bees. After a while, the "flower" is crowded with bees.

Karl von Frisch

The Austrian scientist Karl von Frisch (1886–1982) spent many years investigating animal behavior. He discovered that honeybees can pass on information about the position of nectar-rich flowers through scent and a special dance performed on the honeycomb inside the hive. There are two kinds of dance. In the "round dance," a worker bee signals that the flowers are near the hive. The "waggle dance" means they are farther away, but it pinpoints their position. In this dance, the bee moves in a circle, but then crosses the circle waggling its abdomen. Von Frisch discovered that the angle at which the bee crosses the circle — against gravity — tells others the direction of the flowers in relation to the Sun. The faster the dance, the farther the food. This intricate form of communication was widely disbelieved when von Frisch first described it.

Round dance

A worker bee tells others that food can be found near the hive. Unlike the waggle dance, the round dance does not give a precise position, and the bees fan out in all directions in search of food.

Bees are rarely attracted to green flowers

A bee investigates a pink flower, but finds nothing

Bees cluster around the blue flower, but the food has gone

Responding to the environment

COMPARED WITH BIRDS OR MAMMALS, most invertebrate animals have very simple nervous systems. But this does not mean that they cannot respond to the world around them. Just like animals with backbones, they have to reproduce, find food, and avoid being eaten. The way they behave is just as important to their survival as their size and shape.

In any animal's life, there are constant decisions to be made. For example, the animal may have to decide whether to move in one direction or another, whether to court a mate or chase it away, or whether to feed its young or feed itself. The study of animal behavior in nature — known as ethology — is based on observing the many choices that an animal makes. Even simple animals such as snails and wood lice can behave in quite a complex way.

EXPERIMENT
Tracking snails

Marking and tracking animals is an important way of following their behavior over a set period. A small pot of enamel paint can help you to discover a great deal about snails' private lives.

YOU WILL NEED
- enamel paint • paintbrush
- garden snails • flowerpot

Marking a snail
Hold the snail gently by its shell, and carefully paint a number on it. Make sure that no paint gets on the snail's body.

Ruling the roost
Snails like to roost in damp places. Put a large clay flowerpot upside down in a garden, and prop up one edge. Early the next morning, remove any snails, mark them, then put them back in the flowerpot.

Coming and going
You can now see how many snails return to the flowerpot the following night. Do the same snails always return each night? Mark any new arrivals, and see how often new snails appear.

EXPERIMENT
Choosing a chamber

In a choice chamber, wood lice decide between two sets of conditions, such as variations in light and humidity. The chamber has two compartments, and the wood lice move from one compartment to the other through small doorways.

1 Screw the side strips to the base. Cut three "doorways" in the dividing wall, large enough for wood lice to crawl through. Fix the wall to the base so that it divides the box in two.

2 Place some wood lice in the box, and cover with the lid. Check after a day to see that the wood lice are equally distributed between the compartments. This is important — if they are not, see if there is anything irregular about your box or its position that could be influencing the wood lice.

YOU WILL NEED

● screws ● panel pins ● small hand saw **A** plywood base and cover, both 10 in (24 cm) square **B** 2 hard clear plastic covers

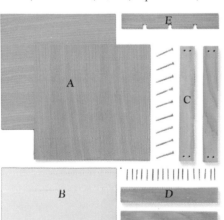

10 in (24 cm) square and 10 in x 5 in (24 cm x 12 cm) **C** 2 side strips 10 in x 1 in x $^3/_4$ in (24 cm x 3 cm x 2 cm) **D** 2 side strips $8^1/_2$ in x 1 in x $^3/_4$ in (20cm x 3 cm x 2 cm) **E** dividing wall $8^1/_2$ in x 1 in x $^1/_2$ in (20 cm x 3 cm x 1 cm)

Collecting wood lice
Wood lice can often be found under rocks and pieces of wood. They are quite harmless, and can be picked up and put into a petri dish for use in the choice chamber.

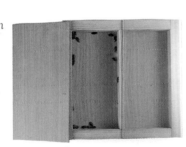

Dry or moist?
To see if wood lice respond to humidity, place a piece of moistened cotton wool in one of the compartments. Add the wood lice, and cover the whole box. Next day, look to see how the wood lice are distributed between the compartments.

Light or dark?
Cover one compartment with clear plastic, and the other with the wooden lid. Leave them for one day, and then see where the wood lice are. You can now check whether darkness or humidity is more important by making one chamber moist but light (wet cotton wool with the plastic lid) and the other dark but dry (wooden lid only).

Gauging growth
How quickly does a snail grow in the wild? Find out by weighing individual numbered snails every week over a two-month period, and drawing a graph to show when they grow the fastest. With an axis for weight and one for time, plot a separate line for each snail.

Favorite foods
Feed two sets of marked snails on different plants that you are growing outside. After a few days, release the snails outside, midway between the two plants. Which plants do the snails prefer?

Camouflage and mimicry

THE WORLD OF INSECTS is full of deception and trickery. For many insects, being seen and recognized can be fatal. In order to escape their predators, they conceal themselves by looking like something else. What could be less appetizing than a pebble or a dead leaf? This camouflage works only if an insect keeps still. As soon as a "pebble" or "leaf" starts to move, the game is up. But some insects have other ways of keeping predators at bay. One of these is warning coloration. Some insects are so boldly colored that they are almost impossible to miss. Their bright colors advertise the fact that they are poisonous, and predators learn to avoid them. So effective is this that some harmless insects mimic them, gaining protection by bluffing.

Sitting prickly
The similarity in color makes it difficult to discern between moth and prickly thistle.

■ Living by bluff

Early on in their lives, most birds learn to avoid bees and wasps and link them with the chance of a painful sting. Over millions of years, quite harmless insects have come to look like bees and wasps by mimicking both their color and shape. Wasp and bee mimics are common almost everywhere — yards are a particularly good place to see them.

Bee-fly
The furry, plump bee-fly looks and sounds just like a bumble bee, but has no sting.

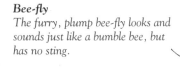

Tricky colors
The bright warning colors of the wasplike hoverfly (syrphus or syrphid fly) are a trick.

Revealing wings
Hoverflies (syrphus or syrphid flies) have no sting, and a close look shows that they have only one pair of wings, whereas real wasps have two pairs.

EXPERIMENT
Hiding a human

Few things are more guaranteed to send animals rushing for cover than the sight of a moving human. By camouflaging yourself, or building a blind (p. 141), and then keeping as still as possible, you can watch animals without them noticing you. Camouflage cream, or stage makeup, and a face veil will help to break up the outlines of your face.

YOU WILL NEED
● *camouflage cream or greasepaint* ● *face veil*

Merging with the background
By hiding in thick vegetation, you can conceal most of your body. Your camouflaged face will be difficult for animals to recognize as human.

■ Background blending

Butterflies and moths have evolved a wide range of disguises to hide them from their predators. Many moth caterpillars look like dead twigs, while the caterpillars of some butterflies look exactly like bird droppings. Adult butterflies and moths often have camouflaged wings. With their wings closed, they can look exactly like a leaf.

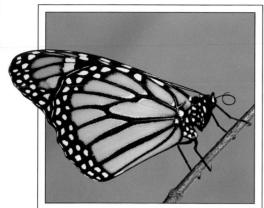

Warning coloration

A passing butterfly makes a tempting prospect for a hungry bird, but the North American monarch is a meal worth missing. Its bright colors warn that its body is packed with poisons, and any bird that unwisely eats a monarch is violently sick. The bird learns a lesson from this experience, and never touches the brightly colored monarchs again. The caterpillar of the monarch stores poisons, which it derives from some of the plants it eats. These are passed on to the adult butterfly. By using such effective means of camouflage, the monarch can sometimes become the victim of deception. Another butterfly, the viceroy, has evolved colors that mimic the monarch. The viceroy is quite harmless, but it gains protection by looking like its poisonous counterpart.

A living "leaf"

The Indian leaf butterfly looks just like a dead leaf. The stripe across the wings imitates a leaf's middle vein.

Hidden in the reeds

The bittern is a striking example of camouflage in the bird world. It lives in dense reedbeds, where its brown and black plumage makes it almost impossible to see. When alarmed, the bittern "freezes" with its head pointing upward, but with its eyes firmly fixed on the intruder. When the intruder moves, the bittern silently swivels around to face it. If the wind is blowing, the bittern will sway gently like the reeds around it to make its disguise even more effective.

Still and silent

Pick somewhere that is concealed and comfortable. Keeping very still and quiet is just as important a part of camouflage as color and shape.

Hugging the ground

Height makes humans very conspicuous. If you keep low down and hide behind raised ground, there is less of you for animals to see.

Life in the soil

THE SOIL BENEATH YOUR FEET teems with life. Even in dry, inhospitable places such as deserts, microscopic forms of life can be found on and beneath the surface. In more fertile regions, a tablespoon of soil contains millions of organisms. These include bacteria and fungi (pp. 68-69), as well as many different kinds of animals. Some, such as earthworms (pp. 124-125) and wingless insects, are big enough to see, but many more, such as roundworms and mites, are much smaller.

Soil organisms are nature's recyclers, and are essential to other forms of life. They break down dead plants and the bodies of animals, and release the nutrients they contain. Most soil organisms need oxygen to survive. Digging a garden gets oxygen into the soil, and so helps to promote the natural processes of decay.

EXPERIMENT

Testing the acidity or alkalinity of soil

The life in soil depends on its chemistry and composition. Wet, acid soil, for example, harbors relatively few organisms, while alkaline soil tends to be rich in minerals that support many kinds of life. You can test the acidity or alkalinity of soil (its "pH") by using colored litmus paper, which can be bought at most drugstores or school supply stores.

YOU WILL NEED
- *plastic spoon*
- *distilled or de-ionized water*
- *soil* ● *jar with lid*
- *red litmus paper*
- *blue litmus paper*

1 COLLECT A SAMPLE of the soil you want to test. Put a spoonful of soil into the jar, and stir it to break up the particles and loosen any lumps.

2 NOW ADD DISTILLED or de-ionized water to the prepared soil until the jar is about half full. Screw the lid of the jar on tightly.

3 SHAKE THE JAR GENTLY for about one minute to mix the soil and water. Leave it on a flat surface until the soil starts to settle again.

EXPERIMENT
Tullgren funnel

To see animals that live in soil, you first need to separate them from their environment. Most soil organisms live in cool, dark conditions, and will move away from light and heat. The Tullgren funnel uses a strong light to drive small animals out of a sample of soil. They fall into a jar, making it easy to collect and examine them.

You Will Need
- soil ● angled lamp ● kitchen sieve
- plastic funnel ● tweezers ● jar
- hand lens ● petri dish or saucer

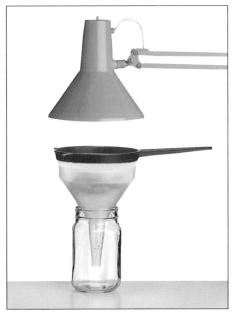

1 PLACE THE FUNNEL in the jar. Put the sieve in the funnel, and add a small amount of soil. Position the lamp so that it is close to the funnel, but not actually making contact with it. Switch on the lamp, and leave for about one hour. The tiny animals in the soil will move away from the light, drop through the sieve, and fall into the jar.

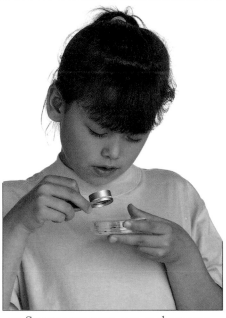

2 SWITCH OFF THE LAMP, and remove the sieve and funnel. The animals in the jar can be tipped into a petri dish or saucer. Separate the tiny animals with the tweezers, then examine them with a hand lens. Try repeating the experiment with soil from different habitats, to find out which kind of soil has the most prolific animal life.

4 UNSCREW THE LID, and dip the handle of the plastic spoon into the water above the soil. Take the spoon out of the water slowly.

5 NOW DAB THE STRIPS of blue and red litmus paper with the spoon handle, so that both strips of paper absorb some of the water.

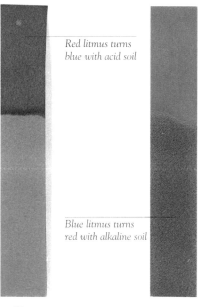

Red litmus turns blue with acid soil

Blue litmus turns red with alkaline soil

6 ONE OF THE TWO LITMUS PAPERS will now change color, telling you whether the soil in your test sample is acidic or alkaline.

Earthworms

ANNELIDS — THE GROUP OF ANIMALS to which earthworms belong — do not have hard skeletons. Their bodies are divided into segments, and they move along by stretching and contracting. Their muscles push and pull against a fluid-filled chamber called the coelom.

Earthworms feed on decaying organic matter. They collect their food by eating soil, and digesting the nutrients it contains. The rest of the soil passes through their bodies, and either fills their tunnels as they move or is brought to the surface. Here it forms little piles called "casts." In this way, soil from deep down in the ground is brought to the surface.

In many parts of the world, earthworms are vital to life in the soil. They mix up the soil, bringing minerals to the surface, and they also carry dead plant matter underground. Their tunnels let the soil "breathe," and they also help rainwater to penetrate the soil. Without earthworms, the soil would become hard and airless.

EXPERIMENT
Making a wormery

Earthworms can be kept in a wormery — a special cage, filled with soil, that has transparent sides. A wormery lets you see the tunnels that earthworms form, and it also lets you watch the way they mix up the soil. You can find some worms by digging up a few shovelfuls of dampish earth. Put the worms that you collect into a jar until the wormery is ready for them.

YOU WILL NEED
● *2 sheets of hard, clear plastic 10 in x 10 in (25 cm x 25 cm)*
● *a piece of wood* $^3/_4$ *in x 1*$^1/_2$ *in (2 cm x 3.5 cm) long, cut into 2 lengths of 10 in (25 cm), 1 length of 8*$^1/_2$ *in (21 cm), and 2 lengths of 2*$^1/_2$ *in (6 cm)* ● *leaves*
● *saw* ● *screwdriver*
● *18 screws*
● *soil of different types from around where you live*

■ Mating earthworms

An earthworm has both male and female reproductive organs. It cannot mate with itself, but has to find a partner. Mating worms lie next to each other in opposite directions, and each one produces eggs and sperm. Most earthworms mate underground, but some species mate on the surface, on warm, humid nights. You can sometimes see them if you look in the yard at night. Use a flashlight with a red plastic cover over the light. Worms are sensitive to vibrations, so walk softly.

Earthworm sizes
Most earthworms are no more than 1 ft (30 cm) long. Giant earthworms from Australia and southern Africa can reach over 6 ft (2 m) when stretched out.

The worm has two sets of muscles that make it move. Ring-shaped muscles inside each segment make the body lengthen. Muscles running along the body make it contract.

4 Add the different soils to the wormery so that they form contrasting layers. The wormery should be about three-quarters full. Put some leaves on top, and add water to make the soil damp but not wet. Carefully add the worms. Cover the wormery with a dark cloth, and put it somewhere cool and dark. Check every day to make sure that the soil is moist.

5 After a few days, you will begin to see tunnels as the earthworms eat their way through the soil. The layers of soil will gradually start to get mixed up. If your worms do not seem to be tunneling, make sure that the soil has not dried out, and that the worms are not too warm or too cold.

1 Cut five pieces of wood to the sizes specified.

2 Use the drill to make three equally spaced holes along opposite edges of each sheet of plastic, two holes along a third edge of each sheet, and a hole through the middle of the two smallest pieces of wood.

3 Use these holes to screw the plastic sheets to the three pieces of wood that make up the frame. Screw on the wooden feet at the base.

The clitellum, or saddle, produces a sticky jacket when the worm mates. The worm lays its eggs into the jacket and slips free of it. The jacket then hardens to form a cocoon for the eggs

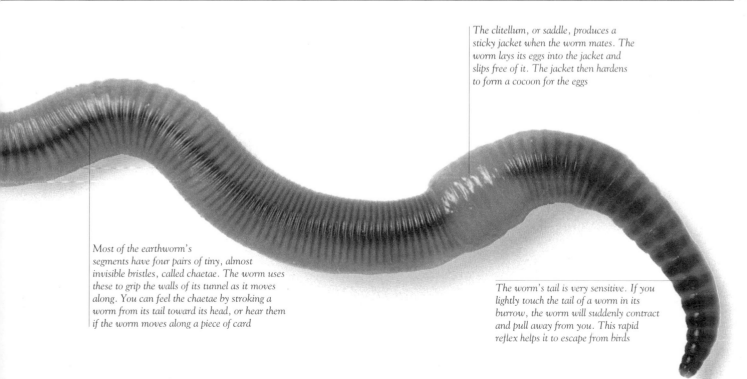

Most of the earthworm's segments have four pairs of tiny, almost invisible bristles, called chaetae. The worm uses these to grip the walls of its tunnel as it moves along. You can feel the chaetae by stroking a worm from its tail toward its head, or hear them if the worm moves along a piece of card

The worm's tail is very sensitive. If you lightly touch the tail of a worm in its burrow, the worm will suddenly contract and pull away from you. This rapid reflex helps it to escape from birds

BIRDS

Feathered for flight
*Feathers (above) are not merely decorative parts
of birds' plumage; they are essential for the
miracle of flight. In their rain-forest home,
brilliantly colored gold and blue macaws (left)
can fly high over the trees in search of seeds
and fruit.*

INSECTS, BIRDS, AND BATS are
the only groups of animals that
have managed to conquer the
air with powered flight. Of
these three, birds are the
supreme aviators. Equipped
with the perfect hardware —
feathers — they can soar high
up into the sky, dart through
the treetops, or hover over the
ground. Some birds never
venture far themselves, but
others can circle the Earth in
the course of a lifetime.

THE SCIENCE OF FLIGHT

THERE ARE MORE THAN 8,500 SPECIES of birds on Earth. The heaviest of them, the flightless African ostrich, can weigh up to 275 lb (125 kg) — about as much as two adult humans. The lightest — tiny hummingbirds that live in Central America — can weigh less than $^7/_{100}$ oz (2 g), which is about the same as a sugar cube.

Birds have always fascinated humans, and they were one of the first groups of animals to be studied in detail by early naturalists. One of the most important conservation movements in the world — the Audubon Society — takes its name from the American artist John James Audubon (1785–1851). His famous collection of paintings, *Birds of America*, included more than 1,000 birds, which were shown accurately for the first time. Audubon's paintings were almost all life size, and were far too big and precious to be taken outside. Today, field guides small enough to fit into a pocket can help you to identify birds in their natural habitats.

Archaeopteryx,
part bird, part reptile, was a fossil discovered in Solnhofen, Germany.

■ Origins of birds

Our knowledge of how bird life on Earth began goes back to 1861, when a dramatic discovery was made at a mine in Solnhofen in the heart of southern Germany. If you were to visit this part of Europe today, you would see a hilly, forest-covered landscape, cut by rivers that run northward to join the upper waters of the Danube. But millions of years ago, the scene was very different.

A nest box encourages birds to breed where they can be watched.

In the place of hills, there was a huge, shallow sea. The lime-rich skeletons of tiny animals living in this sea gradually built up a thick layer of sediment on the sea floor. As one layer became compressed by the next, the sediment turned into the rock that we know as limestone.

The limestone formed in the Solnhofen region is very smooth — so smooth that in the nineteenth century it was split into slabs and used for printing. The limestone slab would be inked, and then the image formed by the ink would be transferred onto paper, in a process known as lithography, meaning "stone drawing." To produce these printing slabs, workmen split the limestone into thin sheets. As the stone parted, it often revealed the fossilized remains of animals that had died and been covered by the sea-floor sediment.

Solnhofen was so well known for its fossils that their discovery was almost a matter of routine. But one day, a freshly split slab revealed something quite different. Entombed in the rock was the complete fossilized

An owl's pellet can show exactly what it feeds on.

Feathers have evolved many shapes and colors.

skeleton of a small bird, and, preserved by the fine grains of this special limestone, something never seen before in a fossil — the unmistakable outline of feathers.

■ A puzzling past

The fossils found in Solnhofen were named *Archaeopteryx lithographica* (*Archaeopteryx* means "ancient wings"). When first described in detail, they caused a sensation among scientists. Just two years previously, Charles Darwin (pp. 20-21) had published *The Origin of Species*, outlining the theory of evolution. Here was a classic "missing link" — part bird, part reptile — that bore out Darwin's ideas that species changed or "evolved" as time went by.

Like modern reptiles (pp. 144-145), *Archaeopteryx* had teeth, claws on its front legs, and a long tail. But, at the same time, it had feathers just like a bird. You might think from looking at the fossil that it flew like a bird as well, but on this point, scientists are still not sure. Flight needs strong muscles. In a bird, these muscles are anchored to a projecting breastbone, called a keel. But the skeleton of *Archaeopteryx* does not have a keel, and so it is difficult to see how it could

A chick's body heat is conserved by feathers.

produce enough power to stay in the air for long.

Some scientists believe that *Archaeopteryx* may have spent much of its time in trees, using its wings to glide from one to another. Others believe that it was a ground dweller. It is possible that it used its wings to help it leap after insects, or to scoop up its prey.

■ Flight and feathers

Although no one knows for certain how the first birds used their feathers, without doubt feathers are the key that has enabled birds to become supreme in the air. Feathers are strong and light, but also flexible. Because a bird has so many of them, it does not matter too much if some get damaged. All birds replace most of their feathers at least once a year, and many replace them twice or even three times. You can often find old and worn feathers that have been "molted," or shed, as new ones take their place. By contrast, insect or bat wings must last a lifetime: if they are damaged, they cannot usually be repaired.

Feathers do more than just help a bird to fly. Feathers also streamline the body and keep it warm. Since the days of *Archaeopteryx*, over 150 million years ago, feathers have evolved many different shapes and a huge range of sizes. A male peacock's display feathers can be 5 ft (1.5 m) long, while the feathers on a bird's

eyelids are rarely more than $\frac{1}{20}$ in (1 mm) in length.

■ Shaped for flight

Over millions of years, natural selection has tailored birds' bodies much as an aircraft engineer shapes a plane. A bird's wings and feathers are the essential hardware that it needs for flight, but if you could look inside its body, you would see other changes that help to keep the bird in the air.

Flight requires a great amount of power. Like an aircraft's engines, a bird's "power plant" — the large muscles that flap its wings — burn fuel at a great rate, up to 20 times faster than the muscles of a mammal. This requires a large supply of oxygen, and a bird's lungs have extra compartments that extend deep into the body. As a result, they extract oxygen from air much more efficiently than ours.

Birds have different-shaped wings, depending on their needs. In general, birds that fly rapidly have pointed wings to provide lift without drag. Broad, rounded wings are best for short distances — either taking off quickly in pursuit of prey or escaping predators.

In order to fly, a bird's muscles must generate enough lift to counteract its weight. Birds' bodies

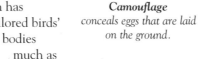

Camouflage
conceals eggs that are laid on the ground.

Konrad Lorenz
(1903–1989) was a scientist who investigated "imprinting" in birds.

Keep a notebook
to record your observations of birds.

have lost anything that is "excess baggage." Compared with their reptile ancestors, they have fewer bones, and many of them are hollow. Instead of having teeth, which are heavy, they have lightweight beaks. In most birds, the legs and feet have also become slender and light. Even waste disposal has been modified to save weight — most birds do not have a bladder.

■ A visual world

Just like the pilot of a high-speed aircraft, a flying bird needs to be very well co-ordinated. When a small bird flies through a tangled thicket, it adjusts the positions of its wings and tail with split-second timing to avoid hitting any branches or twigs in its way. To do this, it relies on its most important sense — its keen eyesight.

In many species of birds, the eyes are as heavy as the brain, and in some, they are so big that they almost touch inside the skull. Birds use vision not only for flying but also for finding food, spotting predators, courting a partner, and searching for a nest site.

During the past few years, scientists have discovered that birds are sensitive to visible light and also to light that is "polarized," or filtered so that its waves vibrate only in certain planes. Although we cannot detect it, sunlight reflected from some parts of the sky is partially polarized, and experiments have shown that birds use polarized light as one way of navigating if they set out after sunset, before the stars are shining brightly.

Binoculars
allow you to look closely at birds without disturbing them.

Interlocking barbs
make feathers strong but flexible.

Wings

IF YOU THROW A PAPER PLANE into the air, sooner or later, it will fall to the ground. Unless you are an expert, the chances are that it will crash-land. But when an eagle or a vulture takes to the air, it can stay aloft for hours, with only the slightest flick of its wings. It will land with perfect control, exactly where it wants.

Birds' wings are specially sculpted for flight — they have a "camber" or curve. As the wing travels through the air, this curve produces an upward force called lift. If lift is greater than the force of gravity, the bird rises into the air.

Pigeon wing
The feathers on a wing overlap to make a smooth surface that cuts its way through the air.

A marathon migration
The short-tailed shearwater has one of the longest migrations of all birds, encircling the Pacific Ocean in a figure-of-eight path up to 20,000 miles (32,000 km) long. It breeds on islands in the Bass Strait, between Australia and Tasmania, before setting off on its epic voyage around the ocean, and then returning months later to the same island from which it set off. Many other birds fly long distances every year. The Arctic tern travels from the Arctic to the Antarctic and back, feeding in the continual daylight of the summer in the far north and south.

■ Equipped for flight

These are the feathers that the pigeon uses in flight. Pigeons are strong fliers, and much of their body weight is made up of powerful pectoral muscles that link the wingbones with the keel. The largest feathers help with lift; the smaller ones insulate the body and smooth the airflow.

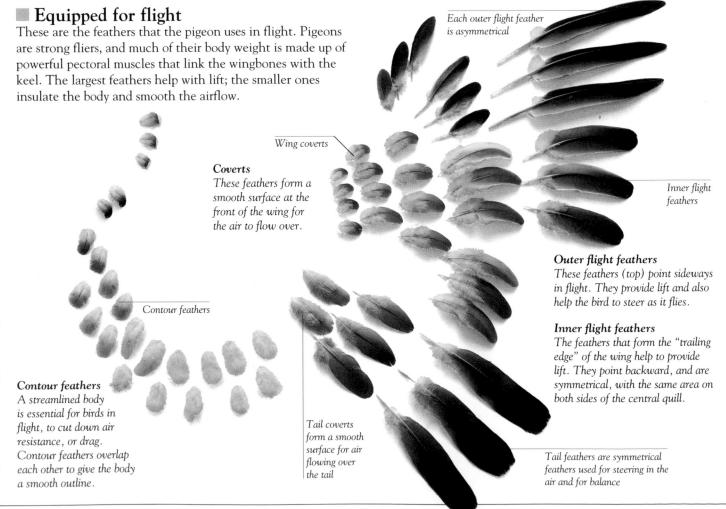

Each outer flight feather is asymmetrical

Wing coverts

Coverts
These feathers form a smooth surface at the front of the wing for the air to flow over.

Inner flight feathers

Contour feathers

Contour feathers
A streamlined body is essential for birds in flight, to cut down air resistance, or drag. Contour feathers overlap each other to give the body a smooth outline.

Tail coverts form a smooth surface for air flowing over the tail

Outer flight feathers
These feathers (top) point sideways in flight. They provide lift and also help the bird to steer as it flies.

Inner flight feathers
The feathers that form the "trailing edge" of the wing help to provide lift. They point backward, and are symmetrical, with the same area on both sides of the central quill.

Tail feathers are symmetrical feathers used for steering in the air and for balance

■ Feather types

Feathers have evolved int[...]
their use. Young birds are [...]
known as down, which h[...]
adult birds, many feather[...]
ends are firm and broad. [...]
covered by the broad pa[...]

*Macaw
flight
feathers*

How f[...]

If you look at a fe[...]
tip of a bird's win[...]
surface is curved. [...]
also shared by th[...]
lift. When a fligh[...]
the air, the air fl[...]
upper surface m[...]
underneath it. T[...]
speed above and [...]
pushes the feath[...]
this for yourself [...]
blow air at a fea[...]

■ Patterns of flight

An experienced birdwatcher can often tell a bird's species just by seeing a tiny silhouette in flight. This is because birds have very characteristic ways of flying, which depend on the shape of their wings. Birds that stay in the air for hours at a time, such as eagles and albatrosses, have long wings that allow them to soar and glide. They cannot change direction very easily, but in the open air, this does not matter. Birds that fly short distances need to be able to avoid obstacles and predators. They have shorter, more rounded wings — ideal for sudden changes of direction.

Vulture

For vultures and many other large birds, flying involves little effort. They hold their wings out and rise high into the sky by soaring — circling upward on columns of rising warm air called thermals. At the top of one thermal, they glide gently down in search of the next.

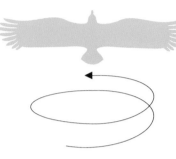

Swift

A swift's narrow, backswept wings have evolved for flying at high speed. Because they have a small area and are fairly flat, they do not produce much drag, which would slow the bird down. Swifts fly by a combination of quick flaps interspersed with short, shallow glides.

Penguin

The plump-bodied penguins have lost the ability to fly in air, but instead they "fly" underwater. A penguin's wings are short and stiff, and they work like flippers, speeding the bird along at over 25 mph (40 kmh) — faster than most ships. Penguin feathers trap a layer of air, which keeps in the body's heat. The wings are short, but they are quite strong and can deliver a well-aimed blow to anyone who comes too close on land.

Gull

If you watch a gull, you will see that it uses a mixture of gliding and flapping to stay in the air. A gull's narrow, pointed wings are like those of a glider, and they provide enough lift for it to hang motionless in a strong sea breeze. If a gull wants to change position, it can do this with a burst of flapping flight.

Finch

Most finches live in woodland or grassland, and their wings have evolved for short bursts of flight between perches. Their wings are slightly oval, a shape that provides lift and maneuverability, but uses considerable energy in overcoming drag. In the open, finches can often be recognized by their bobbing flight, with the wings beating, then closing for a while.

Hovering hummingbirds
Specialists in the art of hovering, hummingbirds can stay in one place in windless air. Their tiny wings can beat nearly 100 times in a second — far too fast for the human eye to see. Hovering flight burns up energy very quickly. Hummingbirds are able to hover for long periods only because they are "fueled" by nectar, a food that is made up of energy-rich sugars.

Birds that cannot fly
The kiwi, a flightless bird from New Zealand, has wings only 2 in (5 cm) long. Unlike most other birds, it has a good sense of smell, which it uses to find worms and insects. Evolution is an unpredictable process, and it often "backtracks" on itself. Having evolved the ability to fly, birds like the kiwi have since lost it again. For them, flying has stopped being important as a way of finding food or escaping predators, and their wings have become reduced until they are too small and weak for flight. Many flightless birds, such as the emu and ostrich, rely on size and strength to overcome danger. Smaller ones, such as the kiwi and kakapo, live on islands where there are few large predators.

Feather

FEATHERS ARE T
mammals — a
body heat. But
role in flying.
scales of dinos
ancestors of bi
keratin, the sa
that forms hu
Reptile scales
but feathers l
too heavy to
up of many t
barbs) attach
quill. Even w

Bird pellets

BIRDS CAN PECK, but they cannot chew. Because of this, they have to swallow mouthfuls of food whole. When an owl eats a mouse, it consumes everything — even the bones and fur. The owl's stomach digests the soft parts of the mouse, while the unwanted leftovers form a pellet. This is a tightly packed lump that the bird then coughs up.

Many birds produce pellets. You can sometimes find piles of them under places where a pellet-producing bird, such as an owl, has roosted. Pellets quickly dry out, and they do not smell. It is quite safe to pick them up, as long as you wash your hands afterward. Having collected the pellets, you can begin some fascinating detective work to find out what the bird has been eating.

Hunter of the night
The barn owl is a nocturnal hunter. It is found throughout the world on every continent except Antarctica. Barn owl pellets contain the remains of small mammals and birds.

EXPERIMENT
Examining owl pellets

You can pick apart dry pellets with tweezers, but the smallest bones will often break. A better way to examine an owl pellet is to soak it in a solution of water and dishwashing liquid, then carefully prize out the bones from the soft matter.

YOU WILL NEED
- card ● glue ● hand lens
- sieve ● screw-top jar

- tweezers
- dishwashing liquid ● pellet

1 HALF-FILL THE JAR with water, and add one drop of dishwashing liquid. Drop the pellet into the jar. Screw the lid on tightly, and shake the jar vigorously for about 30 seconds.

2 LEAVE THE JAR to stand for about five minutes, and then briefly shake it again. The dishwashing liquid will help the water to soak into the fur in the pellet, and it will start to fall apart. When the pellet has completely disintegrated, pour the contents of the jar into the sieve. You should now be able to pick out the bones using tweezers. The bones from each animal will be scattered throughout the remains of the pellet. Skulls, jaw bones, leg bones, and ribs are the easiest ones to single out, but keep a lookout also for teeth. The teeth of shrews, mice, and voles have characteristic surfaces, which you can examine using a hand lens.

■ Different types of pellet

All kinds of bird produce pellets, as a way of getting rid of the parts of their food that they cannot digest. Birds of prey and owls produce pellets that are made up almost entirely of animal remains. Most eagles and hawks tear meat from bones before swallowing it — unlike owls, their pellets either contain no bones, or just small pieces. Crows and gulls also make pellets. These contain a mixture of remains from plants, including hard seed coats, and the shells of animals such as crabs.

Shrew skull
Shrews have very small skulls, with narrow jaws and forward-pointing front teeth. Be careful when handling shrew skulls, because they break easily.

Mouse skull
The skull of a mouse is easy to identify because of the large gap between the front teeth (incisors) and cheek teeth (molars).

Vole skull
The cheek teeth (molars) have flat surfaces, which are used for chewing plant food.

Barn owl pellet
These are big, rounded, and gray or black. Small bones can sometimes be seen on the surface.

Wader pellets
These often contain fragments of broken shells.

Crow pellet
Insect remains are often found in crow pellets. Crows eat both plant and animal matter, especially insects.

Songbird pellet
Small birds sometimes produce pellets containing hard, indigestible seeds.

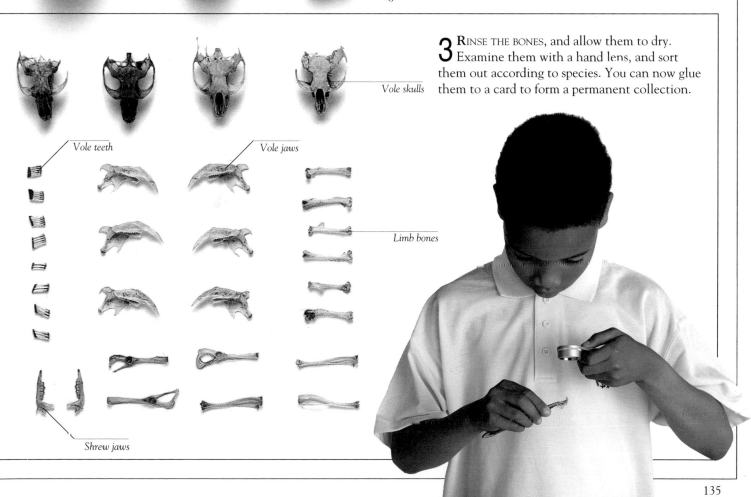

Vole skulls

Vole teeth

Vole jaws

Limb bones

Shrew jaws

3 Rinse the bones, and allow them to dry. Examine them with a hand lens, and sort them out according to species. You can now glue them to a card to form a permanent collection.

Eggs

A BIRD'S EGG IS RATHER LIKE A SPACESHIP. Inside, there is a living thing — a chick — which has to survive in the hostile environment outside its mother's body. The shell of its "space capsule" provides protection, and inside is all the food and water that the living inhabitant requires. The egg is also equipped to store the waste products of its occupant in a special sac. The only major way in which an egg differs from a spaceship is that it is permeable to gases. Oxygen can travel in from the air outside, but the tiny pores through which it passes are too small to let much water out. When the chick has reached the right stage of development, it breaks open the shell and struggles free into the outside world.

Camouflaged clutch
Eggs are a valuable source of food for predators, and are quickly eaten if left unguarded or unconcealed. These quail's eggs are laid on the ground. When they are not being incubated, they depend on camouflage to escape being noticed. The eggs can be identified by the blotches of color that merge with grasses or pebbles.

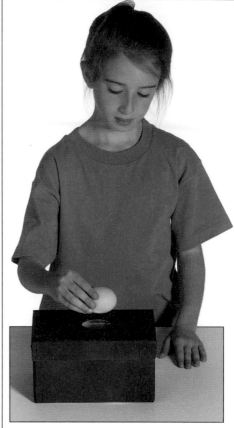

Using the viewer
The light from a flashlight illuminates the egg.

■ From chick to chicken

When it is first formed, a hen's egg is a single cell. After fertilization, the original single cell divides into many smaller cells. When it is laid, the hen sits on the egg, or "incubates" it. Unless it is kept at a constantly warm temperature in this way, the chick will not develop properly. About three weeks after laying, the chick inside the egg is fully developed and is ready to hatch. At first, the chick obtains oxygen from its blood vessels which come into contact with air flowing through the shell. But as the egg is incubated, it loses some water, and an airspace develops at its blunt end between the shell lining's two membranes. The chick pushes its beak into this airspace a few days before it hatches.

1 WHEN THE EGG'S AIR supply is used up, another oxygen source is needed. The chick pokes a hole in the eggshell and breathes fresh air from outside. When it is ready to emerge, the chick pecks out a circle of holes in the blunt end of the egg. It has a special chalky tip to its beak, known as an egg tooth, to enable it to crack through the hard shell.

2 USING ITS FEET, the chick forces away the blunt end of the eggshell and completes the hatching process. A young chicken is "precocial" — it can run about and feed itself within a few hours of hatching. The young of "altricial" birds, such as house sparrows, are helpless at hatching. They are reared in nests by their parents.

When the circle of holes is complete, the end of the egg flips off like a lid from a box, and the chick emerges

EXPERIMENT
Making an egg-viewing box

You can make a special viewing box to see inside an egg. Paint the inside of the box a dark color, cut out an egg-shaped hole, and place a flashlight, pointing upward, inside the box. When you put an egg onto the hole, you should be able to see the outline of the yolk inside. This way of looking into eggs is often used to separate fertilized from unfertilized eggs. Only fertilized eggs contain developing chicks, which appear as dark silhouettes when seen against the light.

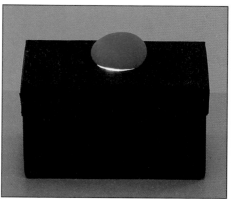

YOU WILL NEED
● *shoe box painted a dark color inside* ● *egg* ● *flashlight or a bicycle light*

A bird's eye view
For the best results, use the viewer in a darkened room.

■ Inside an egg

Albumen (egg white)

Double membrane

Yolk

Shell

Air-space

Chalazae

Area that will develop into chick

At the center of an egg is the yolk, the young bird's food supply. The yolk is held in the middle of the egg by two twisted cords made of protein, called the chalazae. When the parent bird rolls the egg during incubation (to warm it evenly), the chalazae move the yolk back to its original position, keeping the developing chick on top. The white of the egg, or albumen, contains water reserves for the chick. In this diagram, the egg is shown from above.

3 YOUNG CHICKS HAVE well developed heads and feet, but small, stubby wings. They cannot fly, but they can run quickly to escape danger. They can find all their own food because when they hatch, they have a strong instinct to peck at anything that might be edible.

Soon after hatching, the egg tooth drops off

Newborn chicks are covered with wet down that soon dries out

4 YOUNG CHICKENS LEARN THE SOUND of their mother's call while they are still in the egg, and they follow her as soon as they can walk. They quickly learn to recognize her by sight as well, a process known as imprinting (p. 140). If eggs are incubated artificially, the chicks will imprint on the first moving being they see when they emerge from the egg.

Watching birds

WHEREVER YOU LIVE — in the city or in the country — birds are likely to be the most conspicuous animals around you. They are highly active, and always on the lookout for food or for danger. Bird behavior is partly a matter of instinct, and partly a matter of learning. When a sparrow builds a nest, for example, it is acting by instinct. Although its first efforts may not be very impressive, it does not have to be shown the basic steps. In the same way, birds are driven by instinct to set up territories, to repel intruders, or to migrate in a set direction at a particular time of year. Equipped with just a pair of binoculars and a notebook, you can quickly learn to recognize these patterns of behavior. For more detailed study, building and using a blind will give you a close look at birds' daily activities, without their being aware of your presence.

Ringing birds
Ornithologists investigate the behavior of migratory birds by fastening tiny identification rings around the birds' legs. They can monitor the birds' movements by checking these regularly. Ringing birds requires great skill and care.

■ DISCOVERY ■

Konrad Lorenz

The Austrian scientist Konrad Lorenz (1903–1989) was an important figure in the study of animal behavior. Much of his work was concerned with the interplay of instinctive and learned behavior. In a series of experiments on birds, Lorenz investigated "imprinting" — the process by which a young animal instinctively becomes attached to a parent.

Working with goslings and ducklings, Lorenz found that imprinting took place during a critical period — usually between 5 and 24 hours after hatching. If he took the eggs of a greylag goose away from their mother, and stood near them as they hatched and during the critical period, the goslings would

immediately take him for their mother. He found that if the critical period had passed, imprinting did not take place.

■ Bird territories

Many birds set up territories with clearly defined boundaries. The maps below are from a famous study of robin territories by the English ornithologist, David Lack (1910–1973). By watching the same piece of ground for four years, he was able to find out exactly how the robins' territories changed with the passing seasons.

Early spring
Robins rarely live for more than a year, as many die of starvation in the winter. By the time spring arrives, the numbers of robins are at their lowest. Here seven surviving male robins have each set up a large territory.

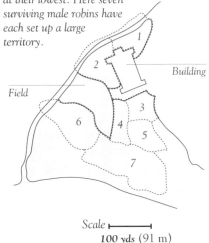

Scale ┣━━━━┫
100 yds (91 m)

Early winter
Nine months later, more robins are competing for the same piece of ground. Some males have been forced to give up parts of their territories to others. In most species it is only the male that defends territories, but robins are unusual — during the fall and winter, the females have territories of their own.

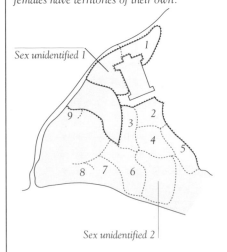

EXPERIMENT
Making a bird blind

This blind gives you an all-around view, and can be completely camouflaged. Two people are needed to put it up. Hammer a nail into the top of each upright, leaving at least 2 in (5 cm) projecting. Screw the eyes into the ends of the crossbars, and use wood glue for extra security.

YOU WILL NEED
● *4 poles about 5ft (1.5 m) long (the uprights)* ● *4 poles about 3 ft (1 m) long (the crossbars)* ● *4 nails 4 in (10 cm) long* ● *8 metal eyes* ● *10 tent pegs* ● *4 guy ropes* ● *wood glue* ● *camouflaged netting* ● *hammer*

■ Birdwatching equipment
No birdwatching trip is complete without these two pieces of equipment — a pair of binoculars, and a notebook to record any details you may wish to look up later.

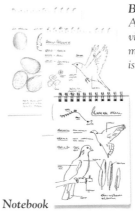

Binoculars
A wide field of view and high magnification is important.

Notebook
Keep a notebook for your field sketches of bird shapes, feathers, flight, and behavior.

1 LAY THE POLES on the ground, and attach a crossbar to each pair of legs, putting the nails through the metal eyes. Lift the poles and the crossbars upright.

2 MAKE SURE that the legs stand in a square. While one person holds the first two crossbars, the other fixes the remaining two crossbars in position.

3 TIE A GUY ROPE to the top of each leg, making sure that it is at 45° to the corner of the frame. Use a tent peg to anchor each guy rope to the ground.

4 MAKE SURE THE FRAME is square, and the guy ropes tight. Now arrange the netting centrally over the frame. Decide on the best side for entry to the blind.

5 PEG DOWN three sides of the net, leaving the entry side free. Insert more twigs and leaves into the net to camouflage the blind in its surroundings.

6 FROM INSIDE THE BLIND, clear several holes in the camouflage to enable you to see out on all sides. The blind is now ready for use.

REPTILES

The diversity of reptiles
The tortoise (above) has an armor plating that protects it from predators. Like many lizards, chameleons (left) are able to change color to signal to each other or to match their background and avoid danger.

FOR ABOUT 200 MILLION YEARS, reptiles were the dominant form of life on land. During the age of the dinosaurs, reptiles evolved to produce the largest animals that ever walked on Earth. But with the disappearance of the dinosaurs, the long reign of the reptiles came to a close. Today, their modern descendants, which include snakes, lizards, and turtles, are living reminders of the reptiles' past supremacy.

REPTILES OF THE WORLD

AT LEAST 300 MILLION YEARS AGO, reptiles appeared on Earth. They evolved from amphibians, animals much larger than their modern counterparts (pp. 78-79). Unlike amphibians, reptiles developed eggs with tough, leathery shells. This enabled them to break the link with water, and so become true creatures of the land.

Of all of the land animals, reptiles are the largest ones to have no internal heating system of their own — in other words, they are "cold-blooded." Reptiles need the heat of the sun to warm them up in the mornings and to help them digest their food after a meal. For this reason, most of the world's reptiles are found in the tropics, with fewer found toward the higher latitudes.

Wherever there is the warmth that they need, reptiles are found in most habitats. In the sea there are turtles and sea snakes, and there are even a few oceangoing lizards, such as the marine iguana of the Galápagos Islands. Fresh water is the haunt of terrapins, crocodiles, alligators, and giant snakes such as the anaconda of South America and the evocatively named elephant-trunk snake of Asia, whose baggy gray body cannot move about at all on dry land.

One lizard has even taken to the air. The flying dragon of Southeast Asian rain forests has extensions to its ribs that it can spread out on either side of its body like two fans. Because they are covered by a large flap of skin, these ribs act like the wings of a glider, allowing the lizard to swoop from tree to tree.

All reptiles have a covering of scales, giving them a tough, well-protected surface. The scales are made of keratin, the same protein that makes up our skin, hair, fingernails, and toenails. Since they are not warm-blooded, reptiles do not need an insulating layer of fur or feathers with which to retain their body heat. Their thick, scaly skin protects them from their enemies by making them difficult to attack, and unappetizing as well.

■ Reptile eggs

Unlike the eggs of amphibians, reptile eggs keep most of their moisture in but allow oxygen in and carbon dioxide out. Eggs like this can be left to hatch on land, where they are usually covered by soil or sand. Although some amphibians can breed without water, by keeping the eggs inside their bodies, most have to return to a pool or swamp for breeding. By breaking the link with water, reptiles are able to live in drier habitats, such as deserts, where they are particularly successful.

Most reptiles abandon their eggs once they are laid. Unlike birds' eggs,

they do not need to be kept constantly warm, although a few snakes do coil their bodies around the eggs and quiver their muscles to warm them up a little. Other snakes keep their eggs inside their bodies and give birth to live young. Crocodiles (pp. 148-149) guard their nests and carry the young to water when they hatch, but turtles abandon their eggs to the hands of fate. Like baby birds, young reptiles are equipped with a special egg tooth, which they use to hack their way out of the egg when they are ready to emerge. This tooth falls off shortly after hatching.

■ Reptiles of the past

There are three main groups of reptiles in existence today: they are the snakes and lizards, the crocodiles and alligators, and the turtles and tortoises. In the past, there were many more reptiles, and during the age of dinosaurs they were large and highly successful creatures.

Some scientists now believe that the dinosaurs could not have been entirely cold-blooded, because they were too large to have depended on external heat. The fossils of some pterosaurs, flying reptiles that had wingspans of up to 42 ft (13 m), show the impression of what looks like

Snakes are "cold-blooded" and can only move about once they have absorbed enough heat.

Tiny, gripping bristles on a gecko's toes enable it to walk up walls and across ceilings.

Crocodiles and alligators are among the closest living relatives of the dinosaurs.

If threatened by danger, a terrapin can pull its head and legs into the safety of its shell.

The shells of tortoises, turtles, and terrapins are made of bone, covered with hard scales.

fur. Fur is used to keep in body heat, meaning that those reptiles were warm-blooded.

The Gila monster is the largest lizard in the United States, and one of only two species of poisonous lizards in the world.

Although the dinosaurs have all died out, they have left descendants on Earth in the form of birds. If you look at a chicken's legs, you will see that they have a scaly skin — a reminder that its ancestors were reptiles. The chicken egg, which is similar internally to that of a reptile egg, is another reminder.

Two other large groups of reptiles have also died out: the seagoing plesiosaurs and ichthyosaurs. These were descended from land reptiles, although the ichthyosaurs had paddlelike flippers and looked very similar to fish or dolphins. The plesiosaurs were rather like long-necked reptilian seals. Both of these groups became extinct at about the same time as the dinosaurs, 65 million years ago.

■ Turtles and tortoises

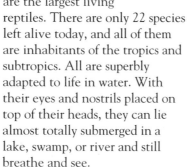

Of all the reptiles alive on Earth today, the turtles and tortoises (p. 150-151) are the most ancient group. About 260 million years ago they developed a heavy armored shell for protection, and this has ensured their survival to the present day.

The eye sockets in this lizard's skull show the importance of vision in finding food.

In a few species, the shell seems to have become redundant. The leatherback, a massive oceangoing turtle, has a shell that is no more than a thick, rubbery jacket. The leatherback lives mainly on jellyfish. Since these

Long-legged anole lizards change color for camouflage.

provide little of the calcium needed for building a shell and bones, the leatherback has had to economize on its bony parts. But at 10 ft (3 m) long — the largest turtle — the leatherback escapes most predators.

A group of river turtles, known as softshells, have abandoned their bony armor for the sake of speed in pursuing their prey. But what is left of the shell still gives them protection, since it is perfectly round and smooth, making it difficult for a predator to get hold of.

■ Crocodiles and alligators

Apart from birds, the animals most closely related to dinosaurs are crocodiles and alligators (pp. 148-149). They are the largest living reptiles. There are only 22 species left alive today, and all of them are inhabitants of the tropics and subtropics. All are superbly adapted to life in water. With their eyes and nostrils placed on top of their heads, they can lie almost totally submerged in a lake, swamp, or river and still breathe and see.

Tortoises have no teeth, and instead use their hard gums to tear at food.

■ Lizards of all sizes

The largest single group of modern reptiles is made up of lizards (pp. 148-149) and snakes (pp. 146-147). Lizards range in size from tiny geckos only 2 in (5 cm) long to the gigantic Komodo dragon, found on only four small islands in

Southeast Asia. This ferocious predator can grow to 10 ft (3 m) and preys on deer and wild boar. Geckos take much smaller prey — flies and other insects. Most have small, light bodies that help them to climb tree trunks and even the smooth walls of houses.

A few geckos can run across ceilings, using special pads on their feet. Each of their toes is broad and flat, like the petals of a flower, and on the underside there are dozens of tiny ridges. These ridges grip onto tiny irregularities in the surface on which the gecko is climbing. In tropical countries, geckos are often welcome inhabitants of houses because they prey on insect pests.

The Australian thorny devil, despite its fierce appearance, is quite harmless and lives on ants.

■ Living without legs

Snakes evolved from their lizardlike ancestors over 100 million years ago. Unlike lizards, they have no eyelids — instead their eyes are protected by a transparent permanent covering, which gives a snake its glassy stare. Another important difference between snakes and lizards is that snakes do not have external ears.

Many groups of lizards also include animals without any legs. Although they can look quite similar to snakes, their bodies are actually much more like those of lizards than snakes. It is clear to scientists that these legless creatures evolved from lizards with legs in relatively recent times — and in evolutionary terms, that means within a few million years.

Snakes and lizards periodically shed paper-thin layers of scaly skin as their bodies grow.

Snakes

WORLDWIDE, THERE ARE ABOUT 2,400 species of snake. Most snakes have poisonous venom, but only some species are dangerous to humans. In the course of evolution, snakes have lost their legs — they are descended from lizardlike reptiles with four legs. It used to be thought that because they have legless bodies, snakes were once burrowing animals. But biologists have found that long, thin lizards with small legs move through burrows much more easily than snakes, and so exactly why snakes became legless is still a mystery.

■ The skeletal snake

A snake's skeleton consists of a skull, a spine, and up to 450 pairs of ribs, which extend the full length of the body. The more primitive snakes — boas and pythons — have remnants of a hip girdle halfway along their bodies.

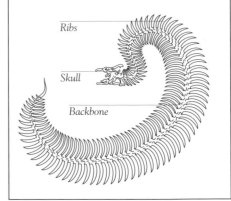

Ribs

Skull

Backbone

Snake scales are hard and dry. Some snakes have large belly scales that can be raised or lowered by muscles. They use these scales to get a grip on the ground as they slither along

Snakes smell by using their tongues to collect scent molecules from the air

Snake in the grass

The grass snake is common in northern Europe and, although venomous, is harmless to humans. Like many snakes, it is persecuted by people who mistakenly think that all snakes are dangerous.

One working lung

Most snakes have only one lung that actually works (usually the right lung). It extends both forward and backward inside the body.

■ The anatomy of a snake

Everything inside a snake's body is as long and thin as it can possibly be, and the organs are packed tightly together to economize on space. Despite this, snakes can still eat large animals such as deer. Loose, detachable bones in the skull, and ribs that can "swing open," enable the snake to swallow its prey. This is an advantage in harsh environments such as deserts, where meals may be few and far between. Most snakes eat once a week or less, and many eat only once a month.

Poison fangs allow poisonous snakes to inject their prey with venom, a modified form of saliva. Some snakes inject their venom through hollow fangs like hypodermic needles

Tracheal lung

Heart

Left lung

Right lung

Trachea (windpipe)

Liver

■ Shedding skins

As it grows, a snake's scaly skin becomes too small for its body. Like insects and lizards, a snake periodically sheds or "sloughs" its old skin. The new, larger skin underneath is then ready to take the old skin's place.

Head

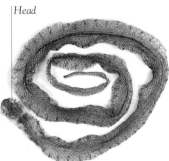

Head

Head

Egg-eating snake
This snake eats eggs whole. They break inside its body, and the shell is regurgitated.

Grass snake
Compare this skin with the grass snake opposite. The skin covers the snake's whole body — even its eyes.

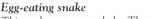

Large scales on underside

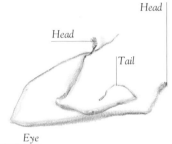

Head

Head

Tail

Eye

Adult rat snake
This large skin has been shed by an adult snake. It shows the large scales on the snake's underside.

Hatchling rat snake
These two tiny skins were shed by rat snakes not long after they were hatched from eggs.

■ Constricting snakes

After seizing its prey in its jaws, a python or boa coils its powerful body around the victim and squeezes hard. The animal dies of lack of oxygen — it simply cannot breathe in the snake's deadly embrace. A python can kill several small animals at once with this technique, crushing one in each coil of their bodies.

Reticulated python
Boas and pythons are among the largest of all snakes, the record being 36 ft (11 m) for an anaconda. Large pythons can kill crocodiles, and many species feed on prey such as deer and wild pigs.

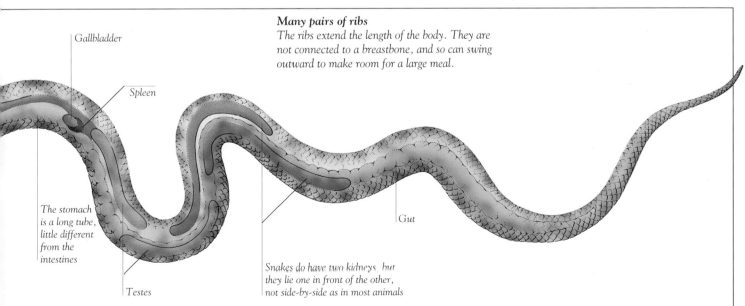

Gallbladder

Spleen

Many pairs of ribs
The ribs extend the length of the body. They are not connected to a breastbone, and so can swing outward to make room for a large meal.

The stomach is a long tube, little different from the intestines

Gut

Testes

Snakes do have two kidneys, but they lie one in front of the other, not side-by-side as in most animals

Crocodiles, alligators, and lizards

THE GIANTS AMONG REPTILES are crocodiles and alligators. The largest species, the estuarine crocodile of Asia, occasionally grows to over 20 ft (6 m) long. All crocodiles and alligators have special features to help them live in water — a transparent eyelid allows them to see while submerged, and flaps close their ears and nostrils when they dive. Another flap closes off the windpipe, so that they can eat their prey underwater without drowning.

The gharial crocodile and the mugger alligator live in parts of India and Nepal that have quite cold winters. These two species have an extraordinary way of surviving frosty nights, when being cold-blooded (p. 144) is a great liability. Sinking to the bottom of a river or lake, they let their metabolism drop to a very low level. This means that they need very little oxygen, so rarely have to come up to the cold surface to breathe.

Dwarf crocodile
The West African dwarf crocodile is only 5 ft (1.5 m) long, and has unusually short jaws.

■ Lizards
The lizards' closest relatives are not the crocodiles, as you might expect, but the snakes (pp. 146-147). Lizards and crocodiles look similar because they are covered by small overlapping scales. Most lizards have four legs, but there are some legless varieties too.

Lizards are relatively small reptiles that eat insects, although a few, such as the Komodo dragon, hunt bigger prey. Only two species, the Mexican beaded lizard from Central America and the Gila monster of North America, are known to be venomous.

Long tail breaks off easily if held

■ How a crocodile looks after its young
In comparison to other reptiles, crocodiles and alligators take great care of their young. The females make a nest for their eggs and remain close by until they hatch. Saltwater crocodiles build a huge mound of vegetation on land, which rots and warms up like a compost heap, keeping the eggs warm. When the young hatch, they call to their mother, who picks them up in her mouth and carries them to water. Some stay with their mother for up to three years.

Armored skin
The crocodile has heavy armor plating, made of bone, along its back. Adult crocodiles have little need for this cumbersome protection, but it probably helps young ones to survive the attacks of birds and lizards.

Young crocodile in mother's jaws

Crocodile eggs

Nest excavated by mother crocodile

Powerful tail used for swimming

Rainbow lizard
Like many lizards, this species from tropical America uses its tail as a defense. If a predator catches the lizard by its tail, the tail breaks off, and the lizard makes its escape. It soon grows another one.

Southeastern five-lined skink
There are more than 1,200 species of skink, and they make up one of the largest families of lizards. Most species of skink have very tiny limbs, and with their ultra-smooth bodies, are easily mistaken for snakes.

Anole lizard
Anoles are tree-dwelling lizards, related to the iguanas. Their bright green body color is a useful camouflage against leaves, and when they clamber down a tree trunk or cross open ground, they can rapidly change color from green to brown.

Skin can change color

■ Alligators

Although they are physically similar, alligators and crocodiles belong to separate families. Like crocodiles, alligators have a complex type of heart, more advanced than those of other reptiles, and similar to those of birds. Alligators are the closest living relatives of the dinosaurs. They possess the biggest and most complex brains, making them the most intelligent of the reptiles.

■ Nile crocodile

The Nile crocodile measures up to 16 ft (5 m) long. When hunting, it can lie very still in the water, with only its eyes and nostrils exposed. Antelope and other animals come down to the water to drink without noticing the crocodile lurking close by. Seizing the head of its prey, the giant reptile drags it underwater, where it drowns. Crocodiles cannot chew chunks from their prey — they wedge their victim under a rock in the water, sink their teeth into a leg, and then twist themselves around in the water until the leg is torn off.

Webbed back feet

Crocodile's body is slung low between its legs

Peglike teeth

Crocodile tears
According to legend, crocodiles cry when eating their prey, and to "shed crocodile tears" is to pretend to be sad about something you are really quite pleased about. The truth behind the legend is that some crocodiles have to get rid of excess salt from their bodies, and they excrete this in their tears. Sometimes this happens while the crocodile eats.

Turtles and tortoises

OVER 260 MILLION YEARS AGO, turtles and tortoises
evolved — long before their larger relatives, the
dinosaurs. The armor plating of these fascinating animals
protects them against most predators when adult, but
they are vulnerable when young because they reproduce
by laying eggs. Particularly threatened are the seagoing
turtles that lay their eggs at night on sandy beaches.
They have to cope not only with people digging up their
eggs for food but also with the bright lights and noise
from tourist hotels. Some species are now
seriously endangered.

Into the unknown
*A young tortoise hatching from its egg. Some
turtles and tortoises lay hard-shelled eggs like
those of birds, but others lay eggs with more
flexible leathery shells. The eggs are not guarded
or cared for, and the hatchling must fend for itself
from the moment it is born.*

Growth rings visible on
keratin plate or scute

Bony plate revealed where
scute has fallen off

Joint between
bony plates

Basking terrapins
*Two European pond terrapins sunning themselves on a log. Unlike
tortoises, which are vegetarians, terrapins are mainly carnivorous, and will
eat fish, large insects and worms, frogs, and newts.*

Layered shell
Where tortoises live in the
wild, you may find
fragments of their shells. If
you examine these
carefully, you will see a
layer of white bone
underneath, with a layer of
brown keratin over the top.
(Keratin is the same protein that
makes up our skin and
fingernails.) This two-layered shell
is very strong. The joints between the
keratin plates (or scutes) do not lie
directly above the joints in the bony plates.
This means that the weakest points in the bony
layer are bridged by the keratin layer, and vice versa. The wiggly joints
between the bony plates add to the strength of the shell, being more
difficult to crack open than straight joints. The same kind of joint is
found between the skull plates of animals.

Protect the natural world
In some countries tortoises are no longer
sold as pets. In the United
States terrapins are a
protected species.
Some states
prohibit their
captivity.

Keratin plates

Legs covered
by scales

Live-in armor

A turtle or tortoise's backbone and ribs are fused to the shell, and so are the hip girdle and the shoulder girdle. The shell itself is made up of about 60 separate bones. When a turtle or tortoise hatches, the shell bones are not fused together, just as the sections of the skull are not yet connected in a newborn human baby. The bony plates grow together and become tightly joined as the reptile matures. Some turtle species have soft shells, making their bodies lighter for faster swimming.

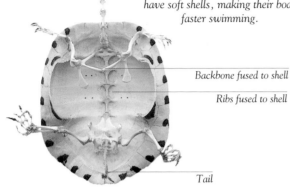

Backbone fused to shell

Ribs fused to shell

Tail

Laying eggs

A female turtle laying eggs into a specially prepared pit that she has dug on a sandy beach. Some turtles lay over 200 eggs in their nests. By contrast, the African pancake tortoise (so named because its very flat shell enables it to hide in rock crevices) lays just one.

■ Keeping a terrapin

Terrapins can be kept successfully in an aquarium tank. However, before you buy a terrapin, ask where it has come from. Never buy specimens that have been collected in the wild, as they die in huge numbers when collected and transported. Keep the tank water clean by changing it regularly, and remove any scraps of food before the terrapins have left (the scraps will decompose and contaminate the water).

Arranging the tank

Terrapins need both water and "dry land" in their tank. In cold weather, keep small terrapins warm with a light bulb suspended above the tank.

Cleaning a terrapin

If algae build up on the terrapins' shells, scrub them lightly with a toothbrush. Always handle your terrapins gently, and wash your hands well afterward, as they can carry diseases.

Landscaping the tank

Place a flowerpot on its side to provide an underwater shelter for the terrapins.

fire to keep themselves warm. If they had migrated much more slowly, natural selection (pp. 22-23) might have brought fur back again. For modern humans living in cold climates such as Europe and North America, a coat of fur would be far more useful than sweat glands.

Humans are not the only mammals to have lost their fur. So have the elephant, rhinoceros, and hippopotamus, all large animals that live in hot climates. The larger an animal is, the more difficulty it has in cooling off, because the core of the body is a long way from the surface. Fur would be a nuisance for an African elephant, whereas the woolly mammoths of the last Ice Age still found their coats useful. The aquatic mammals — whales and dolphins — have also lost their fur because it would interfere with swimming. If you have ever tried to swim with your clothes on, you will know how heavy and slow it feels.

Echidnas and duck-billed *platypuses are the only mammals that lay eggs.*

■ Placental mammals

There are three groups of mammals in the world. In the group of mammals that we belong to — the placental mammals — the young do a lot of growing while still inside the mother. In its mother's womb, the baby gets all the food it needs from its mother's blood. But the blood of the baby and that of the mother do not mix. Instead there is an area on the side of the womb, called the placenta, where the baby's blood runs through a maze of tiny blood vessels. Food

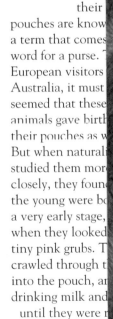

A mammal's *body is propped up by its legs.*

molecules and ox[ygen]
from the mother [
through the bloo[d
Carbon dioxide a[nd
products can mov[e
opposite direction[s

The baby is link[ed
placenta through [
cord, which carrie[s
black and forth. W[hen
baby is born the u[
has t[
the w[
mam[
chew[
cord. [
mark[
where[
cord [

■ M[

Mam[
their [
pouches are know[n
a term that comes[
word for a purse. [
European visitors [
Australia, it must [
seemed that these[
animals gave birth[
their pouches as w[
But when naturali[
studied them more[
closely, they foun[d
the young were bo[rn
a very early stage, [
when they looked [
tiny pink grubs. T[
crawled through t[he
into the pouch, a[nd
drinking milk and[
until they were r[
In certain w[
marsupial ma[
better system[
than the place[
They can have [
at different stage[
development —[
inside th[
small on[
and one [
leave the[
are very [
either fo[

Designed for survival
Young house mice in their nest (above) look helpless, but, as with all mammals, their life cycle and behavior are designed to promote the survival of the species. Self-protection is the aim of these meerkats from southern Africa (left), keeping a lookout for danger.

MAMMALS

THERE ARE ABOUT 4,000 SPECIES OF MAMMALS IN THE WORLD. They include the largest animals on land and in the sea — the elephants and whales — and also many animals that graze and browse, as well as the stealthy and quick-witted predators that hunt them. This group of animals also includes one species that has had a greater effect on the planet than any other — ourselves.

THE MA[...]

THE FIRST MAMMALS
they lived at a time
When the dinosaurs
evolved to take thei[...]
they live in habitats

The first European explorers t[...]
reach Australia were amazed a[...]
the animals they found.
Instead of deer and antelope
grazing on the grass, there
were kangaroos and
wallabies, which
bounded away on their
back legs when alarmed.
In the eucalypt trees they
saw koalas, and on the
ground, bandicoots,
lumbering wombats, and
other extraordinary
animals. To add to their
astonishment,
they saw that
these animals carrie[...]
their young in speci[...]
pouches made by fo[...]
of skin.
    Although they we[...]
looking at a whole [...]
world of animal life[...]
these visitors from a[...]
would have found a[...]
things at least that
were reassuringly
familiar. Despite th[...]
often extraordinary
shapes, these anima[...]
had fur. They also f[...]
milk to their young[...]
and were warm-
blooded. These characteristic[...]
were enough to
identify them as
mammals —
members of a group of
animals that has spread
over almost all the Earth.

■ The human mammal

You are a mammal.
For the first few
weeks or months of
life, mammals are

The young of marsupial
mammals develop in the safety
of the mother's pouch.

Skeletons

THE SKELETON OF A CRAB or a locust is on the outside of
its body, forming a hard case that has to be shed as the
animal grows. In mammals, as in all other vertebrates,
things are the other way around. The skeleton is on the
inside, and it acts like a frame on which the rest of the
body is built.

Before birth, the skeleton is made up entirely of a
substance called cartilage, which is rather like plastic. It
is strong and flexible, but not hard enough to support a
heavy body moving about on land. As an animal grows
up, the cartilage in its skeleton has to be reinforced.
Cells inside the cartilage begin to deposit mineral salts,
turning the cartilage into bone, a much harder
substance. In humans, this process, known as
calcification, takes about 20 years. An average skeleton
eventually contains about 11 lb (5 kg) of mineral salts.

■ A skeleton's story

Even if you have never seen a hare
before, its skeleton alone tells you that it
is a plant-eater that relies on good vision
and speed to escape from danger. Its
teeth are adapted to tearing up plants
and chewing them. Its large, sideways-
facing eye sockets show that it has big
eyes and a wide field of view. The long,
slender legs show that it
can run at high
speed.

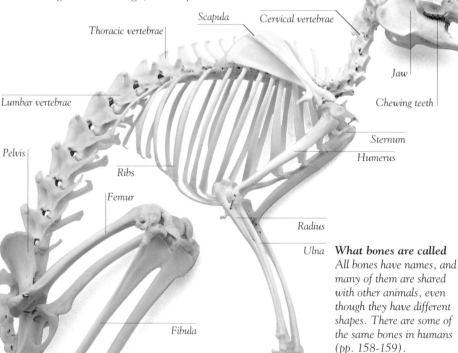

Thoracic vertebrae
Scapula
Cervical vertebrae
Skull
Jaw
Chewing teeth
Lumbar vertebrae
Sternum
Humerus
Pelvis
Ribs
Femur
Radius
Ulna
Fibula
Tibia
Tarsals
Metatarsals
Phalanges

What bones are called
All bones have names, and
many of them are shared
with other animals, even
though they have different
shapes. There are some of
the same bones in humans
(pp. 158-159).

EXPERIMENT
Stripping skulls

Adult supervision is advised for this
experiment
Skulls are fascinating objects to collect,
but they often need cleaning if you
want to keep them. There are several
ways of going about this. This method
uses natural decay, followed by
chemical cleaning. Bury the skull in a
flowerpot filled with soil, and sink it in
the ground. Leave it there for at least
two months if the weather is warm, and
longer if it is cold.

YOU WILL NEED
● *beaker* ● *bleach* ● *flowerpot* ● *pencil*
● *string* ● *sal soda* ● *soil* ● *spoon*

■ Limb shapes

Mammals live in almost every habitat
on Earth, including the air and the
oceans. To move and feed, they have
evolved different limbs, ranging
from hands to wings.

Good pickings
The aye-aye lives on trees in Madagascar.
It uses its extremely long second finger for
finding and stabbing insects.

Squirrel skull

Jaw bones

Incisor teeth

1 SIFT THROUGH THE SOIL to remove the skull. Check that the flesh has decayed. Wash the bones thoroughly.

2 TIE THE SKULL to a pencil, and lower it into a warm solution of sal soda. Leave for four hours.

3 RINSE THE BONES. Leave them for two hours in water with a little bleach. Remove, rinse, then dry them.

Whale flipper

Digit 1

Digit 5

Digit 4

Digit 2

Digit 3

The five-fingered limb

All vertebrates have the basic bones in their limbs, with five "digits," or fingers. In mammals, the limbs have evolved into many different shapes and sizes.

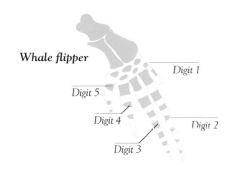

Bat wing

Digit 1

Digit 2

Digit 5

Digit 4

Digit 3

Looking at skulls

A skull is a complicated collection of many bones, some of which are joined tightly together. Examining the jaws and teeth will tell you what the animal feeds on (p. 163). The position of the eye sockets will tell you if an animal has binocular vision (p. 166), a feature found in many predators.

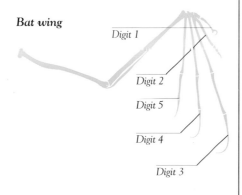

You can use a blunt metal probe, or "seeker," to lever out a molar tooth, showing you how it is rooted in the jaw

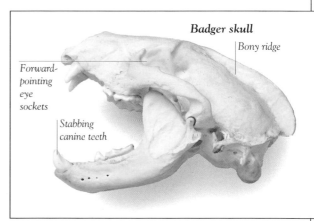

Badger skull

Bony ridge

Forward-pointing eye sockets

Stabbing canine teeth

A badger's brain case

The tall ridge that runs down the center of a badger's cranium, or brain case, anchors the muscles that it uses to bite. The badger has particularly powerful jaws, which it uses for tearing up meat and chewing plant food.

Weasel skull

Despite its diminutive size, the weasel is an effective hunter. Its skull is very small, allowing it to enter burrows in search of prey. It has powerful jaws, and its teeth can tear or chew.

Lizard skull

Most lizards have well-developed eyes, and hunt by sight. Their skulls can be recognized by the large eye sockets. Unlike mammals, they have simple, peglike teeth that are similar to each other.

Joints and movement

THE ADULT HUMAN SKELETON consists of over 200 bones. Neighboring bones meet in places known as joints. Some joints are locked together, but many more are able to move. Those in your backbone move only slightly, while others, like those in your fingers, are much more flexible.

Joints need to be lubricated to stop them seizing up. In mobile joints, the bones are covered by a layer of cartilage where they meet. The cartilage is quite slippery and is "oiled" by synovial fluid. The whole joint is held together by ligaments, and is encased in a flexible membrane which stops the synovial fluid from leaking out.

EXPERIMENT
Making model joints

Adult supervision is advised for this experiment
You can see the principles behind the body's joints by making wooden models. These consist of simple joints with two bones.

YOU WILL NEED
- rubber bands
- G-clamp ● hinge
- jigsaw ● paint
- sandpaper
- screws ● set square
- tenon saw
- dishwashing sponge
- wood

Phalanges (finger bones)

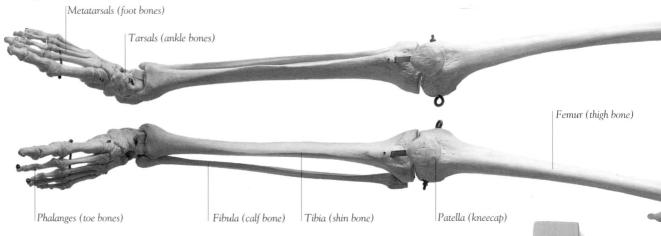

Metatarsals (foot bones)

Tarsals (ankle bones)

Phalanges (toe bones)

Fibula (calf bone)

Tibia (shin bone)

Patella (kneecap)

Femur (thigh bone)

Humerus

■ Elbow

The hingelike elbow joint connects the humerus of the upper arm and the paired radius and the ulna of the lower arm. It can only move in one plane.

Arm bent
The hinge at the elbow can fully close to allow your arm to bend inward.

Arm straight
The hinge can open up to 180° but no farther, unless your elbows are "double-jointed."

Bones of lower arm

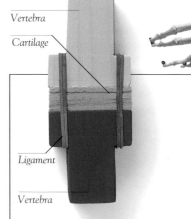

Vertebra

Cartilage

Ligament

Vertebra

■ Vertebrae

A backbone, made up of 26 bones called vertebrae, is linked together by joints.

■ Cranium

The eight separate bones that protect your brain are locked together by joints that cannot move. This model shows one of these joints in close-up. The joints in the cranium do not form until after you are born. As you grow, the bones gradually get larger and meet. In adults, the bones eventually fuse and the joints disappear.

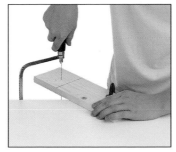

Making the joint
Clamp a square of wood firmly to a working surface. Use a jigsaw to cut a vertical, wavy line. Separate the two halves, and sand and paint them before putting them back together.

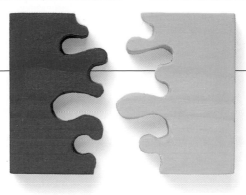

Locked together
The bones fit together just like two pieces in a jigsaw puzzle. The complicated curves prevent any movement between the two bones.

Cranial bone

Cranial bone

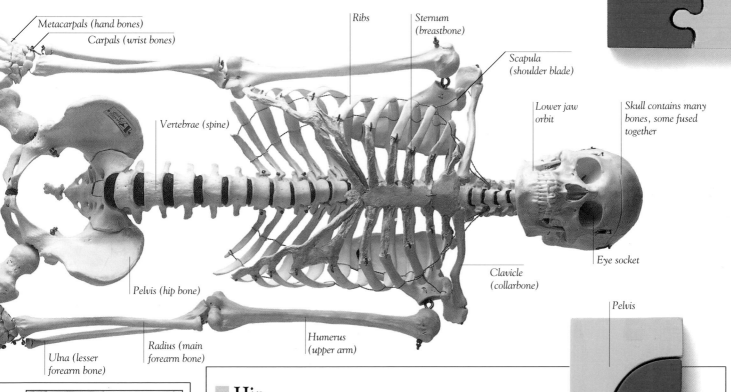

Metacarpals (hand bones)

Carpals (wrist bones)

Ribs

Sternum (breastbone)

Scapula (shoulder blade)

Vertebrae (spine)

Lower jaw orbit

Skull contains many bones, some fused together

Eye socket

Pelvis (hip bone)

Clavicle (collarbone)

Ulna (lesser forearm bone)

Radius (main forearm bone)

Humerus (upper arm)

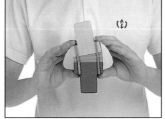

Bending the backbone
The bones are separated by a pad of cartilage and held in place by strong muscles and ligaments. Each joint moves a small distance. But there are many joints, so your spine can bend quite far.

■ Hip

In this two-dimensional model of the hip, the yellow part is the pelvis (the socket), and the blue part is the femur (the ball).

Leg swinging outward
Looking down to the hip, the ball is seen rotating in the socket to let the leg swing outward.

Leg swinging inward
The ball rotates in the other direction to let the leg swing inward.

Pelvis

Femur (thigh bone)

Muscle power

MUSCLES ARE PARTS OF THE BODY that make things move. The largest muscles — those in your legs — are so strong that together they can move the whole body. The smallest are so tiny that you may not realize that they are there. When you feel cold, you will know the feeling of getting "goose-flesh." Tiny muscles attached to your hairs contract, pulling the hairs upright.

Not all the body's muscles work in the same way. Skeletal muscles are the ones that you use to move your legs, arms, and other parts of your body. They are known as "voluntary" muscles, because you have complete control over them. But not all types of muscle are voluntary. Cardiac muscle, for example, keeps your heart beating, and smooth muscle moves food along your digestive system. These kinds of muscle keep your body working, and they do this without your having to tell them to.

Under the skin
Early anatomists made very precise drawings of the muscles, but they had no idea what made them move.

EXPERIMENT
Measuring muscles

Arm extended
Measure the distance around the upper arm at its widest point.

■ Making muscles move

Motor neurons are nerve cells that make your body move. Each one works by conducting an electrical signal to a set of muscle fibers. When the motor neuron "fires," the muscle fibers contract. The signal that travels down a motor neuron is not quite the same as a current flowing through a wire, but it does move very quickly. Some motor neurons can be over 3 ft (1 m) long, but even so, a signal can travel from one end of the nerve to the other in just $1/100$ of a second. The motor neuron shown here has been shortened to fit onto the page.

Node of Ranvier
These tiny gaps in the myelin sheath act like relay stations, passing the electrical signal down the axon.

Myelin sheath
The axon is surrounded by special cells that wrap themselves around the nerve cell. These cells act like insulating tape.

Axon
The axon is a thin filament, the longest part of the nerve cell. It can conduct an electrical signal.

Muscle fiber
The muscles that make your body move consist of bundles of fibers. Within each fiber are protein molecules that can slide over each other to make the muscle contract.

Nerve endings
A motor neuron ends in tiny pads (synapses), which lie beside the muscle fibers. When a signal travels down the nerve, these pads release a substance that makes the muscle contract.

When a muscle contracts, it gets shorter and fatter. In your upper arm, there are two sets of muscles — one contracts as the other expands.

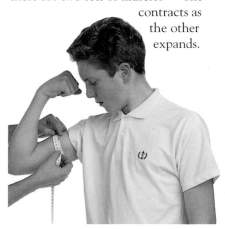

Arm flexed
Measure again. Is there any difference? What happens if you measure just the front or back?

Pulling in pairs

Muscles can pull, but they cannot push. To make your limbs move, your muscles are arranged in "antagonistic" pairs or sets. One muscle — the flexor — bends up the joint, while another muscle — the extensor — straightens it out. In the model of the arm below, springs take the place of muscles, and pieces of string make up the tendons that attach the muscles to the skeleton.

YOU WILL NEED
- *hinge* ● *4 hooks*
- *4 screws* ● *2 springs*
- *string* ● *2 pieces of wood*

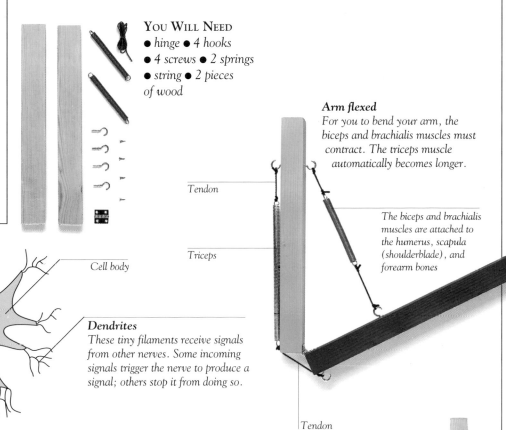

Arm flexed
For you to bend your arm, the biceps and brachialis muscles must contract. The triceps muscle automatically becomes longer.

The biceps and brachialis muscles are attached to the humerus, scapula (shoulderblade), and forearm bones

Tendon

Triceps

Tendon

Nucleus

Cell body

Dendrites
These tiny filaments receive signals from other nerves. Some incoming signals trigger the nerve to produce a signal; others stop it from doing so.

The triceps muscle is attached to the humerus, the scapula (shoulderblade), and the ulna (one of the two bones in the lower arm)

Biceps

Arm extended
The triceps muscle contracts to extend the arm, and the biceps and brachialis muscles become longer.

Luigi Galvani

The Italian professor of anatomy Luigi Galvani (1737–1798) was the first to realize that electricity plays a part in animal movement. He made this discovery accidentally. A machine that generated electrical sparks was being used next to the leg of a frog, which had been dissected to reveal its muscles. The frog's leg suddenly contracted, and by further experiments, Galvani proved that electricity from the machine had caused the movement. Galvani's name lives on in the process of "galvanizing," in which electricity is used to deposit zinc on iron, making it rust-proof.

Teeth

THE HARDEST PARTS of your body are not your bones, as you might expect, but your teeth. Bone is very hard, but it cannot cope with years of cutting and chewing. To eat your food, you rely on enamel — the mineral coating of your teeth that is so hard that it can last a lifetime.

Your teeth, like those of most hunting mammals, do not grow once they have been formed. To make up for this, you change teeth as you get older. Your first set, called "baby teeth," starts to appear when you are about six months old. They are quite small, and are gradually replaced by your adult or permanent teeth, which are much bigger. Sometimes your first adult teeth can look much too big for you, but the rest of your body eventually catches up in size.

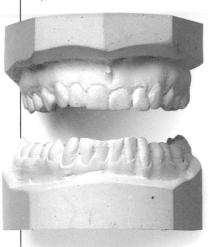

Full set
This is a dentist's plaster cast of a set of adult, or permanent, teeth.

■ Types of teeth

Humans have three different types of teeth. Each plays a separate part in helping you to process your food.

Incisors
These teeth have flat sides and a sharp edge. When you bite, the sharp edges of your top and bottom teeth meet to cut your food.

Canines
Canine teeth are sharp and pointed for gripping and tearing meat. Since knives and forks were invented, we have used our canines far less.

Premolars and molars
These teeth have peaks, or cusps, that fit into hollows in the tooth opposite. The cusps pierce food, and grind it up during chewing.

■ Above and below

When all your adult teeth have appeared, you should have 16 teeth in each jaw (four incisors, two canines, four premolars, and six molars), making 32 teeth altogether. Your "wisdom teeth," right at the back of the jaw, may not appear until you are in your twenties, and sometimes they don't appear at all.

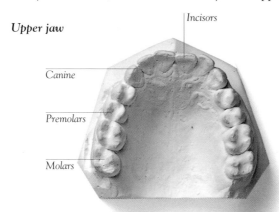

Upper jaw

Incisors
Canine
Premolars
Molars

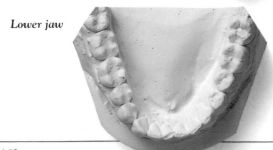

Lower jaw

■ Inside a tooth

Next time you eat ice cream, see what happens if you stop in mid-bite. In a short while, your teeth will begin to feel very cold and uncomfortable! This happens because your teeth contain nerve endings. Together with tiny blood vessels, these lie in the "pulp cavity" — the spongy center of each tooth. The pulp cavity is surrounded by a bonelike substance called dentine. The part of the tooth that does the biting is covered with enamel, which is extremely tough.

Cross-section of a molar tooth

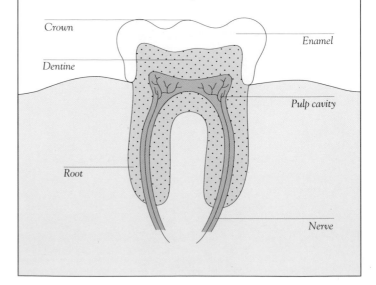

Crown
Dentine
Root
Enamel
Pulp cavity
Nerve

■ A plant-eater's teeth

The skull shown below belongs to a deer — one of many kinds of mammals that feed entirely on plants. It needs to be able to cut and grind its food. In the front of the mouth are the cutters — the incisor and canine teeth — found *only* in the lower jaw. When the deer closes its mouth, these teeth are pressed against a hard pad on the upper jaw. Behind the cutters, a gap, called the diastema, gives the deer's tongue room to move the food around. Then come the grinders — the large premolars and molars at the back of the mouth. As the deer chews, its lower jaw moves from side to side, and ridges on the surface of the teeth grind the food into a pulp.

Skull of a deer

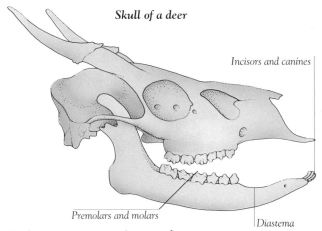

Incisors and canines

Premolars and molars

Diastema

■ A meat-eater's teeth

Many mammals live mainly on meat. They include wolves, foxes, and cats of all sizes, from the ones we keep as pets to lions and tigers. The skull shown below belongs to a fox. It has sharp, closely set incisors for cutting and scraping meat. The long canines are useful for grabbing and holding prey, and for tearing at meat ("canine" comes from the Latin word *canis*, meaning a dog). The teeth at the back of its jaw are designed for cutting. Unlike our molars, they have long, sharp edges. Teeth like these are called "carnassials." Because they are near the hinge of the jaw, they can exert a pressure that is great enough to crack open bones.

Skull of a fox

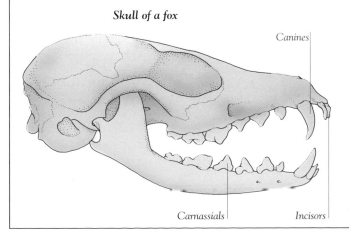

Canines

Carnassials

Incisors

EXPERIMENT

A tooth under attack

The enamel that covers your teeth is very tough, but it is not good at coping with chemical attack. If you eat a lot of sugar, bacteria in your mouth turn it into acid, which attacks the enamel. Cola drinks attack tooth enamel directly. Either way, bacteria get into the dentine beneath, and the result is tooth decay. Put the tooth in the cola, and watch what happens. Leave it, and take it out of the cola 24 hours later. Can you see any difference?

YOU WILL NEED
● *a discarded tooth (yours, or an animal's)* ● *cola* ● *drinking glass*

Endangered by its teeth

An elephant's tusks are specialized teeth that are used for scraping, or to dig for roots, lever the bark off trees, fight off enemies, and impress other elephants. Tusks keep growing throughout an elephant's life, so the longer the tusk, the older the elephant. They are also the source of ivory, and huge numbers of African elephants have been killed for their tusks. The trade in ivory is now banned, but it remains to be seen if the elephant will survive.

Hollow base

Solid tip

Lungs and breathing

LIKE ALL OTHER ANIMALS, you need oxygen in order to live. Your body absorbs oxygen from the air around you through the lungs. These are rather like sponges, full of tiny channels and chambers that fill up with air when you breathe in. The oxygen in the air passes across the membranes of the lungs and into the blood vessels that surround them. At the same time this is happening, carbon dioxide, a waste product of metabolism, passes in the other direction.

When your body is working hard, your heart pumps faster, and you breathe more quickly. Unlike your heartbeat, breathing is not fully "automatic." You can control your breathing, but usually your body does this for you.

Testing your lung capacity

Find out how much air your lungs can hold with this home-made "spirometer."

YOU WILL NEED
● *large plastic or glass jar with lid* ● *kitchen bowl* ● *tubing* ● *marker* ● *measuring jug*

1 Fill the jug with an exact amount of water, and then pour it into the jar. Mark the height of the water on the jar. Keep filling and marking until the jar is full.

2 Half-fill the bowl with water, screw the lid on the jar, turn the jar upside down, and place it in the bowl. Remove the lid.

3 Carefully place one end of the tube in the jar without letting in any air, then blow as hard as you can into the other end of the tube. The air from your lungs will force the water out of the jar. Use the markers to measure the air's volume.

Pour in the liquid, and mark the volume, until the jar is full

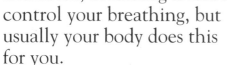

Ask a friend to hold the jar still as you blow

Add food coloring to the water to make it easier to see

Making a model lung

By making this model, you can see how your diaphragm (a sheet of muscle in your chest) helps to make your lungs fill up or empty. With a rubber band, fasten one balloon to the end of the ballpoint pen barrel. This is the "lung." Position the tube in the neck of the bottle, and make an airtight seal with modeling clay. Cut across the other balloon, and use it to seal the bottom of the bottle — this is the "diaphragm." Fasten the string to the balloon with the tape.

YOU WILL NEED
● *top half of a plastic bottle* ● *ballpoint pen barrel* ● *2 balloons* ● *rubber band* ● *string* ● *modeling clay* ● *tape* ● *scissors*

1 WHEN YOU PULL GENTLY on the string, the air pressure inside the bottle falls. Air from the outside then flows into the intact balloon, and it begins to inflate. This is just what happens to your lungs when your diaphragm contracts.

Trachea (windpipe)

Ribcage

Breathing in
When you breathe in, muscles attached to your ribcage and diaphragm have to work to draw air through your windpipe into your lungs.

Lung

Diaphragm

2 IF YOU LET GO OF THE STRING, air pressure inside the bottle rises. Air is forced out of the balloon. It quickly deflates, just as your lungs do when you breathe out.

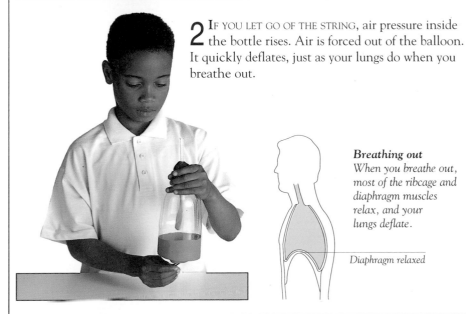

Breathing out
When you breathe out, most of the ribcage and diaphragm muscles relax, and your lungs deflate.

Diaphragm relaxed

Instant breath-test

This simple experiment using limewater shows that the air you breathe out is rich in carbon dioxide. Limewater is not dangerous, but it doesn't taste pleasant.

YOU WILL NEED
● *jar* ● *drinking straw* ● *limewater (made by dissolving an antacid tablet in water)*

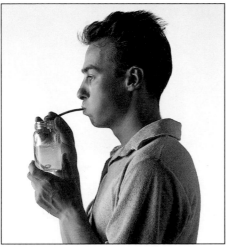

1 HALF-FILL THE JAR with limewater. When you breathe out through the straw, the carbon dioxide in your breath starts to react with the limewater. Tiny specks of insoluble calcium carbonate — or chalk — are produced.

2 AS MORE AND MORE calcium carbonate is formed, the water starts to turn cloudy, and eventually becomes white. This shows that your breath contains carbon dioxide.

Vision

THE SENSITIVITY OF YOUR EYES is remarkable. They can detect the feeble glimmer of a distant star but, within seconds, they can adjust to seeing in a brightly lighted room, where the light energy is millions of times greater. Your eyes collect light, convert it into electrical messages, then send them to the brain. Unlike the eyes of some mammals, your eyes can see in detail and in color. Their forward-pointing position enables you to see in depth, but at the same time, you can also see to either side without moving your head. Some mammals have a wider "field of vision" — their eyes look to either side so they can spot approaching predators.

■ Looking inside the eye

When light strikes your eyes, the lens focuses it onto the retina. This is a thin "screen," made of millions of sensitive cells, called rods and cones. Rods are sensitive to different light levels, but cannot distinguish colors. Cones are less sensitive, but give color vision. The blind spot, where the optic nerve emerges onto the retina, cannot see at all.

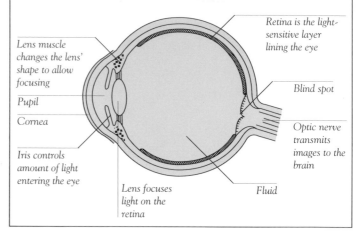

Lens muscle changes the lens' shape to allow focusing

Pupil

Cornea

Iris controls amount of light entering the eye

Lens focuses light on the retina

Retina is the light-sensitive layer lining the eye

Blind spot

Optic nerve transmits images to the brain

Fluid

EXPERIMENT
Binocular vision

Why do we need two eyes? "Binocular" vision — two eyes working together — lets you judge distances.

YOU WILL NEED
● *heavy-gauge wire* ● *insulated electrical cord* ● *electric bell*

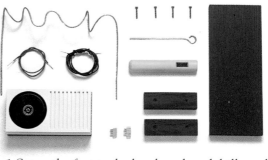

● *2 small plastic circuit junctions*
● *screws*
● *wooden handle*
● *wooden baseboard*

1 Screw the feet to the baseboard, and drill two holes in it. Drill a hole through the handle, and cut out a space large enough to house a circuit junction. Twist a 2 ft (60 cm) piece of wire, leaving straight ends. Feed the ends through the holes in the baseboard. Connect one end to the cord, and connect this to the bell.

2 Cut a 4 in (10 cm) length of wire for the handle; make an open loop at one end. Insert the wire into the handle, using a circuit junction to connect it to the cord. Put the loop around the twisted wire. Move it along the wire without ringing the bell. Try with one eye closed.

Identifying your dominant eye

Although your brain receives images from both eyes, it pays more attention to the image from your "dominant" eye. This quick test shows which of your eyes is dominant. Look at an object such as an upright piece of wood. With both eyes open, hold up one of your fingers to line up with the object. Now cover each eye in turn. When you cover the dominant eye, your finger will suddenly seem to move, so that it is no longer lined up with the object.

YOU WILL NEED
● *one piece of wood*

1 **WHEN YOUR DOMINANT EYE** is uncovered, the piece of wood seems to line up with your finger.

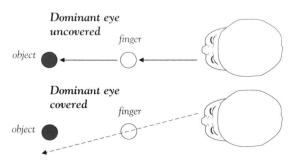

2 **WHEN YOUR DOMINANT EYE** is covered, your brain can only receive the image from the other eye.

Because your uncovered eye is not in line with your finger and the object, your finger seems to jump.

Dominant eye uncovered

object ← ◯ *finger*

Dominant eye covered

object ◯ *finger*

Try this with your friends, to see if the dominant eye is different in right- and left-handed people.

Testing your peripheral vision

Even when you are looking straight ahead, your eyes can see objects at your side. How far back this "peripheral" vision extends depends partly on the object's color.

YOU WILL NEED
● *pairs of different colored cards, about 4 in (10 cm) square*

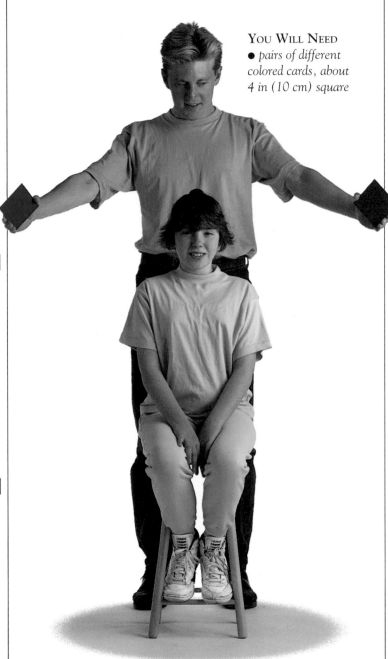

Sit on a chair, looking straight ahead. Now ask a friend to stand behind you, holding a card of the same color in each hand, and gradually bring them forward, until you can see them. Make a note of the position where the cards were first visible. Now repeat the experiment with a pair of cards of a different color to see how your peripheral vision varies.

Touch

IF YOU HAVE EVER TOUCHED something very hot, you will know the importance of your sense of touch. When the nerve endings in your hand detect heat, they flash a warning message through your nervous system. You do not even have to think what to do next, because an automatic reaction, or "reflex," takes emergency action. Almost before you know it, muscles in your arm contract, and your hand is pulled away from danger.

Touch works mostly through the skin, your largest sense organ. It has millions of nerve endings, which are sensitive to light and heavy pressure, heat, cold, and pain. Some parts of the body, such as the hands, are crammed with nerve endings, making them more sensitive than other parts.

■ DISCOVERY ■
Healing with pins

Acupuncture is an ancient form of medical treatment that was developed in China. An acupuncturist pushes fine needles into a patient's skin, choosing one or more of the special points shown on these maps of the body. Nobody is exactly sure how acupuncture works, but it helps many people to overcome pain and recover from illnesses.

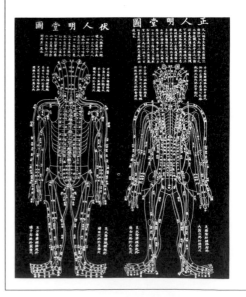

EXPERIMENT
Mapping your sense of touch

Adult supervision is advised for this experiment
Tiny nerve endings are scattered just beneath the skin's surface. Touching your hand with hot and cold paperclips will reveal the position of nerve endings that detect heat and cold. In the same way, a blunt crayon and a pin will show the position of nerves that detect pressure and pain.

YOU WILL NEED
● *2 plastic cups*
● *crayon* ● *fine-tipped pen*
● *hot water* ● *ice cubes* ● *metal paperclips* ● *pin*
● *ruler*
● *squared paper*

EXPERIMENT
Heat and habituation

Adult supervision is advised for this experiment
The signals that you receive from your sense organs are processed by your brain. If a signal is produced for long enough, your brain begins to get used to it. This is called "habituation."

1 POUR OUT THREE jars of water — one just hot enough to touch, one warm, and one cold. Put one forefinger in the hot jar, and the other in the cold jar, and leave them for a minute.

Your brain will gradually get used to the two different temperatures

1 HEAT ONE PAPERCLIP, and cool another. Draw a grid on the hand as below.

2 TOUCH EACH SQUARE with both clips, the crayon, and pins. Record the findings.

3 AT THE END OF the experiment, you will have four skin maps, showing nerve endings that can detect heat, cold, pressure, and pain. Which has the most nerve endings?

Testing the sensitivity of skin

Adult supervision is advised for this experiment
See how your skin separates two "stimuli" when they occur close together. Gently touch a friend's skin with pairs of pins, and ask how many pins your friend can feel. Be very careful — you must not draw your friend's blood.

YOU WILL NEED
- *6 pieces of balsa wood*
- *paper* ● *pencil* ● *pins* ● *ruler*

1 Carefully push two pins through each of the balsa wood strips. Position the pins so that they are the following distances apart: 1 in (2.5 cm); $^3/_4$ in (2 cm); $^3/_5$ in (15 mm); $^2/_5$ in (10 mm); $^1/_5$ in (5 mm); $^1/_{10}$ in (2 mm).

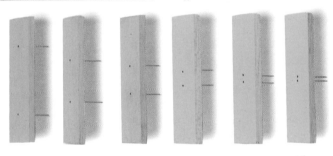

2 Ask the person you are experimenting on to look away. Now lightly touch his or her forearm with the pins that are farthest apart. Ask how many pins the person can feel.

3 Repeat step 2 with the other strips until only one pin can be felt. Record the result each time. Try this on the front and back of the arm to see which side is the more sensitive.

2 NOW PUT both fingers in the warm water. What can you feel? Your fingers are at almost the same temperature, but your brain seems to think otherwise.

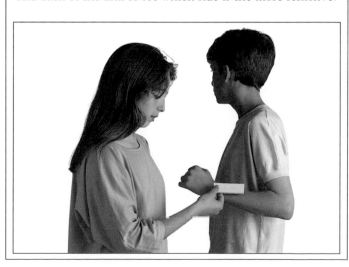

Taste and smell

THE TWO SENSES that can detect chemicals are taste and smell. Although you can tell the difference between many kinds of food, you can only sense four separate tastes — sweet, sour, salty, and bitter. When you eat, your sense of smell is also at work. It can distinguish between hundreds of different kinds of chemicals. Together with taste, it helps you to sense the flavor of a food. If you have a cold, you often cannot smell your food, which is why it seems to have little flavor.

The human sense of smell is more highly developed than the sense of taste. Although our noses are not nearly as sensitive as those of dogs, for example, we can detect some strong-smelling chemicals when they make up just one 30-billionth of the air around us. Substances that we can taste have to be in a much more concentrated form. They are sensed by organs on the tongue called taste buds.

Mapping your tongue

By touching a substance with the tip of your tongue, you can tell if it is sweet, but not bitter. This is because the groups of taste buds that detect the four different tastes — sweet, sour, salty, and bitter — are in different areas of your tongue.

1 Cut the lemon in half, and squeeze some juice into a glass. Make a strong solution of the other three substances (sugar, salt, and tea or coffee) by putting a small spoonful of each into a glass and adding just enough water to dissolve it.

2 Draw a small amount of one of the liquids into the dropper. Choose a point on the person's tongue, and touch it with a small spot of the liquid, but do not say what it is. Ask the person to identify the taste, and to rinse his or her mouth.

YOU WILL NEED
- *4 glasses*
- *dropper* ● *spoon*
- *water* ● *lemon*
- *sugar* ● *salt* ● *tea or coffee* ● *pencil*
- *paper*

3 If the person can identify the taste, note the position you touched on a sketch map of the tongue.

4 Clean the dropper by flushing it with water, and repeat steps 2 and 3, choosing the substance and position at random each time. Test the whole tongue a number of times with each taste to build up the map.

■ A matter of taste

The taste buds are clusters of cells that can sense chemicals, and are connected to nerves that travel from the tongue to the brain. When you eat, substances in food trigger the cells to send messages along the nerves. The resulting taste, combined with smell, produces the food's flavor.

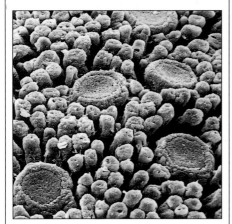

Tongue under a microscope
Taste buds are tiny sensory organs — in the picture they are around the circular structures. The spaghettilike projections are papillae, which cover the upper surface of the tongue, but are not involved in taste. Taste-bud cells last a very short time — some are replaced every 24 hours.

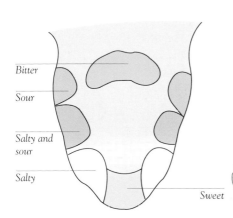

Bitter

Sour

Salty and sour

Salty

Sweet

The tongue map
After carrying out the mapping experiment, you should find that different parts of the tongue are sensitive to different flavors. The central part of your tongue can hardly taste at all, because most of the taste buds are concentrated at the back and along the edges.

EXPERIMENT
Testing your taste threshold

How strong does a taste have to be before you can detect it? In this experiment, you can test your ability to taste salt. By making up six different strengths of salty water, you can find out your "threshold" taste level. The strongest solution contains $1/2$ oz of salt per pint of water (25 g per liter). The concentration of the other solutions is half as strong as the next one up.

YOU WILL NEED
● *large measuring jug* ● *water* ● *6 glasses*
● *spoon* ● *salt* ● *kitchen scales* ● *food color (optional)*

1 WEIGH OUT $1/2$ oz of salt and dissolve in 1 pint of water (25 g in a liter) in a jug. This produces a salt solution which you can gradually dilute. You can add a few drops of food coloring to make the dilution visible.

2 MARK THE LEVEL ON THE JUG that corresponds to half the solution. Now fill the first glass. Pour away some solution until it is on the halfway mark. Top up with water to make a pint or a liter to halve the salt concentration.

3 FILL THE SECOND GLASS with the diluted solution. Repeat step 2, which again reduces the salt content by half, and fill the third glass. Repeat step 2 until all six glasses are filled with salt solutions of different strengths.

4 STARTING with the most dilute solution, take a small sip to see if you can taste the salt. If not, move to the next glass and take a small sip from that. When you can taste the salt, you have reached your threshold level.

Hearing

SOUND IS CREATED when something vibrates. When you switch on a radio, for example, it converts radio signals into movement. Although you cannot see it, the radio's speaker vibrates rapidly, and this sends pulses of energy into the air around it. Your ears detect these pulses, and the result is what you experience as sound.

Your ears work very much like a radio set in reverse. Each of them channels the vibrating air into an opening in your skull. There, the vibrations strike the eardrum, a tiny membrane that lies at the entrance to the inner ear. The eardrum moves backward and forward, and three tiny bones connected to it carry the movement to the cochlea, a spiral-shaped chamber. The cochlea is filled with fluid, and is lined with nerves that are sensitive to changes in pressure. As the eardrum vibrates, it squeezes the fluid, and the nerves produce electrical signals that travel to the brain, which translates them into sounds.

Seeing by sound
Some animals can use sound instead of sight to find their way about. When a bat hunts insects after dark, it produces bursts of high-pitched sound as it flies. The sound bounces back off any objects around it. The bat hears these echoes through its sensitive ears, and uses the echoes to pinpoint its prey.

EXPERIMENT
Hearing without ears

Sound does not only reach your ears through the air. In fact, the vibrations that make up sound travel better through a solid object, such as your body. You can prove this by using the sound produced by a tuning fork. The sound from a tuning fork is a pure note, meaning that the vibrations it produces occur at a single rate, or frequency.

YOU WILL NEED
● *tuning fork*

1 STRIKE THE END of the tuning fork against a hard surface, such as a tabletop. This will make it vibrate and produce its pure, single-frequency note.

2 HOLD THE TUNING FORK near your ear. At first, the sound will be loud. As the energy stored in the fork is passed to the air, the sound will start to die away.

3 WAIT UNTIL YOU CAN no longer hear the sound. Now move the tuning fork so that its base just touches your teeth. What sound can you hear now?

4 REPEAT STEPS 1 AND 2, and then hold the base of the fork against your head. Try moving it to different positions, to see where it sounds loudest.

EXPERIMENT
Changing ears

Having two eyes enables you to judge depth (pp. 166-167) very precisely. In a similar way, having two ears enables you to tell exactly where a sound is coming from. When you hear a sound, your brain compares the signals from your two ears. It can detect the tiny difference in the time the sound takes to reach each ear, and it uses this to pinpoint the sound's origin.

In this experiment, you can trick your brain by reversing the signals coming from your ears. Each of your ears is connected to a funnel that collects sound, but the tubes linking the funnels are crossed over. Now see if you can listen without believing what you hear.

YOU WILL NEED
- *2 lengths of plastic or rubber tubing*
- *2 plastic funnels*
- *piece of wood*
- *insulating tape*
- *adhesive tape*
- *small piece of fabric*

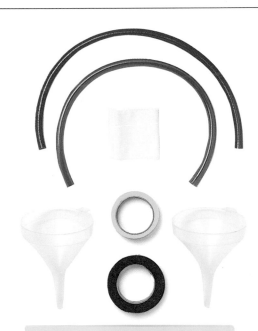

1 CONNECT ONE TUBE to each funnel, and fix the funnels to the piece of wood, so they lie in opposite directions. Tape some fabric over the end of each tube. It is very important to make sure that the tubes fit snugly enough into your ear to prevent any outside sounds from "leaking" in.

2 NOW CLOSE YOUR EYES, and ask a friend to clap at different positions around you. See if you can pinpoint the sound. What happens if you use a high-pitched sound, such as a whistle, instead of clapping? Is it easier or more difficult to tell where the sound is coming from?

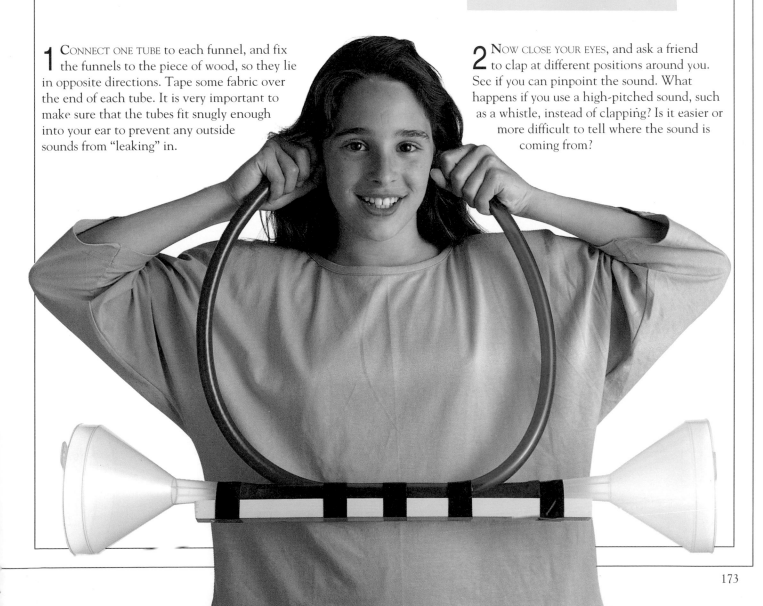

Mammals in the wild

STUDYING MAMMALS can be challenging, because many of them are secretive and highly intelligent creatures. Even in the African savanna, which teems with mammals of all sizes, animals as big as elephants have an uncanny ability to move silently and avoid being seen. Tracks and feeding signs (pp. 180-183) can tell us quite a lot about an animal's behavior, but biologists can now discover even more using modern electronics. Tiny radio transmitters, together with cameras that can "see" in the dark, reveal mammalian secrets that are normally hidden.

Top of the tree
In their natural habitat, lions are "top predators," and have no natural enemies. The male lion, the legendary "king of the beasts," is not actually a great hunter. Most of the work of tracking and catching large prey is carried out by the females, which hunt in groups. At one time, lions were found in many parts of the Old World, including Africa, the Middle East, and even parts of southern Europe. Today, they are found in the African savanna.

■ Mammalian defenses

Many mammals use their teeth or horns to fight off predators, or to ward off rivals. A few have evolved special weapons that can come to the rescue if they get into difficulties.

Crested porcupine quills

A porcupine can easily detach its sharp quills

Backing out of trouble
The porcupine's reaction to an aggressor is to back into it, leaving its opponent with a skinful of sharp quills. The porcupine keeps growing new quills to replace any that are lost.

■ Tracking mammals

The miniaturized radio transmitter is a device that lets biologists follow every step that a mammal takes. The transmitter is usually housed in a collar. This is fastened in position while the animal is temporarily "knocked out" by a tranquilizer.

Sending signals
A radio collar gives out signals at a particular frequency and rate. By using a directional antenna, a biologist can pinpoint the animal without having to go near it. Large land animals, such as bears, and animals at sea can also be tracked by radio. The radio signals can be picked up by satellite and the animal's position shown on a computer screen.

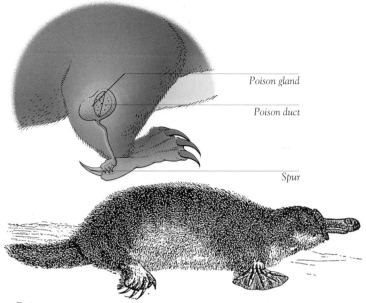

Poison gland

Poison duct

Spur

Poisonous spurs

The male duck-billed platypus is one of the few poisonous mammals. The ankles on its back legs each have a spur that can inject venom. The platypus can use these spurs to fight off predators, but their main function may be to deter rival males. The poison is strong enough to kill small animals, and can partially paralyze a human. Female platypuses do not have spurs.

Chemical defenses

Many mammals use strong scents to mark their territories. In skunks, this has evolved into a means of defense. When cornered, a skunk can squirt a foul-smelling liquid at a would-be predator, making it think twice before attacking. The skunk's boldly striped coat is another example of warning coloration (pp. 118-119). Instead of blending with its background, it stands out, making it clear to other animals that it is perfectly capable of looking after itself in a skirmish.

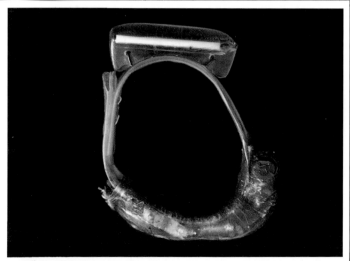

Seeing in the dark

Badgers are among the many mammals that spend most of their lives out of sight. During the day, they sleep in deep burrows, or "sets," emerging above ground at dusk. They find their way about in the dark mainly by smell, following well-used runs. Radio tracking can show where an individual badger is, but it cannot reveal exactly what it is doing. To find out, biologists can use a special device, called an image intensifier. This lets you "see in the dark" by amplifying what little light there is. As long as the biologist keeps downwind, the animals go about their nightly routine, unaware that they are being studied.

Tracking collar

This collar is designed to fit around the neck of a small mammal. The transmitter's battery will keep it working for about six months. The collar either is removed before the battery fails or else it is designed to fall off once the study has finished. As well as a transmitter, the collar contains a tiny "betalight" — a small glass tube that contains a light powered by low-level radioactivity. The radiation is too feeble to pass through the glass, but the beam of the light makes the animal easy to track at short range, when using radio signals becomes cumbersome. Betalights have to be used with care, because they can reveal an animal's position to hungry predators

Mammalian reproduction

ANIMALS PRODUCE THEIR YOUNG in two ways. In asexual reproduction, there is just one parent, and the offspring grow up to be identical to it. This happens, for example, in aphids (p. 34). In sexual reproduction, there are two parents, and the young have different combinations of their characteristics (p. 48). Mammals, including humans, can only reproduce sexually. When two mammals mate, sperm cells from the male's body fertilize the egg cells inside the female. Each egg then develops into an embryo, which is nourished by the mother. In placental mammals, such as cats, the embryo stays inside the mother's body until it is well developed. In marsupials, such as the wallaby, the young finish their development outside the mother's body.

■ How an egg is fertilized

When two mammals mate, millions of sperm cells pass from the male to the female, starting a journey that few of them will manage to complete. Lashing their tiny tails, or filaments, they swim inside the female's body toward the fallopian tubes, where the eggs are waiting. Several sperm cells may meet an egg, but only one gets through the membrane around it. The membrane then changes so no more sperm can get in. The two nuclei — one from the sperm and one from the egg — join, and the egg becomes fertilized. The egg's single cell is ready to divide and grow.

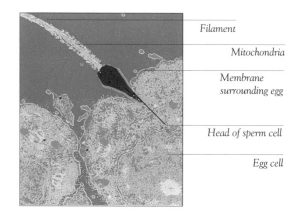

Filament

Mitochondria

Membrane surrounding egg

Head of sperm cell

Egg cell

■ Reproduction in placental mammals

Placental mammals — a group that includes such diverse members as mice and humans — have a special way of nurturing their young while it is still inside the mother's body. After the egg has been fertilized, it settles on the inner lining of the womb, or uterus. Here it becomes "implanted," or surrounded by cells from the womb lining of the mother. On one side, a spongy layer of cells called the placenta develops, where the blood vessels of the embryo and those of the mother lie close together. Food and oxygen can pass from the mother's blood into the embryo's through the umbilical cord, while waste products from the embryo pass in the other direction.

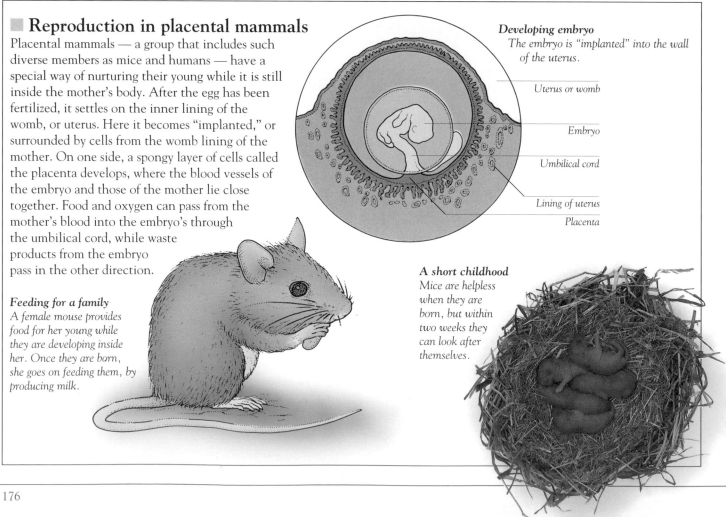

Developing embryo
The embryo is "implanted" into the wall of the uterus.

Uterus or womb

Embryo

Umbilical cord

Lining of uterus

Placenta

Feeding for a family
A female mouse provides food for her young while they are developing inside her. Once they are born, she goes on feeding them, by producing milk.

A short childhood
Mice are helpless when they are born, but within two weeks they can look after themselves.

▪ Reproduction in marsupials

The most dangerous moment in a young wallaby's life is the period between being born and entering its mother's pouch. Like other marsupials, it is tiny, blind, deaf, and hairless at birth. Only its front legs work fully, and it uses these to clamber slowly through its mother's fur toward her pouch. It finds its way by scent, and also by an instinct to move upwards, against the pull of gravity. When the young wallaby reaches the pouch, it climbs inside, and immediately clamps its mouth onto one of the teats. There it can feed and grow in safety, while the next embryo starts to develop inside the mother's body.

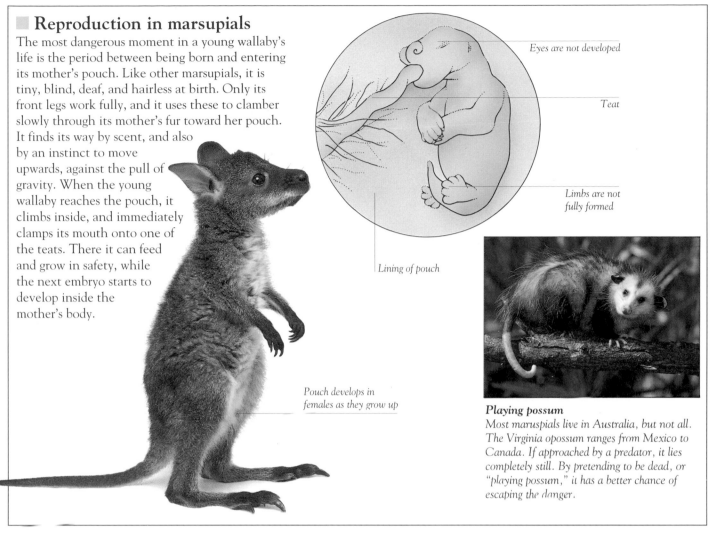

Eyes are not developed

Teat

Limbs are not fully formed

Lining of pouch

Pouch develops in females as they grow up

Playing possum
Most marsupials live in Australia, but not all. The Virginia opossum ranges from Mexico to Canada. If approached by a predator, it lies completely still. By pretending to be dead, or "playing possum," it has a better chance of escaping the danger.

▪ Reproduction in monotremes

The monotremes are the rarest, and strangest, of mammals. There are only three species — the duck-billed platypus and two spiny anteaters, or echidnas. They are the only mammals to lay eggs. The platypus lays two leathery eggs, and incubates them in a nest. The echidnas lay a single egg, which they carry in a small pouch.

As well as laying eggs, monotremes have several other primitive features. Although they produce milk, they have no nipples for their young to suck on. The milk simply flows out onto the fur, where the young animal laps it up. The monotremes are not wholly warm-blooded either. They keep their bodies at a much lower temperature than other mammals, and it fluctuates considerably. The body temperature of a spiny anteater varies between 77°F and 99°F (25°C–37°C).

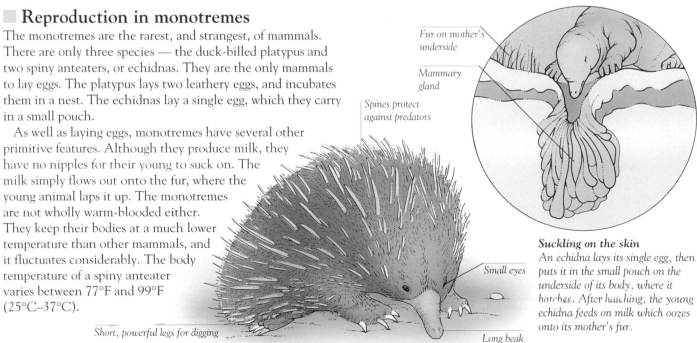

Fur on mother's underside

Mammary gland

Spines protect against predators

Small eyes

Short, powerful legs for digging

Long beak

Suckling on the skin
An echidna lays its single egg, then puts it in the small pouch on the underside of its body, where it hatches. After hatching, the young echidna feeds on milk which oozes onto its mother's fur.

Living by night

UNLIKE US, MANY MAMMALS are nocturnal, which means that they are active by night and sleep through the day. Long ago, the first mammals moved about under the cover of darkness to escape predatory dinosaurs. Many of the smaller mammals have remained nocturnal, and mammalian predators, such as foxes, are active at night in order to catch them.

Possums
Distant cousins of the Western Hemisphere opossum, brush-tailed possums are among the few marsupial mammals to have benefited from the spread of houses and gardens in Australia. These cat-sized creatures show little fear of humans, and they like suburban gardens for the rich supply of fruit, leaves, and flowers. The possum is tree-dwelling, but it often makes its home in the roof space of a house, and its noisy comings and goings may disturb people sleeping below. It is sometimes referred to as "silver-gray" because of its fur. During the 19th century, brush-tailed possums were released in New Zealand, where they are now a pest, as they have few natural enemies.

■ Fast-food foxes

Although foxes are largely nocturnal animals, you may see them in the daytime, especially during the summer, when the nights are short. Foxes follow regular routes when moving about, and these are often clearly visible: well-worn paths with gaps in hedgerows and tall vegetation show where foxes have pushed through. They produce a pungent smell with secretions from their anal glands, and these can be smelt at intervals on their trails. It may be possible to see a fox if you conceal yourself near one of these thoroughfares at dusk or dawn — do not go alone, but ask an adult to accompany you. In some parts of the world, particularly in Britain, you may see foxes in towns and cities. As well as their usual prey, these urban foxes raid garbage cans for the remains of "fast food" takeaways. Although they seem to take care in crossing roads, many are killed by cars and they have a much shorter lifespan than country foxes.

■ Keeping a gerbil

Creating the habitat
Gerbils live in deserts and dry grasslands from Africa to China. To make an artificial habitat for them, fill a tank with a layer of sand.

Sand enables gerbils to burrow

Wood for gnawing
Like other rodents, a gerbil has constantly growing teeth. To keep them in check, it must have something to gnaw, so place some pieces of wood in the tank.

In training
Playing teaches fox cubs how to catch and keep hold of their prey.

Raccoons
Natural inhabitants of wooded streamsides in North America, raccoons often live in towns and cities because that is where food is easily found. The clang of an overturned garbage can, for example, or tracks in snow or mud are clear signs that they are around. If you hear a raccoon feeding at night, you may find it if you venture out with a flashlight (take an adult with you).

Feeding
Seeds are a wild gerbil's main source of food. Dried corn, oats, canary seed, wheat grains, and even cornflakes make up a good basic diet. Green foods are also needed. You can even try out different wild plants.

Long back legs to shovel sand

Food is held by the paws, and gnawed

Long tail for balance

The finished tank
The tank is now ready for its occupants. Keep the tank in a warm, dry place, but do not leave it in direct sunlight for too long. Clean the tank out every week.

Making tracks

MANY MAMMALS ARE SECRETIVE creatures. Always on the alert for sounds or smells that might spell danger, they can slip away long before you have a chance to see them. But by keeping a keen eye on the ground, you can use their tracks to find out quite a lot about their behavior.

The best place to look for tracks is where the ground is damp but firm. Here, the tracks will show you some important differences in the way mammals move. Hoofed mammals, such as deer, leave very sharp tracks, because all their weight is borne on one or two small, hard toes on each foot. Animals that walk only on their toes are known as "digitigrade," and they are usually quick and nimble. Less speedy mammals — animals such as badgers, bears, and raccoons — have bigger tracks in proportion to their size. These "plantigrade" animals have a more lumbering movement, and their tracks are often close together.

When examining tracks, look carefully to see how many toes there are, and whether there are claw marks. In dogs and foxes, the claws are always extended, but in cats they are retracted into the paws when the animal walks, so leaving no trace.

Front foot

Hind foot

Raccoon tracks
The raccoon's weight is shared between its toes and its main pads. The toes of the front feet, used for holding food, spread more widely than those on the back feet.

Tracks in the snow
In parts of the world that have cold winters, many animals either hibernate or fly south. Most mammals, however, remain active, and after snow has fallen their tracks are easy to see. These tracks were left by a lynx. The lynx's front paws are armed with sharp claws that it uses for catching its prey. Its food includes small rodents that live in tunnels under the snowy blanket.

Because fresh snow is very light, tracks form in it quite easily. If you follow the tracks of a predator, such as a fox, you may see signs in the snow showing where it has made a kill

EXPERIMENT
Using sand to collect tracks

A layer of sand placed on the ground will reveal the tracks of animals both large and small.

1 POUR SOME DAMP SAND onto the ground or a tray. Sand with very fine grains gives the best results.

2 SMOOTH THE SAND into a thin layer, and then place the tray on the ground so the edge is at ground level.

3 HERE THE CAT'S distinctive paw marks will show up on the sand.

EXPERIMENT
Making a cast of tracks

You can use plaster of Paris to create a permanent record of an animal's tracks. This technique works best in damp, firm mud, such as that at the edge of a lake or on a path in shady woodlands. It will not work in snow, because plaster of Paris gets warm as it sets, and will melt the tracks.

YOU WILL NEED
- cardboard ● jug ● mixing bowl ● paperclips
- plaster of Paris ● scissors ● spoon

3 MIX SOME PLASTER with water to make it slightly runny. Pour it onto the tracks, and smooth the surface.

Raised casts of tracks

1 CLEAR AWAY any loose soil or leaves from the tracks, so that these do not stick to the plaster.

2 USING THE PAPERCLIPS, make a cardboard ring and fit it over the tracks, leaving no gaps around the bottom.

4 AFTER THE PLASTER has set, lift it up complete with its collar. Let it dry for a day, then remove the collar.

■ Other animal tracks

The sand tray method will record the tracks of many different kinds of animals, not only mammals but also reptiles, amphibians, birds, and invertebrates. Try putting the tray in the same place by day and by night, to see how the tracks differ.

Streaked tracks produced by crawling

Parallel lines of "footprints"

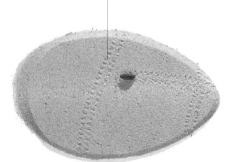

Frogs and toads
As this frog crawls over the sand, its feet leave long tracks. Frogs and toads are amphibians (pp. 78-79), and can move by crawling or by hopping. They usually crawl when looking for food, and hop to escape from danger. Nearly all frogs and toads are nocturnal, so leave the sand out at night to see their tracks.

Invertebrates
Here a woodlouse leaves its delicate but distinctive tracks as it crawls across the sand. The heavy-bodied woodlouse is one of the many invertebrates that feeds on the ground by night. Other invertebrates that are large enough to leave clean tracks include beetles, crickets, millipedes, centipedes, and scorpions.

A natural impression
The sidewinder snake leaves unmistakable tracks in the sand. It arches its body sideways through the air so that only two or three points of its body touch the ground at any one time.

Feeding signs

SPOTTING AND RECOGNIZING ANIMAL feeding signs is like detective work. From the clues that lie scattered around you, you can build a picture of the animal life in an area. Scattered feathers, frayed bark, droppings, broken shells, and chewed seeds are just some of the many clues that you can follow.

The number of signs you can find depends on how an animal feeds. Many plant-eating mammals, such as rabbits and deer, spend much of their waking lives eating, often in places that they visit again and again. You can tell that they have been around a certain area by chewed vegetation, and also by droppings. Many mammals, including rabbits and badgers, leave their droppings in particular places, called latrines. These act as markers to show other animals of the same species that a patch of ground has already been claimed. The feeding signs left by meat-eating animals are fewer and farther apart; they eat less often, and they sometimes eat their prey whole. When a fox attacks a bird, the site is often marked by feathers. When it digs up the nest of a mouse, there will be no signs of its prey, just a depression in the ground.

Stripped cones

Signaling by scent
Rabbit droppings are often piled up on mounds of grass. Their scent tells other rabbits that the area is occupied. Rabbits are plant-eaters, and like many other herbivores, their droppings are rounded and fibrous. Deer eat lots of low-nutrient food and leave large amounts of droppings. The droppings of carnivorous animals are usually pointed, and often contain fur and pieces of bone. Carnivores also use droppings to mark their territories.

Rabbit droppings

Feeding on cones
Many animals attack the scales of cones to reach the seeds.

Hazelnut shells

Breaking into a nut
You can often tell what sort of animal has eaten a nut by the way it has been opened. These hazelnuts were eaten by a vole.

■ Other leftovers
Most creatures, both large and small, leave feeding signs. Birds tend to have favorite places that they always return to when feeding. If you examine the remains in these places, you can find out what the birds have been eating.

Insect leftovers
This pile of butterfly wings has been left by a bird that fed on their soft bodies.

A shrike's larder
Shrikes are small birds that eat insects, small mammals, and sometimes other birds. One of the methods they use to catch their prey is to impale it on the long thorns of plants, or on the spikes of barbed wire. This holds the prey while the shrike tears off pieces to eat. It also serves as a "larder" to store food.

Barking up a tree
In Africa, trees with smashed branches and stripped or torn bark are signs that elephants have been feeding. Throughout the world, many other mammals feed on the bark of trees, especially where cold winters reduce the supply of more nutritious food.

Prey to a fox
This jay's wing marks the spot where a fox made a kill. Because the wing contains little meat, the fox has left it behind.

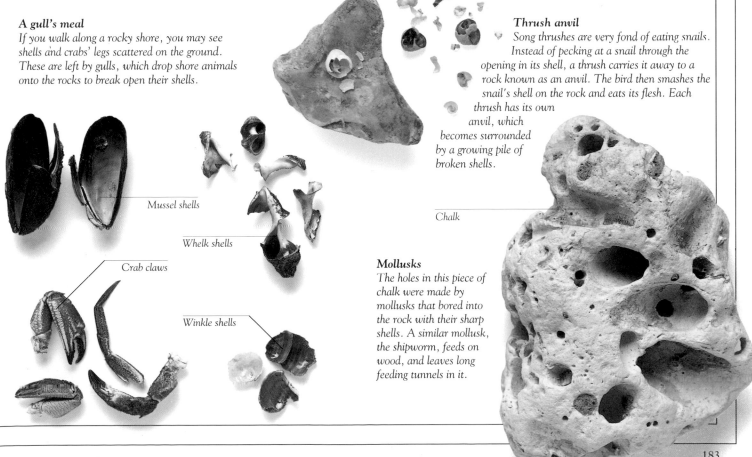

A gull's meal
If you walk along a rocky shore, you may see shells and crabs' legs scattered on the ground. These are left by gulls, which drop shore animals onto the rocks to break open their shells.

Mussel shells

Whelk shells

Crab claws

Winkle shells

Thrush anvil
Song thrushes are very fond of eating snails. Instead of pecking at a snail through the opening in its shell, a thrush carries it away to a rock known as an anvil. The bird then smashes the snail's shell on the rock and eats its flesh. Each thrush has its own anvil, which becomes surrounded by a growing pile of broken shells.

Chalk

Mollusks
The holes in this piece of chalk were made by mollusks that bored into the rock with their sharp shells. A similar mollusk, the shipworm, feeds on wood, and leaves long feeding tunnels in it.

183

Glossary

THE FOLLOWING FOUR PAGES are designed to give you a quick reference to many of the biological terms used in this book. This glossary explains terms that are important to living things as a whole; it does not include all the many parts of living organisms. If you want to look these up, turn to the index (pp. 188-191). Use the index, too, if you want to read about a particular group of organisms, such as reptiles.

ABDOMEN In insects, spiders, and crustaceans, the section of the body farthest away from the head. It is attached to the thorax.

ALTRICIAL (birds) Hatching in a poorly developed state, often unable to see and without feathers. *See also Precocial.*

AMINO ACIDS The building blocks of proteins. There are 20 common types of amino acids. They join together in special sequences to form different proteins.

ANTENNA (biology) One of the paired sense organs, sometimes known as "feelers," on the head of an invertebrate. An animal uses its antennae to feel or to taste.

ASEXUAL REPRODUCTION Reproduction in which there is only one parent. The young have exactly the same chromosomes as the parent, and therefore the same characteristics. *See also Sexual reproduction.*

ATOM A very tiny particle that cannot easily be split into anything smaller. Everything is made up of atoms. Elements consist of one type of atom only, but most things you see consist of many types of atoms, combined into molecules. Some molecules have only one type of atom.

BASIDIUM A group of spore-forming cells found in many fungi. A toadstool may have millions of basidia.

BINOCULAR VISION Vision using two eyes to gauge depth.

BIOSPHERE All the parts of the Earth that are inhabited by living things.

CALCIFICATION The process of hardening that happens when calcium carbonate (chalk) is laid down by cells.

CAMBIUM (trees) A layer of cells just beneath the bark that divides to produce outward growth of the trunk. Branches and roots of trees also have a cambium layer.

CARBOHYDRATES Compounds of carbon, hydrogen, and oxygen formed by photosynthesis and stored in plants. They include sugars, starch, and cellulose.

CARNIVORE An animal that eats other animals.

CARTILAGE A rubbery protein that makes up our skeletons; calcification hardens the cartilage into bone.

CATERPILLAR The larva of a butterfly or moth.

CELLS The living units that make up most organisms.

Chemical bridges making up genetic code

DNA molecule
The distinctive "double helix" structure of the molecule looks like a twisted ladder.

They consist of jellylike cytoplasm held in by a membrane. At the center of most cells is a nucleus.

CELLULOSE A tough carbohydrate that makes up the cell walls of plants.

CHITIN A tough carbohydrate found in the external skeleton of insects, crustaceans, and spiders, and in the cell walls of fungi.

CHLOROPHYLL The main chemical that plants use to trap the energy of light for photosynthesis.

CHLOROPLAST An organelle in plant cells. The chloroplasts are like tiny factories, carrying out photosynthesis.

CHROMOSOMES Strands consisting mainly of DNA found inside cells. They contain the chemical code needed to control the structure and development of the cell. Most cells have two copies of each chromosome.

CHRYSALIS Another name for the pupa of a butterfly or moth. *See also Pupa.*

COELOM A cavity (hollow area) found inside the body of earthworms, insects, starfish, and other animals. In earthworms it contains a fluid and helps the worm to move about by giving the muscles something to push against.

COLD-BLOODED ANIMAL One that cannot warm itself, as a warm-blooded animal can. Its temperature depends on its surroundings, so in warm sunshine, cold-blooded animals are warm.

COLONY A group of related living things, all belonging to the same species, that live or breed with one another.

CONSUMER (ecology) A living thing that eats other living things. Apart from plants, which make their own food, most living things are consumers.

CONVERGENT EVOLUTION The process by which two living things of different lines of descent gradually evolve similar structures through living in a similar way.

CYTOPLASM The contents of a cell, including the organelles, but not the nucleus.

CYTOSOL The jellylike part of the cytoplasm, in which organelles are suspended.

DECOMPOSER A saprophyte which, by feeding on dead things, breaks them down into simpler substances.

DIURNAL Active by day.

DNA Abbreviation for deoxyribonucleic acid. This important substance carries all the information needed to build a living thing and to keep it alive.

DOUBLE-JOINTED Having joints that can move through a greater angle than most people's. Despite this term, double-jointed people do not have more joints than everyone else.

ECOLOGY The study of how living things fit into the world around them.

ECOSYSTEM All the living things in a particular region (such as a forest, lake, or river), as well as the soil, water, and nonliving things they use.

EGG CELL A female sex cell, in both animals and plants. *See also Sexual reproduction.*

ELEMENT A simple substance that is made up of one kind of atom only.

EMBRYO A very young plant or animal, still inside the mother (in mammals), its egg (in birds and reptiles), or its seed (in plants).

ENAMEL The very hard substance that covers the surface of teeth.

ENDOPLASMIC RETICULUM A large bag, made of membrane, inside plant and animal cells. The membrane is folded up like an accordion. Many different proteins are stored safely inside the bag, away from the rest of the cell, until they are needed.

ENZYME A special type of protein. Enzymes control all the chemical reactions that happen inside living things.

EVOLUTION A very slow process of change that affects all living things. It can gradually change the characteristics of a species, and produce new species from existing ones. The main driving force behind it is natural selection.

FATS A family of energy-rich chemicals that do not mix with water. The group includes solids (fats) and liquids (oils).

FERTILIZATION In sexual reproduction, the stage at which male and female sex cells join together to form a single cell.

FOOD CHAIN A diagram that shows how food, and therefore energy, passes from one living thing to another in an ecosystem.

FOSSIL The ancient remains of an animal or plant found preserved in rock.

FRUIT In the botanical sense, any seed-bearing structure. A fruit is often brightly colored, juicy, and pleasantly sweet to taste.

GENE A unit of inheritance, passed on from parent to offspring. Some genes have clear effects — they can make the eyes blue or brown. A gene is made up of a length of DNA inside a cell. Each gene controls the assembly of a particular protein.

GERMINATION The process in which a seed, spore, or pollen grain starts to develop.

GILL (fish) Feathery structures in fish and other aquatic animals that extract oxygen from water for the purposes of respiration.

GILL (fungi) A flap, usually hanging downward, on which a fungus's spores are produced.

GLUCOSE A type of sugar, or carbohydrate, used by most living things for energy.

HABITAT The environment needed by a particular species for its survival.

HABITUATION The process of becoming used to, or tolerant of a drug, or activity. Not the same as addiction.

HERBIVORE An animal that feeds on plants.

HOLDFAST The anchor that attaches a seaweed to a solid surface such as a rock.

HORMONE An internally secreted chemical produced by one part of the body to trigger changes in the functions of another.

HUMUS The remains of plants and animals, found in the upper layers of soil.

HYPHA (plural hyphae) One of the feeding threads that make up a fungus.

IMPRINTING A special form of learning shown by very young animals, in which they learn to recognize their parents. Once triggered, imprinting cannot usually be reversed.

INVERTEBRATE An animal without a backbone, or vertebral column.

JOINT Part of the skeleton where two bones meet.

KERATIN The protein that makes up skin, hair, fur, nails, and hooves.

LARVA The young stage of an insect or other invertebrate, which looks quite different from its parent.

LATERAL LINE A line of pressure sensors found along the side of a fish's body.

LIGAMENT A strong, flexible material that holds two bones together where they meet in movable joints.

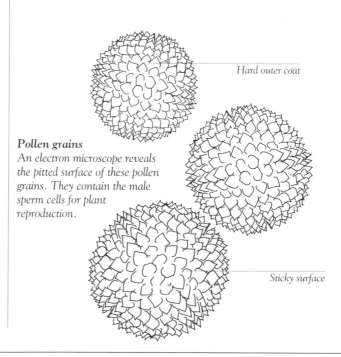

Hard outer coat

Pollen grains
An electron microscope reveals the pitted surface of these pollen grains. They contain the male sperm cells for plant reproduction.

Sticky surface

LIGNIN A substance found in plants, particularly trees. It is this that makes them woody.

MANTLE (biology) In snails, oysters, and other mollusks, a layer of the body that produces calcium carbonate (chalk) to build up the shell.

MEMBRANE A very thin flexible sheet, made up of two layers of fat molecules. Membranes surround all cells.

METABOLISM All the chemical reactions that occur inside a living organism.

METAMORPHOSIS A complete change in body shape, as when a caterpillar changes into a chrysalis and then into a butterfly.

MIGRATION In animals, a regular and well-established journey from one place to another.

MIMICRY Imitation of one living thing by another, in order to gain protection or hide from predators.

MINERAL (biology) A chemical, element, or compound such as iron, that living things need to stay alive.

MITOCHONDRION A small organelle inside cells that releases energy from food.

MOLECULE The smallest particle of a substance made up of two or more atoms. Even the largest molecules can only just be seen with the most powerful microscopes.

MOLTING The process of shedding skin, feathers, or fur.

NATURAL SELECTION The process by which many different natural factors, from climate to food supply, steer the course of evolution. Living things that are best suited to their environment have more young ones.

NECTAR A sugary liquid produced by plants, usually in their flowers.

NEMATOCYST A stinging cell found in sea anemones and related animals.

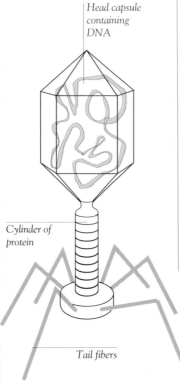

Head capsule containing DNA

Cylinder of protein

Tail fibers

Virus
Looking like a minute spacecraft, this tiny "bacteriophage" virus reproduces by injecting its DNA into a bacterium. The tail fibers attach the virus to the wall of the host cell.

NECTAR A sugary liquid produced by plants, usually in their flowers.

NEOTENOUS Being able to reproduce when the body is otherwise not fully developed — sexual maturity during the larval stage.

NOCTURNAL Active by night.

NUCLEOLUS A dark part of a cell's nucleus that is involved in making proteins.

NUCLEUS The control center of a cell, which contains the chromosomes.

NYMPH The young stage of an insect, such as a grasshopper, that looks like a small version of its parents.

ORGANELLE A tiny, self-contained structure, such as a mitochondrion, inside a cell.

ORGANISM Any living thing.

OVARY The part of an animal or plant that produces the reproductive egg cells.

PARASITE Any organism that lives on or inside another (its host), and from which it takes all of its food.

PHEROMONE A chemical released by one animal that triggers off a response in another of the same species.

PHOTOSYNTHESIS The process by which plants use the energy in sunlight.

PLACENTA (mammals) A complex layer through which food passes from the mother's blood to her unborn young.

PLANKTON The mass of microscopic plants and animals that floats on the surface of seas and lakes.

POLLEN A powdery substance, often yellow, produced by flowers. It contains the male sex cells.

POLLINATION The passage of pollen from the male part of a flower to the female part, so that fertilization can occur. The flowers are usually on different plants.

POLYP An individual coral or sea anemone.

PRECOCIAL (birds) Hatching in an advanced state of development, and quickly becoming independent. *See also Altricial.*

PREDATOR An animal that hunts other animals.

PRODUCER (ecology) Any organism that produces food for itself. Most producers are plants and bacteria using sunlight to make food.

PROTEIN A complicated chemical made by living cells from amino acids. Proteins are essential to all living organisms. There are many kinds of proteins including enzymes and structural proteins such as keratin.

PUPA The stage in the life cycle of an insect during which the larva turns into an adult. *See also Metamorphosis.*

QUEEN In social insects such as bees and termites, the female that starts a colony. Advanced social insects have only one queen, and she is the only member of the colony to reproduce.

RHIZOMORPH A rootlike thread produced by fungi.

RNA Abbreviation for ribonucleic acid, a substance that helps to make proteins. *See also DNA.*

SAPROPHYTE (saprobe) Anything that feeds on dead and decaying matter.

SEED A tough package containing a plant embryo and food reserves for it to use. Following the process of germination, each seed can develop into a new plant. Seeds are produced by sexual reproduction.

Cell of a plant
A plant cell has rigid walls, made of cellulose. Most of the space inside the walls is taken up by a fluid-filled vacuole. The fluid presses the walls outward.

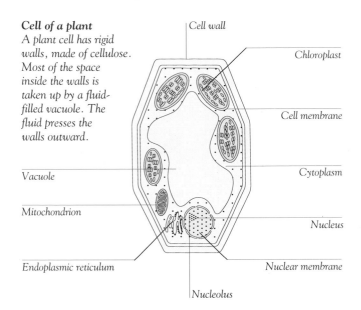

Cell wall

Chloroplast

Cell membrane

Cytoplasm

Nucleus

Nuclear membrane

Nucleolus

Vacuole

Mitochondrion

Endoplasmic reticulum

SESSILE Staying in one place.

SEXUAL REPRODUCTION A way of producing young that needs two parents. One, the female, produces an egg cell, while the other, the male, produces sperm. In sexual reproduction, the young get half of their chromosomes from each parent, and so have some characteristics from each of them. *See also Asexual reproduction.*

SOCIAL Living together in a group and sharing tasks.

SPECIES A group of living things, all of which could breed with each other, if they came together, but could not breed successfully with anything else.

SPERM CELL A male sex cell.

SPIRACLE (insects) An opening in the body which lets air in and out of the tracheae. *See also Trachea.*

SPORANGIUM Part of a plant or fungus that produces spores.

SPORE A very small, tough-coated package of cells that can produce a plant or a fungus. Spores are much smaller than seeds, they do not contain embryos, and they are not produced by sexual reproduction.

SPRING TIDE A tide with a high range. Spring tides occur when the Sun and the Moon lie directly in line with the Earth, so that their gravity combines to pull seawater.

STARCH A carbohydrate used by some plants, such as potatoes, wheat, and rice, as an energy store.

STIPE The stalk of a seaweed.

STOMA (plural stomata) A tiny pore on the surface of a plant's leaves and stems that allows gases to pass into and out of the plant.

STRIDULATION Making a sound by rubbing one surface against another. Many insects create sound in this way.

SUCCESSION (ecology) The process in which one species replaces another when a new habitat is colonized.

SWIMBLADDER A gas-filled bladder in fish which prevents them from rising or sinking.

SYNOVIAL FLUID (synovia) The liquid that lubricates the joints of the skeleton.

TADPOLE The immature stage of a frog, toad, or other amphibian.

TENDON The strong cords that connect muscles to bones.

TENDRIL A long, thin, wiry structure on a climbing plant that grabs onto twigs, walls, or other supports. Tendrils have developed from leaves in the course of evolution.

THORAX In insects, spiders, and crustaceans, the middle part of the body. In insects, it carries the legs and wings.

TRACHEA (insects) One of many tiny tubes that carry air into the body.

TRACHEA (vertebrates) The tube leading from the throat to the lungs.

TRANSPIRATION The process by which a plant draws water (from the soil) up from its roots to its leaves.

TROPISM In plants, a movement toward or away from something, such as light or the pull of gravity.

TUBER In plants, a storage organ that is formed by a swollen stem.

VACUOLE A fluid-filled area inside a plant or animal cell, lined by a membrane.

VERTEBRATE An animal that has a backbone, or vertebral column.

VIRUS A strand of DNA or RNA, surrounded by a protective capsule of protein. It can reproduce only by invading a living cell.

WARM-BLOODED ANIMAL An animal that can make its own heat by burning up food. This means that it can be warm even if its surroundings are cold.

WARNING COLORATION Bright colors that show predators that an animal is dangerous if attacked — for example, the black and yellow stripes on bees and wasps.

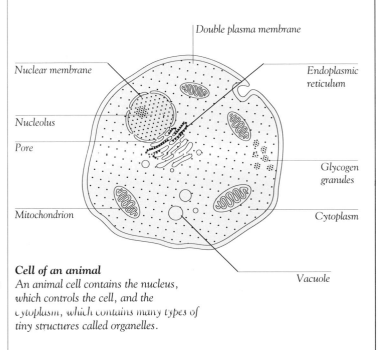

Double plasma membrane

Nuclear membrane

Endoplasmic reticulum

Nucleolus

Pore

Glycogen granules

Mitochondrion

Cytoplasm

Vacuole

Cell of an animal
An animal cell contains the nucleus, which controls the cell, and the cytoplasm, which contains many types of tiny structures called organelles.

Index

Acknowledgments

DAVID BURNIE WOULD LIKE TO THANK the many people whose help, advice, and assistance contributed to the preparation of this book. In particular, I am very grateful to our enthusiastic and imaginative wildlife photographers, Jane Burton and Kim Taylor, and also to the DK photographic team, Tim Ridley, Barnabas Kindersley, Steve Gorton, and Sarah Ashun. Special thanks also go to Ken Day, for expertly designing and constructing much of the equipment, to our educational consultant Richard Scrase, for helping to plan the book and suggesting a number of experiments, and to Steve Parker, for checking the text. I am also grateful to John Gillam for providing a number of subjects for photography.

I would like to give particular thanks to Linda Gamlin, who subjected the book to her invaluable scrutiny and provided a great deal of encouragement, and to the team at Dorling Kindersley — Sharon Lucas, Sally Hibbard, and Gurinder Purewall — whose hard work over many months is reflected in every page.

■ SPECIAL PHOTOGRAPHY

Jane Burton, Kim Taylor: 4-5, 14-15, 16, 20-21, 28-29, 30-31, 44, 65, 69, 72-73, 76-77, 78-79, 80-81, 83, 84-85, 88-89, 93, 99, 100-101, 104-105, 106-107, 108-109, 111, 112-113, 114-115, 116-117, 118-119, 128, 129, 136-137, 141, 143, 144-145, 146-147, 149, 152-153, 154-155, 174-175, 176, 178-179, 180-181.
Peter Chadwick: 51, 127, 133, 135
Richard Davies: 29, 82
Philip Dowell: 151, 155, 158-159, 162
Neil Fletcher: 66-67, 76, 118
Linda Gamlin: 56, 59, 64
Steve Gorton: 6-7, 8-9, 10-11, 14-15, 16-17, 18-19, 20-21, 22-23, 50-51, 86-87, 155, 158-159, 16-161, 162-163, 182-183
David Johnson: 130
Colin Keates: 108, 119
Dave King: 29, 82, 92, 156, 174, 177, 182
Cyril Laubscher: 131
Andrew Lawson: 27
Steven Oliver: 30-31, 32-33, 38-39, 40-41, 44-45, 48-49, 52-53, 120-121, 122-123
Roger Philips: 50
Tim Ridley: 6-7, 14-15, 16-17, 18-19, 24-25, 26-27, 28-29, 34-35, 42-43, 46-47, 48-49, 54-55, 56-57, 58-59, 60-61, 62-63, 64-65, 66-67, 68-69, 74-75, 82-83, 84-85, 90-91, 92, 94-95, 96-97, 100-101, 102-103, 106, 109, 110-111, 112, 117, 118, 124-125, 128-129, 132-133, 134-135, 136-137, 138-139, 141, 144-145, 150, 154, 157, 164-165, 166-167, 168-169, 170-171, 172-173, 180-181
Karl Shone: 4, 27, 61
Matthew Ward: 24, 29, 37, 174
Jerry Young: 28, 29, 144, 145, 147, 150-151

■ PICTURE CREDITS

t top; *c* center; *b* bottom;
r right; *l* left

Heather Angel: 60*bl*, 98-99, 114*cl*
Ardea: Francois Gohier 20*bl*, 21*br*
Biofotos: Andrew Henley 155*tl*
Bruce Coleman Ltd: Jane Burton 78*tr*; Eric Creighton 54*tr*; Jack Dermid 149*tc*; Michael Fogden 55*t*, 179*tr*; Peter Hinchliffe 100*bl*; Gordon Langsbury 30*t*, 140*cl*; John Markham 119*t*; Jan Taylor 93*tl*; Kim Taylor 34*bl*, 125*tl*; John Wallis 178*tl*
Mary Evans Picture Library: 21*c*, 30*b*, 168*bl*.
Horizon: 126-7
Hulton-Deutsch Picture Co: 14*br*, 83*br*, 101*c*, 129*cl*, 140*bc*
Mansell Collection: 15*t*, 22*tr*, 24*c*, 48*bl*, 67*cl*, 161*bl*, 168*bl*
Natural History Photographic Agency: 86*tl*; A.N.T. 131*cr*, 147*tr*; Anthony Bannister 142-143, 183*br*; Stephen Dalton 69*tr*, 172*tl*; Peter Johnson 181*tl*; Stephen Krasemann; John Shaw 119*tl*, 177*cr*
Oxford Scientific Films: H.G. Arndt 182*bc*; Kathie Atkinson 154*cl*; Steve Earley 25*bc*; Michael Fodgen 36-37; Richard Kolar 130*tr*; Lou Lauber 128*cl*; David Macdonald 152-153; Roland Mayr 180*br*; Tom Ullrich 175*tr*
Planet Earth Pictures: 70-71; Walter Deas 151*tr*; D. Perrine 25*br*; James Watt 155*br*.
Premaphotos: K. Preston-Mafham 106*cl*, 124*bl*, 149*tl*, 156*br*
Ann Ronan Picture Library: 17*bl*, 84*tr*, 96*tl*.
Edward Ross: 110*cl*
Science Photo Library: Michael Abbey 28*bl*; Dr. Tony Brain 26*cl*; Dr. Jeremy Burgess 12-13; John Durham 67*bl*; Jan Hinsch 23*tr*; Omikron 171*tl*; Petit Format 176*c*
Tony Stone Associates: 31*cr*, 40*tr*
Ullstein: 115*tr*

■ ILLUSTRATIONS

Kevin Marks: 35, 62, 68, 76, 82-83, 87, 88, 90-91, 94-95, 102, 104, 106, 108-109, 111, 112-113, 137, 146-147, 150, 163, 175, 176-177.
Richard Lewis: 135

■ COMPUTER DRAWINGS

Rik Greenland: conservation symbol, 133, 184-185, 186
Sally Hibbard: 42, 46, 169
Dawn Ryddner: 16-17, 18, 33, 56, 61, 66, 78, 80, 115, 136, 146, 157, 160-161, 162, 165, 166-167, 171, 180, 187
Salvo Tomaselli: 67, 100-101

■ MODEL-MAKING

Ken Day: 33, 103, 109, 111, 117, 125, 139, 168

■ MODELS

Steven Casson: 57
Nancy Graham: 151, 178-179
Arabella Grinstead: 105
Sam Jacobson: 118-119, 141
Sharon Lucas: 141
Jake O'Leary: 2, 125, 132-133
Tim Ridley: 35, 165
Samantha Schneider: 3, 57, 110, 136
Roger Smoothy: 2, 103, 109, 167
Gemma Taylor: 2, 103, 106, 167
Other models supplied by Little Boats Model Agency, Rascals Child Model Agency

■ DORLING KINDERSLEY would like to thank Charyn Jones, Caroline Ollard, Stephanie Jackson, and Susannah Tapper for editorial assistance; Diana Morris for picture research; Karin Woodruff for the index; Clair Lidzey Watson for design help; and Hazel Taylor for photographic assistance. Special thanks to Lynne Jowett for finding so many models.

Microscope from Mirador Limited
Binoculars, Telescopes, and Microscopes
150 West End Lane, London NW6, England.